KarterLeschasin

Natalie Dornian

People and Stories of Canada to 1867

Michele Visser-Wikkerink and E. Leigh Syms

PORTAGE & MAIN PRESS

Portage & Main Press acknowledges the financial support of the Government of Canada through the Book Publishing Industry Development Program (BPIDP) for its activities.

Printed and bound in Canada by Friesens.

LIBRARY AND ARCHIVES CANADA CATALOGUING IN PUBLICATION

Visser-Wikkerink, Michele
    People & stories of Canada to 1867 / Michele Visser-Wikkerink and E. Leigh Syms.

ISBN-13: 978-1-55379-092-1
ISBN-10: 1-55379-092-8

    1. Canada–History–To 1763 (New France)–Juvenile literature. 2. Canada–History–1763-1867–Juvenile literature. 3. Canada–Biography–Juvenile literature. I. Syms, E. Leigh II. Title. III. Title: People and stories of Canada to 1867.

FC172.V57 2007   971   C2006-905050-3

Project editor: Annalee Greenberg
Editor: Leigh Hambly
Production manager: Marcela Mangarelli
Writer, Introduction: Linda McDowell
Photo researcher: Susan Turner
Cartographer: Douglas Fast
Illustrators: David Morrow, Joshua Stanton, Jess Dixon, Tom Bendoni
Cover illustration: David Morrow
Book and cover design: Relish Design Studio Ltd.: Suzanne Braun and Terry Corrigan

ACKNOWLEDGMENTS

The publisher would like to thank the following for their review of the content and their invaluable advice:

Pat Adamson, St. James Assiniboia School Division
Wanda Barker, Manitoba Education
Judith Hudson Beattie, Fur-trade historian
Dr. R. Jarvis Brownlie, University of Manitoba
Margaret Dumas, Fox Lake Cree Nation, Frontier School Division
Gary Evans, Educational consultant
Linda McDowell, Educational consultant
William Norton, University of Manitoba
Greg Pruden, Manitoba Education, William Norton, University of Manitoba
Dr. E. Leigh Syms, Manitoba Museum

Special thanks to Dr. Jack Bumsted, Wendy Owen, Gary Evans, and Matthew Rankin for their original work on this project.

Lyrics from "The Hangman's Eyes," p. 215, are reproduced by permission of Alex Sinclair and SGB Productions.

PORTAGE & MAIN PRESS

100-318 McDermot Avenue
Winnipeg, MB Canada R3A 0A2
Tel. 204-987-3500 • Toll free: 1-800-667-9673
Toll-free fax: 1-866-734-8477
E-mail: books@portageandmainpress.com

printed on 30% PCW paper

Contents

Introduction

What Is Canadian History?

This year, you are going to learn about life in Canada from very early times until 1867, the year that Canada officially became a country. The history of Canada is an endless collection of exciting stories about many different people. These people were hunters, trappers, explorers, fur traders, guides, boatmen, settlers, farmers, soldiers, sailors, storekeepers, boat builders, fishermen, foresters, nuns, priests, doctors, and teachers. They were men, women, girls and boys. They were Aboriginal peoples who came here thousands of years ago. They were newcomers who arrived here from faraway lands. Canada's history is also full of intriguing events, including wars, betrayals, and acts of heroism. So, too, it is the story of everyday people – people like you, your friends, and members of your family.

Figure I.1

Where to Find History

Perhaps someone in your family has a collection of things that are important to everyone. This collection might include photos and birth certificates. It may have birth announcements, cards and letters, and newspaper clippings about people in your family. It could include report cards and school projects. Someone in your family likely knows lots of stories about relatives and family events from times before you were born. All of these things add up to your family's history. Your family's history is part of a bigger story of your community and country.

Like your family, historians use many different kinds of information to tell them about the past. These include the following:

Oral history. Oral history is the oldest way of recording stories of people and events. Long before writing was invented, people kept track of their history by telling stories. Usually, certain people memorized the "history" of the family or group and passed this information on to the next generation.

Visual history. Visual history includes images – photos, paintings, drawings, movies, and videos. In very early times, some people recorded their history by making paintings in caves or on rocks (called "pictographs"). In later times, artists painted portraits of important people and events. However, until the invention of the camera, very few images of "ordinary" people and everyday events were made.

Once the camera was invented, pictures (and, later, videos) of family events and celebrations such as graduations and weddings became common.

Written history. Historians use written records from governments and businesses to learn about the big events of life in the past, such as wars and elections. Newspapers can also tell historians about those events and what some people thought about them. These records are usually found in archives and museums. Many important people, such as premiers or prime ministers, put all of their papers and letters in archives.

Historians also read diaries, letters, and cards to learn about the lives of ordinary people. Newspaper ads, receipts, and bills provide helpful information about the everyday items that people bought and what those items cost.

Artifacts. Historians study things that people from the past made and used. These things are called "artifacts." People called "archaeologists" study objects from the past to learn about life in other times.

Places. Historians look for information in places where important events have occurred, including national parks and historic sites. In Manitoba, The Forks and Lower Fort Garry are historic sites.

Provinces and communities also have special sites. Almost every community in Canada has a war memorial listing the people who died in the world wars.

Why Study History

Where did your ancestors come from? Why did certain groups come to Canada? How did people of long ago live? We study Canadian history to find out the answers to these questions and to understand who we are.

Why do we have the laws that we do? Who decided them? Who decided what kind of government we should have? We study Canadian history to find out how and why people of the past decided what laws we would have and how our country would be governed. The more you know about the history of government and law in Canada, the better you will be able to decide what should be changed and what should be kept.

History is not only about the past. By learning history, you will find it easier to understand what is happening today and what might happen in the future. History is *your* story, too.

Questions to ask

Historians try to explain why an event in history happened and what the results of that event were. Historians are like detectives, because they ask questions about each piece of information that they find.

As you read this textbook (and other history books), ask lots of questions about what you are reading. The five most important questions to ask are called the "5Ws": Who? What? When? Where? Why? How? is another important question to ask.

Here are some questions to ask yourself after you have read about an event in history.

Q: How do I know this is what really happened?

A: It is hard to remember all of the details of an event. For example, imagine you and several of your classmates saw two grade 6 students fighting in the playground. The playground monitor might speak to everyone who watched the fight to find out what happened. You would probably all give a different description of what happened. There are several reasons for this.

- You may be a friend of one of the students.
- You might have missed the beginning of the fight.
- You may have missed something because someone taller than you walked in front of you.

Whatever the reason, it is important to remember that everyone has his or her own point of view.

The monitor would also talk to the students who were fighting. Each student would have a different story, since neither would want to be blamed for starting the fight.

Historians need to look at many different descriptions of an event to get all of the information. Historians also use many different sources to ensure that they have all of the details. Historians then try to find out who is telling the story. They have to decide if the storyteller wants them to think a certain way. From all these different bits of information, the historian can start to put together the pieces of the puzzle.

Q: What evidence or proof do I have that this really happened? Was the historian or storyteller there?

A: Ask for proof that something happened in a certain way or at a certain time. Are there any pictures? Are there any artifacts? Did the information come from someone who was actually present at the event? If the person telling the story was there when it happened, that person has important information. He or she will also know much more about the event than someone who writes about it many years later.

When historians look at sources of information they find out if that information is from a "primary source" or a "secondary source." A primary source is something, such as a picture or a letter, that was made by someone who was at the event. A secondary source is any account recorded by someone who was not at the event. Textbooks, such as this one, are secondary sources.

Q: When was this story written?

A: Find out if the story was written when the event occurred or a long time after the event happened. If the story was written a long time after the actual event, certain parts of the story may have been forgotten.

Sometimes historians find new information that changes the way people and events in history are explained. Finding new pieces of evidence in your role as a history detective is one reason that studying history is so much fun.

Getting to Know Your Book

A textbook can be a helpful tool for students. You will save a lot of time if you know what information is in this book and where to find it. Spend a few minutes just turning the pages and looking at the names and places, the pictures and maps.

You will find many illustrations in this book. Many pictures were created by someone who was alive when the event happened. Sometimes it was impossible to find pictures from a particular time. When that happened, a modern artist used historical information to create an illustration especially for this book. Always

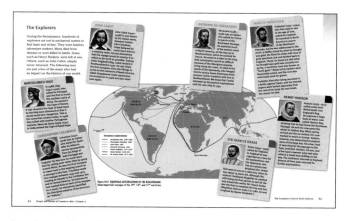

Figure 4.1.? EUROPEAN EXPLORATIONS OF THE RENAISSANCE. Some important voyages of the 15th, 16th, and 17th centuries.

look at the illustrations, because they can give you useful information and help you to remember what you have learned.

You will also find many maps in this book. They show you where the events you are reading about took place. They also show you how the land we now call Canada was divided at different times. Sometimes, they show routes that explorers travelled.

Start at the front of the book

Turn back to the cover of this textbook. What is its title? The title is *People and Stories of Canada to 1867*. What do you think you are going to read about in this book? Now look at the pictures and design on the book cover. Check both the front and the back covers. Have you ever seen pictures of any of these people or places before?

Turn to the title page. Who wrote the textbook? Turn the page over. When and where was the book written? When and where are important questions to ask in social studies. Since this book is about Canada, you will want to know whether it was written in Canada or somewhere else. The date it was published tells you how recent the information is. You may think that a history book does not have to be recent, because all history is old, anyway.

That might be true, but historians, archaeologists, and other scholars are constantly finding new information about history – and sometimes they find out that old information is wrong!

Now turn to the contents page. This page lists 14 chapters in the book and gives you the page number that each chapter starts on. The names of the chapters and of the four parts let you know what you are going to read about. You can tell from the chapter names in this book that you will be reading about topics such as First Peoples, European explorers and settlers, the fur trade, and Confederation.

Go to the back of the book

On the contents page, you will also see the words, *Glossary* and *Index*.

The glossary (p. 232) is a mini-dictionary that explains the meanings of words that you may not know. Words that are in the glossary are in **bold** type the first time they are used. When a word has more than one meaning, you will learn about the meaning used in this book. For example, if you want to find out what an empire is, you can look it up in the glossary.

empire territory ruled by a king or queen

A pronunciation guide (p. 237) will help you pronounce difficult words. The index (p. 238) is an alphabetical list of major topics and names that are mentioned in the textbook and the pages where those topics are explained. If you want to read about Tecumseh, for example, go to the index and look up the word *Tecumseh*. The index gives you the page(s) where you can find the information you are looking for.

Reading Your Book

Reading the part introductions

Every book has a special way of organizing the stories. In this book, the chapters are organized into sections, called parts. At the beginning of each part, you will see a number of pictures. They help you to predict the stories you will read. These pictures are called an "advance organizer." Below the advance organizer is a timeline. A timeline shows you how long ago something took place or when someone was alive. The dates on a timeline are placed in order, from the earliest to most recent.

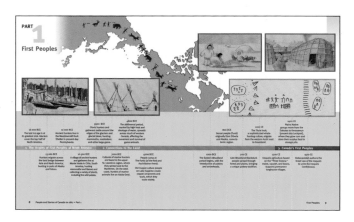

You will find many dates on the timeline and within this book. Sometimes, you will find the term *BCE* beside a date. That means "Before the Common Era," and it signifies the number of years before the year 1. The letters *CE* mean "Common Era," and signify dates from the year 1 onward. Sometimes, no letters appear beside a date. Those dates are from the Common Era (CE), or years after 1. The letter *c.* in front of a date, is short for *circa*, the Latin word for "around."

Reading the chapters

Ben and Sara, two young people who are about your age, introduce you to most chapters. Sara and Ben are very interested in exploring history, here in Manitoba and throughout Canada. You can go with Ben and Sara to museums, on car trips, and even on an archaeological dig.

As you read the chapters, you will find lots of maps, pictures, and coloured boxes. Reading will be easier if you know about the information in the coloured boxes and special sections of the book:

"As you read" information.

This appears in the orange-outlined box at the beginning of each chapter. The information in the box will help you to look for the main ideas in the chapter.

"Did you know?" information.

Light-blue boxes, with the heading "Did you know?" appear in different places in each chapter. They contain interesting and funny facts about people and things in the text.

Gold-coloured information boxes.

These boxes contain important extra information about the main text you are reading. Blue titles tell you what is inside the box. Always check the gold-coloured boxes when you are answering questions or writing paragraphs.

Quotations. These appear in beige-coloured boxes and contain the words that real people said or wrote. When you read them, you will understand what the speakers or writers really thought about the people they met or the events of the time.

Stories. Light-yellow boxes contain historical fiction about pretend people who might have lived in early times. They are based on real information about the events of that time. You can tell that these are make-believe stories by the story icon that appears beside them.

"Imagine" boxes. Light-green boxes contain imaginary interviews, letters, or statements of people who actually lived. A writer has imagined what famous people from history might have said, thought, or written about the times that they lived in. You can tell these are make-believe by the icon that says "Imagine."

The pictures, maps, charts, and diagrams are also helpful when you are reading. Most of them will have titles or captions that tell you what they are about. Remember that the pictures, maps, charts, and diagrams often tell you things that are not in words.

Before you begin reading this book, please read the box at right. Aboriginal peoples are important in Canadian history, so it is important that you know about the correct names for them. The box gives you some information to think about as you read this book.

Names and terms

Aboriginal peoples is the term used to describe the original people of Canada and their descendants. There are three groups of Aboriginal peoples: First Nations, the Métis, and the Inuit.

Canada's Aboriginal peoples are often referred to as *Indians*, but this term is incorrect. Christopher Columbus used it when he mistakenly thought he had landed in India. Today we use other names because First Nations people consider the word *Indian* inaccurate.

In fact, most names used in reports and history texts for various First Nations are not the names that the people used themselves. There are many reasons why this is so. Explorers and early fur traders did not know First Nations' languages well enough and misunderstood the words. Often, they copied down the translators' words incorrectly. In some cases, an unfriendly neighbouring group told the Europeans the wrong name on purpose. Sometimes, Europeans made up their own names for groups. For centuries, the European version of their names has appeared in reports and on maps.

Aboriginal peoples have always had their own names for themselves. The term used by many Aboriginal groups means "the people" or some similar term. The word *Eskimo*, for example, is no longer used. It has been replaced by *Inuit* (meaning "several people") or *Inuk* (meaning "one person"). The members of the five Iroquois nations that made up the famous League of the Iroquois refer to themselves as the *Haudenosaunee* (meaning "the people of the longhouse"). The name *Huron* is from an old French word meaning "boar's head" and refers to the Huron's bristly hairstyles. The Huron refer to themselves as *Wendat* (meaning "Islanders" or "Dwellers on a Peninsula"). The Cree call themselves *Nehiyawak*. Since European names have been so widely used but are gradually being replaced by Aboriginal names, you will find a mixture of terms in this book.

Enjoy reading this book, and remember that the stories here are your stories – about your country.

PART 1
First Peoples

9500 BCE
Clovis hunters and gatherers settle around the edges of the glaciers and glacial lakes, hunting mammoths, mastodons, and other large game.

4800 BCE
The altithermal period, marked by high heat and shortage of water, spreads across much of western Canada, affecting the movement and survival of game animals.

16 000 BCE
The last ice age is at its greatest size. Glaciers cover the top half of North America.

12 000 BCE
Ancient hunters live in the Meadowcroft Rock Shelter in present-day Pennsylvania.

1. The Origins of First Peoples of North America

2. Connections to the Land

13 000 BCE
Hunters migrate across the land bridge between Asia and North America, hunting in parts of Alaska and Yukon.

10 500 BCE
A village of ancient hunters and gatherers live at Monte Verde in Chile, South America, hunting mammoths and llamas and collecting a variety of plants, including the wild potato.

7000 BCE
Cultures of marine hunters are found in the upper St. Lawrence region, where they spread east to the Maritimes. On the west coast, hunters of marine animals live on Haida Gwai.

4000 BCE
People camp at The Forks (of the Red and Assiniboine rivers).

Old Copper culture people on Lake Superior create copper ornaments and tools, which they trade widely.

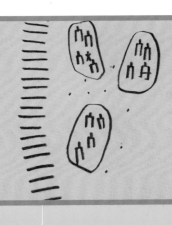

800 BCE
Dorset people (Tunit) originally from Siberia and Alaska, come to Arctic region.

1000 CE
The Thule Inuit, a sophisticated whale-hunting culture, migrate from the western Arctic east to Greenland.

1400 CE
Plains Native groups move from the Dakotas to Kenosewun (present-day Lockport), where they grow maize and store their surplus food in storage pits.

3. Canada's First Peoples

1000 BCE
The Eastern Woodland period begins, with the introduction of pottery and arrowheads.

700 CE
Late Woodland Blackduck people spread through forest and plains, bringing a unique pottery tradition.

1300 CE
Iroquois agriculture based on the "Three Sisters," maize, squash, and beans, supports permanent longhouse villages.

1500 CE
Dekanawidah authors the Great Law of the Iroquois to unite the Iroquois Confederacy.

1 The Origins of First Peoples of North America

Sara and Ben ran up the steps into the museum. In his hand, Ben clutched a strange-shaped stone. That summer, the children's family had been camping near a beach. While gathering stones for her rock collection, Sara had come across the stone with its pointed end. "This doesn't look like just any stone," said her mother. "It looks like something made by people a very long time ago. But we'd have to talk to an expert who knows about those things to find out."

Figure 1.1

Now they were at the museum to see someone who could tell them more. Dr. Leduc, the **archaeologist** at the museum, turned the piece of rock in his hand. "You have found a very old tool called a **projectile point**. Some people call these tools spear points." He walked over to a wall map of Manitoba. "The place where you found this was once the beach of an ancient lake. It was a hunting and camping ground for some of the very first people in this country." Now this odd little rock was becoming more interesting. Dr. Leduc continued, "This tool was used by people to hunt animals a very long time ago. It could be 10 000 years old."

"Ten thousand years!" exclaimed Sara. "That's old!" She felt very proud. But she was puzzled, too. Where did these first people come from? Who were they? How did they live? In this chapter, you will find some answers to Sara's questions.

As you read, think about

- the different ways we can learn about the past
- what our country was like during and just after the last ice age
- how the First Peoples came to the country we now call Canada
- how the First Peoples lived during the last ice age
- how oral tradition tells us about the first peoples' past, beliefs, and values

Learning about the past

People have lived in the land that we now call Canada for at least 11 500 years. To learn about people from very long ago, researchers put together clues from many different sources.

One way to learn about the past is to look at things people left behind. These items are called **artifacts**. They include hunting tools, weapons, and pottery. Artifacts are studied by archaeologists. In chapter 2, you will look at some of the information scientists can get from artifacts.

Another way to learn is by studying languages. Scientists who study languages are called **linguists**. Linguists believe that, a long time ago, there were fewer languages than there are today. When groups of people began to move to different places, each group started to speak a new language. Of course, it took many, many years for a completely new language to develop. Linguists compare different languages to see which words are similar and which words are different. This can tell them where groups of people came from and which other groups they are related to.

A single word in five languages: What do you notice about this word?				
Cree	Anishinabe	Piikani	English	French
ministik	minis	mini	island	île

We can also learn about the past by looking at the land and studying the animals and plants that lived there. For example, special tests can be done on animal bones and plant seeds to find out how old they are.

Another way to find out about the past is through stories. The early people of Canada did not have written languages. Therefore, they could not use writing to pass down their knowledge and wisdom. Each **generation** learned about the past by listening to those who knew the details of each story. This way of passing on information, from fathers to sons, mothers to daughters, is known as **oral tradition**. Many of the stories are still told today. Oral tradition gives us clues to the way people lived long ago and what their beliefs were. From oral traditions, we can find out what the first peoples themselves thought about the land on which they lived.

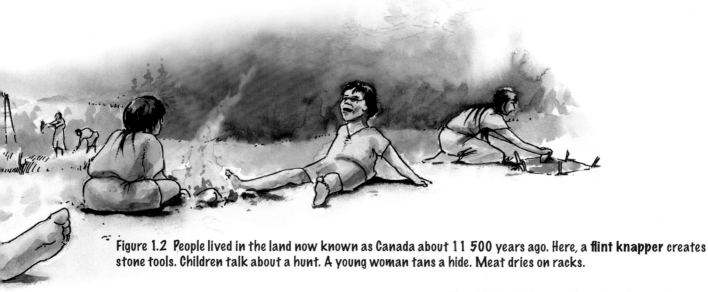

Figure 1.2 People lived in the land now known as Canada about 11 500 years ago. Here, a **flint knapper** creates stone tools. Children talk about a hunt. A young woman tans a hide. Meat dries on racks.

The Last Ice Age

Can you imagine a land where the snow never melts? Where the thermometer hovers at 11 degrees below zero? Manitoba was once like that, day after day and year after year.

The climate of the earth changes over long periods of time. During some periods, the earth is very warm. In other periods, it is very cold. The cold periods are called **ice ages**. The last ice age began more than 25 000 years ago. It reached its peak about 18 000 years ago.

During ice ages, giant **glaciers**, sometimes called "ice sheets" or "continental glaciers," form and cover large areas of low-lying land.

Figure 1.4 This large boulder in northeastern Manitoba was carried south by an ice sheet and deposited far away from its source. You can see the size of this boulder from the person standing beside it.

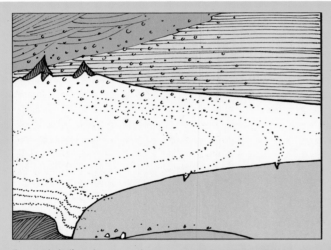

Figure 1.3 The glacier builds up.

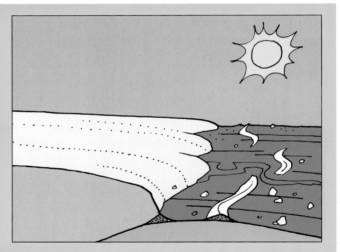

The glacier melts, and **retreats**.

A glacier is formed when, year after year, the weather does not get warm enough in the spring to melt the snow that falls in the winter. The snow piles up, and its weight causes the buried snow to form into huge masses of ice. Imagine how thick some of those sheets of ice were after thousands of years.

Glaciers do not stay in one place, however. Gravity and a glacier's own weight cause it to move. While valley glaciers move down between mountains, continental glaciers spread out in all directions.

As glaciers move, they carry piles of ground-up rocks and debris, known as **till**, with them. This till may be left at the side of a glacier as it moves. It can also be pushed ahead of the glacier or carried beneath it. When this happens, the hard rock acts like a giant piece of sandpaper, carving away the land below the glacier.

Glaciers can also shape the earth because of their immense weight. Glaciers can even cause the earth below them to sink.

As the glaciers from the last ice age melted, the earth below was much different from what it had been before the glaciers. Where the land had been scraped, large rock faces were exposed. In some places, till that had frozen in the ice was dropped on the ground. Some deposits were as huge as boulders, some as tiny as grains of sand, others mixtures of many sizes of particles.

Water became a powerful force in shaping the land. Water from the melting glaciers started flowing, slowly at first, and then in giant torrents. Water that flowed under the glacier carried till with it. This caused the rock below to erode and form great valleys.

In the mountains, valley glaciers spread and often meet each other to cover an area. During the last ice age, the Rocky Mountain region of Canada was covered with valley glaciers. Most of Canada, though, and parts of the northern United States were covered by a continental glacier. In some places, the ice was more than three kilometres thick. Not much can live in such cold conditions, but some plants and animals survived outside the icy areas.

The glaciers began to melt about 16 000 years ago, as the earth entered a warmer period. The glaciers, and the lakes and rivers that flowed from them, carried rich soil. This soil was left behind in some areas, as the water drained into rivers and oceans. Soon airborne seeds landed in the soil and began to sprout, and plants began to grow.

Figure 1.6 These sand dunes, located about 160 kilometres southwest of Winnipeg, were once covered by Lake Agassiz. Known as the Spirit Sands, and located in present-day Spruce Woods Provincial Park, the desertlike area is home to unique reptiles and cacti.

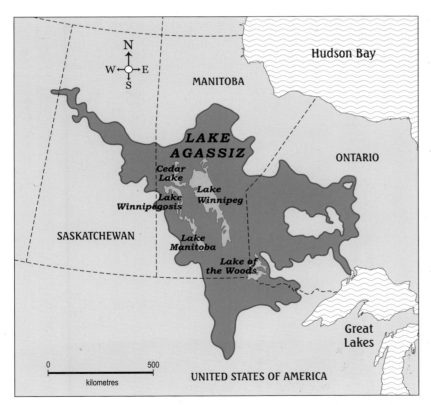

Figure 1.5 LAKE AGASSIZ. Lake Agassiz was a giant lake in the centre of North America. It formed about 12 000 years ago from melting glaciers. It took many forms over the centuries. It drained through the Red River, then east through the Winnipeg River, then northwest through the Mackenzie River. Finally, about 7500 hundred years ago, most of it drained into Hudson Bay. The map above shows the total area of Lake Agassiz over its history.

DID YOU KNOW?

When ice sheets covered Canada, they pressed the land's surface down, just like what happens when a person lies on a foam mattress. When the ice melted, the land started to **rebound,** or bounce back. Every year, the land in the north rises approximately one centimetre. Scientists say that in 10 000 years or so, the land will have risen about 400 metres, the same level as it was before the glaciers.

Animals of the Ice Age

Unusual animals roamed the North American continent for millions of years. Many lived in Canada between ice ages. The animals then moved south as the glaciers covered parts of the earth. When the glaciers retreated, the animals returned, and the people who hunted them followed. But soon after the end of the last ice age, almost half of the large animals in North America, including all the animals in this picture, were extinct. Scientists do not know why this happened, but they have some **theories**.

At the end of the ice age, temperatures became warmer, less rain fell, giant lakes became smaller, and sea levels rose. One theory is that the climate changed so quickly, animals could not **adapt** to the new **environment**. Perhaps some animals could no longer find the kinds of plants or animals they were used to eating. Maybe the warmer weather disrupted the animals' birthing schedules. Perhaps they were destroyed by disease.

Other scientists think that humans hunted certain animals, such as the mammoth, to extinction. Once such an important species was killed off, other species also became extinct. According to this theory, some animals could survive the ice age, but could not escape the destructive ways of humans.

Perhaps it was a combination of all of these factors that caused the extinction of so many animals. With animal species weakened by climate change, hunting finished them off. Whatever the reason, we can see that climate, plants, animals, and humans can all affect one another.

American mastodon

Woolly mammoth

Giant bison

Figure 1.7 All of these animals are now extinct.

Dinosaurs lived and died long before people existed. Dinosaurs first appeared about 250 million years ago. They mysteriously disappeared 65 million years ago.

Most scientists believe that our human species – known as **Homo sapiens sapiens** – originated in Africa, Asia, and Europe about 55 000 years ago and then slowly migrated around the world.

So, while early humans had to share the earth with giant mammals, the giant reptiles known as dinosaurs were long gone.

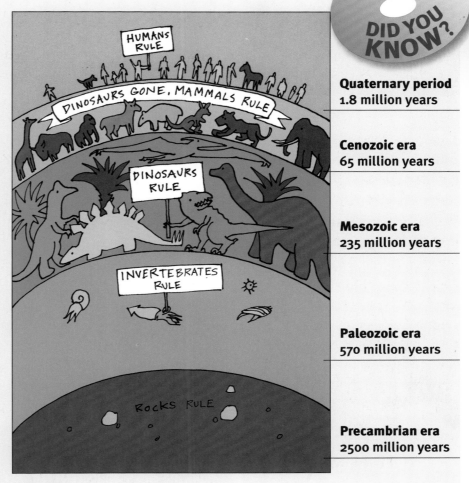

Figure 1.8

DID YOU KNOW?

Quaternary period
1.8 million years

Cenozoic era
65 million years

Mesozoic era
235 million years

Paleozoic era
570 million years

Precambrian era
2500 million years

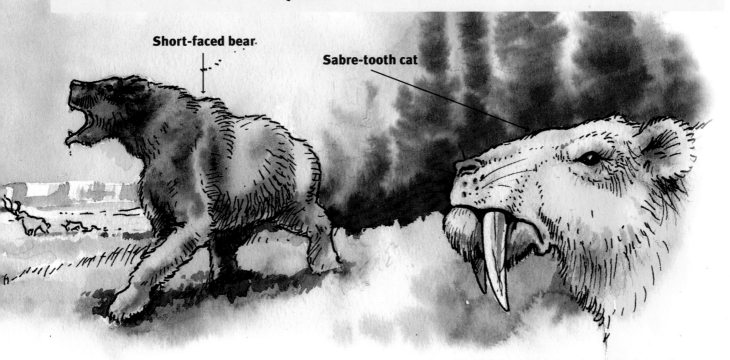

Short-faced bear.

Sabre-tooth cat

Food for Winter

Yesterday, I was gathering seeds and berries in the forest when I heard a scary noise – a weird slurping sound coming from a nearby creek. I was so curious to see what it was, that I left my bundle and crept down to the water's edge. There, through a thicket of grass, I could see a huge woolly mammoth, sucking water through its massive trunk. It must have wandered away from its herd. This mammoth was the biggest, fattest one I'd ever seen! It was more than four metres tall with huge, three-metre tusks and long, reddish hair. I once heard my uncle say that a mammoth can sniff out the scent of humans from far away, except, of course, when its got its nose in a watering hole. Lucky for me!

Quickly, I ran and told my mother what I found. We went straight back to camp to tell the hunters. They would have to move fast. My father had been sharpening his fluted spear collection all morning, and his flint spear points were sharper than the jaws of sabre-tooth cats. He stood and turned to my older brothers, "Your sister has found all of us enough food for the whole winter!" And off they went into the woods.

We didn't hear from them again until nightfall. Finally, one of my brothers emerged from the woods, looking very proud of himself. As we moved our camp to the mammoth carcass, he told me the story.

Figure 1.9

"First we surrounded the mammoth, scorching the grass along the water's edge with fire and smoke. This trapped the beast. Then we skewered it with all 16 of our spears. The mammoth thrashed and raged and nearly killed Father with its trunk. But this beast was so fat that our spears had only managed to wound it. So it galloped off into the woods, knocking over whole trees with its tusks. We followed its tracks for a long time and found it bleeding to death in a clearing. What a fine feast we'll have ourselves tonight!"

When we arrived at the clearing, the hunters had already cut the mammoth's hind quarters into huge slabs of meat. I helped Mother build a firepit, and we began roasting the nicest, fattest strips for the feast to celebrate our great hunt. Mmmm, juicy mammoth steaks.

But today it's back to work. My father and uncles are building a new house out of the mammoth's rib cage with leg bones as doors. Mother is making a roof for the house out of the mammoth hide. I spent the whole day piling strips of meat onto the drying racks. Our whole **clan** is happy. We'll have enough mammoth to eat until spring.

Discovery

Archaeologists discovered these ancient mammoth tracks in a place called Wally's Beach in southern Alberta. The tracks have helped archaeologists learn about mammoth families and how they got their food.

Many other kinds of animal tracks have also been found in the area, including those from horses, camels, bison, caribou, and musk oxen. All of the tracks are from animal species that came from the south. Scientists have also found tools from early hunters. Researchers think that the animals and the people who followed them came from the south before the ice-free corridor opened (see p. 18).

Figure 1.10 Mammoth tracks at Wally's Beach

The First Peoples in North America

Researchers believe that the first peoples in North America came from Asia. What they do not agree on is how these people travelled here and when they arrived. Researchers have found artifacts in ancient villages that date to 12 000 years ago in Monte Verde, Chile, in South America, and 13 000 to 14 000 years ago in Pennsylvania, in the United States.

For many years, scientists believed that groups of people travelled to North America across a piece of land in the far north that connected Asia and North America. These people were following animal herds that were migrating in search of food. This **land bridge**, known as **Beringia**, was above water. That is because during the last ice age, so much of the world's water supply was frozen in glaciers. This made the sea much lower than it is today.

When the glaciers began to melt, and as the land warmed, many of these people moved inland along an ice-free corridor in Alberta. They travelled south or east, following the animals that they depended on.

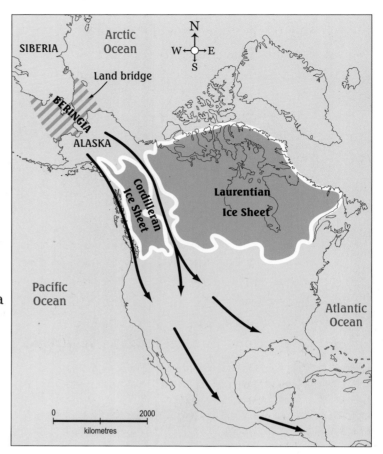

Figure 1.11 POSSIBLE LAND ROUTES OF THE FIRST PEOPLES INTO NORTH AND CENTRAL AMERICA. Different researchers, such as archaeologists, linguists, anthropologists, geologists, and geneticists shared their findings to develop theories about migration into the Americas.

Many scientists now believe that some of the first people to arrive in North America may have used a different route. This happened long before the end of the last ice age, when glaciers still covered most of North America. The ancient hunters travelled down ice-free areas of the west coast of North America to reach land south of the glaciers. With the oceans lower than they are today, people were able to travel across land that is now covered by water. Many of their descendants came north again in search of mammoth (see "Discovery," p. 17) and other large animals. Some scientists also believe that early

> **DID YOU KNOW?**
> Traffic over the Bering land bridge moved both north and south. Some animals, such as camels, originated in North America and, over time, migrated via the land bridge to Asia. Archaeological evidence has also revealed a northward migration of bison, followed by ancient hunters, along the ice-free corridor of Beringia.

people may have come across the Pacific Ocean by boat. This theory is difficult to prove, however, as any evidence for it would be under deep ocean waters.

When the glaciers began to melt and the land warmed, many animals moved north. The people who hunted these animals for food followed them. They arrived in the southern part of Canada about 11 500 years ago. We do not know what language these people spoke or what tribe they belonged to. They are called the "Clovis" people, because evidence of their way of life was first discovered at a now-famous archaeological site near Clovis, New Mexico.

Figure 1.12 This hunting tool, known as a Clovis point, was found in western Manitoba. It is 7.9 centimetres long and is believed to have been used by hunters about 11 000 years ago. Attached to a shaft, this point could pierce the thick hide of a mammoth or mastodon.

Oral Tradition

You have learned how archaeologists and scientists develop theories to learn about the past. Another way to learn about the past is through oral tradition – stories that have been passed down by word of mouth from generation to generation. Among Aboriginal peoples, many stories are told by **Elders** to teach the young about how to live in a community. Many Aboriginal peoples use these stories to explain where they came from. Many Aboriginal peoples believe that their ancestors always lived in North America, and did not travel there from other lands.

There are different kinds of stories. Some are not necessarily based on real things that happened. Sometimes mysterious things occur. Other stories do record events that happened, like battles or meetings with other groups. Some stories mix up the real and fanciful. For example, the Haida people of coastal British Columbia tell about a time when the islands they live on were larger and surrounded by grassy plains. When a supernatural spirit caused the oceans to rise, the people had to move to higher ground. Geologists back up this story. They say that 11 000 years ago the islands were almost twice the size that they are today. When the ice that covered much of North America melted, the oceans rose and covered much of the land.

These stories can tell us about people's **values** and beliefs. They tell us about people's relationships to the creatures they lived with and to the land they lived on. They tell us about the things that were important to people.

Origin stories

Every **culture** in the world has tried to explain how the land was created and how their people came to exist. In Canada, the Mi'kmaq of the east coast provinces tell the story of Glooscap, who came from the sky and created the land, its creatures, and its people. The Iroquois of the Eastern Woodlands tell of a set of twins who created the world on the back of a giant turtle. Among the Inuit of the north is the story of the sea spirit Sedna, whose fingers became the creatures of the sea. Giant, dressed as a Raven, brought daylight through a hole in the sky to the Tsimshian people of the West Coast.

As you read the two origin stories on the next page, think about what you have learned about the early people.

Where the First People Came From

A Cree legend

The other land was above. It was like this land we live in, except that it was cold there. From this land above there came two people, one woman and one man.

Someone said to them, "Do you want to go see yonder land which is below?"

"Yes," they said, "we will go there."

"The land," someone told them, "is different from this one where we dwell. It is cold yonder. And sometimes it is hot. If you wish to go there, however, you must first see the spider at the end of this land."

So they went to see the spider.

He asked them, "Do you want to go and see yonder land, the one which is below?"

"Yes," they said.

"Very well," said the spider. "I shall make a line so that I may lower you."

Then he told them, "There will be someone there who will teach you how to live once you have reached it. He will tell you everything, so you will get along well."

Then he instructed them on what to do during their trip. "Only one must look," he said to them, "until you have made contact with the earth. You may both look then." They were told that if they both looked together, before they came to the land, they would go into the great eagle's nest and would never be able to climb down.

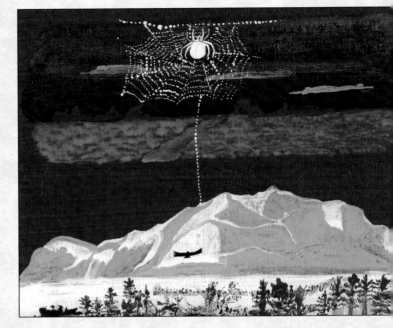

Figure 1.14

As they went along, one looked and the other did not. At last one told the other, "Now the land is in sight. Now the rivers are in sight."

Then one told the other, "Now the lakes are in sight. Now the grass."

Then they both looked before they arrived, as they were right at the top of the trees. They went into the great eagle's nest, having ignored their instructions.

Then the bear arrived at the bottom of the tree. They said to him, "Come and help us."

The bear got up on his hind legs to see them. Then the wolverine came. Together the bear and the wolverine brought the man and woman down.

The bear taught them everything about how to keep alive on the earth.

The people began to multiply from one couple, the persons who had come from another land. They lived giving birth to their children generation after generation. That is us right up until today. That is why we are in this country.

Figure 1.13

Turtle Island

An Anishinabe legend

A long time ago, Kitchi-Manitou put the people on Earth. At first everyone got along. After many years, however, people strayed from their peaceful ways. They began to argue and disagree with their families and friends. Soon, there was no respect for any living thing. Kitchi-Manitou decided to cleanse Earth. He did this with water.

The water came and destroyed all the people except Nanabozho. Some animals that could fly or swim also survived. Nanabozho stayed afloat on a huge log, and he allowed the animals that had survived to take turns resting on the log with him. Nanabozho and the animals looked for land, but they could not find any.

Nanabozho told the animals that he was going to dive into the water, try to reach bottom, and bring up some earth. He said that with the help of Four Winds and Kitchi-Manitou, he would be able to create new land for them all to live on. He dived into the water and was gone for a very long time. When he came up for air, he said the water was too deep for him to reach bottom.

Loon then said he would try. Loon was gone for a long, long time. When he returned, he said that he, too, was unable to reach bottom.

One animal after another tried to reach the bottom and return with some earth. However, all failed, because the water was too deep. Then Wa-zhushk, a little muskrat, said he would try. All the other animals laughed – if they couldn't reach the bottom, surely a little muskrat would not be able to. Nanabozho said if Muskrat wanted to try, he could.

Muskrat took a deep breath and dove into the water. As time went by and he did not come up to the surface, all the animals began to worry that Muskrat had drowned. Then Muskrat floated to the surface. The animals pulled him onto the log. He was no longer breathing. As Nanabozho and the animals began to mourn, one of the animals noticed a ball of soil in one of Muskrat's paws. Muskrat had sacrificed his life so that new life on Earth could begin.

As Nanabozho removed the soil, Turtle offered his back on which to place the soil. When the soil was set on Turtle's back, the winds began to blow, and the tiny ball of soil began to grow. It grew and grew until there was a huge island in the middle of the water. And that is how Turtle Island formed the continent of North America – and the birth place of the Anishinabe.

Figure 1.15

Conclusion

In this chapter, you have learned what the land we live in was like many thousands of years ago. In the next chapter, you will see how ancient people adapted to the land they lived on.

2

Connections to the Land

Sara was very excited. Today was her first day at archaeology camp. Dr. Leduc had told her about it, and she convinced her parents to let her spend a week at the camp's site on the banks of the Red River. Now here she was, with her own toolkit: a trowel, toothbrush, whisk broom, paintbrush, and dental pick, dustpan, and pail. These would help her carefully dig and clean any artifacts she found.

Figure 2.1 Early cultures found food and materials for clothes, tools, and shelter from the land they lived on. This Mi'kmaq wigwam was made from birchbark from the mixed Appalachian forests.

Sara listened as Jamie, the site archaeologist, spoke. "If you were alive 3000 years ago, how would you carry water to your camp from a nearby stream or river? Remember – no one had pails, buckets, bottles, or thermoses back then. What would you use? Where would you find things to use?

"What could you make as a water vessel if you lived in a place where lots of birch trees grew? Near a forest of moss-covered trees? In the north, where there were no trees? What if you lived in the prairies where there were mostly grasslands, or near a riverbank layered with clay? What if you lived in a rocky part of the country, with veins of ore in the ground?

"If I lived in a forest, I could make a container from the tree bark," suggested the girl standing next to Sara.

"Yes," smiled Jamie. "But how would you make the container? You would need some kind of glue or a needle and thread. What would you use? Where would you get these things?"

As you read this chapter, think about how creative and skilled Canada's First Peoples were. They had only the land and what was on it to make the items that you will see on these pages.

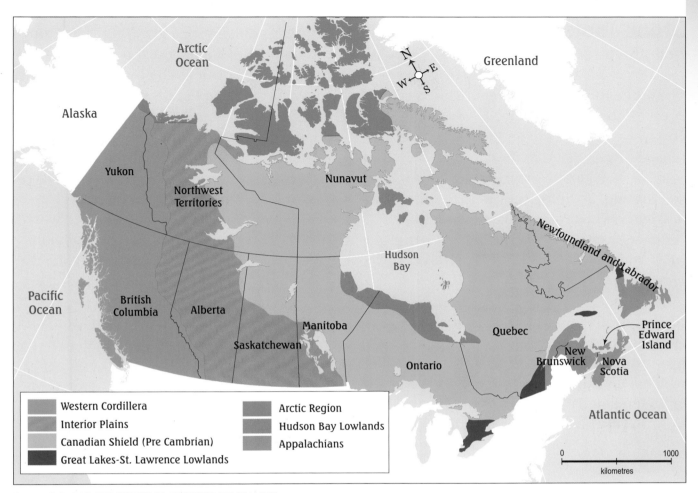

Figure 2.2 MAJOR PHYSICAL REGIONS OF CANADA

Legend:
- Western Cordillera
- Interior Plains
- Canadian Shield (Pre Cambrian)
- Great Lakes-St. Lawrence Lowlands
- Arctic Region
- Hudson Bay Lowlands
- Appalachians

Landforms and vegetation

Western Cordillera: parallel mountain ranges that run southeast to northwest; coniferous trees, Douglas fir, and cedar

Interior Plains: mostly flat or gently rolling area; boreal forests and grasslands in the south, low bushes, mosses, and lichens in the north

Canadian Shield (also called Precambrian Shield): steep and rolling hills of some of the oldest rocks in the world and lots of valuable minerals; boreal forests in the south and tundra in the north

Great Lakes-St. Lawrence Lowlands: rolling hills; mixed forests with oak and maple, fruit trees and grapevines

Arctic Region: mountainous islands with some lowlands; tundra

Hudson Bay Lowlands: poorly drained lowlands (largest wetland in the world); tundra

Appalachians: old, worn-down mountains; mixed forest but mostly coniferous trees and fruit trees in Nova Scotia and P.E.I.

As you read, think about

- how the object was made
- what the object was used for
- what material the object is made from
- what the object tells you about the physical environment it comes from
- what the object tells you about the people who made it

Stone Tools
from the Interior Plains

The stone tools (below) were made by First Peoples about 9000 to 10 000 years ago. Today, we refer to the people who made these tools as Paleo hunters (*paleo* means "old" or "ancient"). Since Paleo hunters lived so long ago, anything they made from wood and leather has rotted and disintegrated. Archaeologists have had to study their stone tools and the animal bones that they threw out to learn about them.

Paleo hunters lived on the plains of western Canada. They hunted types of bison, such as *Bison antiquus*, that are now extinct. Although we do not know which tribes these people belonged to or which languages they spoke, we know they usually hunted in small groups.

Spear points were a very important tool for hunting the animals that people needed for food and clothing. The points were made from many different kinds of stone. Some stone, such as chert and quartz, could be found locally. Knife River flint was mined from pits in western North Dakota.

Paleo hunters also made scrapers for working bison hides and removing tree bark. As well, flat, oval-shaped knives were used to cut materials and butcher animals. Paleo hunters made awls and drills to make holes for sewing clothing and probably for making bark containers. They made a tool called a "spokeshave" to scrape off the bark and smooth the shafts of their dart and knife handles.

Figure 2.3 Paleo hunters made stone spear and dart points (above, left, top 2 artifacts) that they attached to wooden shafts to hunt animals. They used knives to butcher meat and stone scrapers (above, left, bottom artifact) to prepare skins.

Making stone tools

First Peoples used stone to make tools, because stone was hard and **durable**. Paleo hunters were excellent flint knappers who took great pride in their skills.

Boys learned flint knapping from their fathers, uncles, and grandfathers. They spent hundreds of hours learning the basic skills (for example, identifying which stones made the best tools and how to make the various tools). They also spent thousands of hours learning to make tools well.

Figure 2.4 First, the flint knapper needed a chunk of stone to work with. In this illustration, the flint knapper is using a stone hammer to strike large stone pieces off a rock. He would select one of the stone pieces (called flakes) to make the tool.

Figure 2.5 Second, the flint knapper used a tool called the "antler billet" to shape the flake. In this instance, the flint knapper is using the billet to shape the tool into a projectile point.

Figure 2.6 Finally, when the flint knapper had the shape he wanted, he used a tool called the "antler-tine pressure flaker" to make a sharp cutting edge. Here, the flint knapper is taking off very small flakes to sharpen the edges of the point.

Copper Tools
from Lake Superior

About 5000 BCE, hunters from the forests around Lake Superior in the Canadian Shield discovered a material that became soft when it was placed near a hot cooking fire. The way this material responded to heat was quite different from the rocks the hunters used to make tools. Whenever a rock was placed near a fire, it split into many pieces. This new substance (that we now know was copper) remained in one piece. It was also easier than rock to reshape.

The discovery of copper was important. First Peoples learned that heated copper could be used for many different things. It could be hammered into practical tools or decorative jewellery. During the next 4000 years, people dug thousands of pits into the earth to mine copper.

Aboriginal peoples also made copper items for trade. Tools and other items made from Lake Superior copper have been found as far northwest as Thompson, Manitoba, in the northern woodlands, and as far west as southern Alberta. Many First Peoples nations traded for items or materials they did not have. Archaeologists can use the materials that objects are made from to retrace many of the ancient trade routes.

Figure 2.7 Ancient hunters mined copper around Lake Superior and in the Arctic. From these, they made many different items, including dart points, knives, chisels, fish spears, armbands, and pendants. Until the discovery of copper, Aboriginal peoples made most of their tools and other items from stone, antler, bone, wood, and tree bark.

Hunting Tools and Ceremonial Structures
from the Interior Plains

Between about 3000 BCE and 1000 BCE, small **bands** of people lived in camps across the prairies and plains. Archaeologists refer to this period of time in western Canada as the Oxbow culture. Unlike the earlier Paleo people, these hunters hunted small herds of modern bison. They also hunted small numbers of elk, moose, fox, rabbits, and martens.

These early people made a variety of stone tools such as knives, scraping tools,

Majorville Cairn and Medicine Wheel

A medicine wheel is a round, human-made stone structure. More than 40 of them have been found in Alberta. These mysterious structures are thought to represent the traditional spiritual beliefs of First Nations peoples. According to these beliefs, all life is connected and goes in a circle. A medicine wheel, then, was a place to hold certain kinds of ceremonies. Some people think the wheel also marked astronomical events, such as the sunrise at summer solstice.

In 1971, archaeologists began excavation at the Majorville Cairn and Medicine Wheel site on the banks of the Bow River in Alberta. The wheel of stones is 27 metres in diameter. In the centre is a large **cairn** (see figure 2.8), 9 metres around and 2 metres high. The cairn is connected to the circle by 28 spokes. Figure 2.9, at right, shows what the medicine wheel would look like if viewed from above.

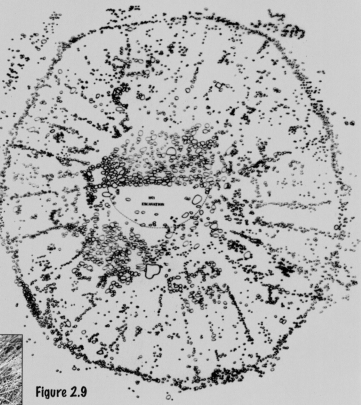

Figure 2.9

Figure 2.8

Archaeologists found thousands of artifacts in the cairn – including several styles of spear and arrow points, stone scrapers, **amulets**, fossil **iniskims** (buffalo stones), and charred bones. From these artifacts, scientists determined that different groups of people had been visiting the site for about 5000 years. The site was first used by people from the Oxbow culture.

awls, and hammerstones. They usually used stone from local sources. Ornaments included **gorgets** made from clam shells and bone beads. A few items of copper, such as beads, were traded from the Great Lakes, and some beads were made from shells from the Atlantic coast.

Figure 2.10

Atlatl and dart – Helpful hunting tools

Oxbow hunters, like hunters before and after them, used the **atlatl** to propel an arrow-shaped dart. The atlatl was a short, flexible carved stick (about 60 centimetres long) with leather finger loops on one end and a hook on the other end. The dart was about 2 metres long. It had feathers on one end and a short, removable foreshaft with the dart point on the other end.

To throw the dart, the hunter aimed it at the animal and forcefully swung his arm over his shoulder. Throwing with an atlatl provided 15 times more power and distance than just throwing the dart by hand. The term *atlatl* comes from the Aztecs of Mexico.

Figure 2.11 These Oxbow period stone points are called "dart points." A dart point was attached to a long, slender shaft, which was thrown with a dart thrower, or atlatl.

Caribou Hunting Tools
of the Subarctic

In the Subarctic region of the Canadian Shield, large caribou herds roamed the barren grounds in summer and migrated to the forested areas in the winter. Since caribou are migratory animals, the people who depended on them for their survival moved about to meet them along their migration routes. People who lived in the Subarctic made use of every part of the caribou, including their meat, bones, blood, and sinews.

Figure 2.12 The stone points at left were used to kill caribou. The stone knife (right) was used for butchering caribou and other animals and cutting hides. It could also be used for whittling wood into tools and toys. The people who made these tools lived in the Subarctic about 2600 years ago. They are known as the Taltheilei culture. They were probably the ancestors of the Dene who lived in the area during the fur-trade era.

Figure 2.13 These people made tools including stone adzes. The adze was used for woodworking, making things such as splints for snowshoes, spear handles, and bows and arrows.

Animal Carvings
from the Arctic

A group of people lived in the Arctic from about 800 BCE to 1000 CE. The Inuit refer to them in their legends as the Tunit, very strong, peaceful people who were driven away and eventually died out. Archaeologists call them the Dorset culture.

The Dorset believed animals had spiritual powers and souls that could be appealed to, to provide help. They viewed animals as equals.

Figure 2.14 People of the Dorset culture are famous for their miniature carvings. This carving of a polar bear head is made from a polar bear tooth. The carving is only a few centimetres in size, not much bigger than the top joint of your thumb. Many Dorset carvings represented only part of an animal.

Most of their carvings are found on small amulets, although the Tunit did carve some small and full-sized masks. Human faces, bears, seals, and birds were common themes.

To the Dorset, the carvings were miniature representations of the spiritual world. The ***angakok*** and people in the community used them in spiritual rituals.

Some tools, such as stone chisels made from jade, were also very small. Jade and other materials were traded widely. The style of the tools and sacred amulets are so similar across the Arctic that there must have been extensive travel, trade, and exchange of ideas.

The Dorset did not appear to have dog sleds, kayaks, or bows and arrows. They did not have floating harpoons to hunt sea life. Yet, with their simple tools, they found ways to live in the Arctic. They followed the migratory routes of the caribou. They built stone **weirs** across the rivers to trap the Arctic char. They hunted caribou and musk oxen with harpoons. They speared walruses, seals, and some small whales such as the beluga and narwhal. They developed ice crampons, or creepers, to attach to the bottom of their mukluks to walk on the slippery ice. They had small sleds that they pulled themselves.

Figure 2.15 Some carvings are so small that many people today need a magnifying glass to see the precise detail in each piece. Like the polar bear head, this carving of a puffin is only a couple of centimetres long.

Figure 2.16 Dorset people made harpoon points from ivory or bone to hunt sea animals. The barbs on each side kept the harpoon from sliding out.

Ceremonial Carvings
from the Coast of the Western Cordillera

On the coast of present-day British Columbia, from about 500 BCE to 500 CE, people lived in large plank houses in permanent villages. Some of them used pointed tools made from bone and stone to hunt deer, bear, and elk. They made harpoons and fish spears to catch salmon, halibut, cod, herring, and dogfish in the nearby waters.

These people were the **ancestors** of the Salish people. Archaeologists call them the Marpole culture. They used many different kinds of stone to make engravings and sculptures. They carved birds, sea monsters, human faces and forms, supernatural beings, bears, and lizards. They made earrings and beads of dentalium shell (small tube-shaped shells) and slate. They carved stone bowls in human shapes that they used for special ceremonies.

These people carved so many objects that archaeologists believe they had specialists who made items for the chiefs and other wealthy members of their nation. If true, it means that they lived in a society that had different social classes.

Figure 2.17 Archaeologists think that this carved human-figure bowl was used for special ceremonies, such as coming of age, birth, marriage, and funerals.

Woodlands Pottery
of the Southern Canadian Shield

About 2800 years ago, First Peoples in Canada learned to make ceramic pots from clay that they dug from riverbanks.

Pottery was an important achievement. With the pots, people began to practise a new kind of cooking. For example, they could now make stews and soups. Before there was pottery, people cooked food such as meat on sticks over campfires or they heated food over hot ash pits. Ceramic

Figure 2.18 Archaeologists have learned about people from the pottery that was made long ago.

pots also made it easier to store food and to carry water and other liquids long distances, because the containers were leakproof. Women were the ones who made the pottery, and they took great pride in what they produced.

Laurel-style pottery

The first pottery made in Manitoba was of a style archaelogists call "Laurel." It was used from about 1 CE to 800 CE. Laurel pottery was cone shaped with small, round indents around the upper part of the vessel. These pots were made by starting with the mouth of the vessel and working to the pointed bottom.

Figure 2.19 Most pottery is found in small pieces called "sherds." If enough sherds from the same original pot are located, archaeologists can put the pot (or parts of the pot) together again. Putting a pot back together is much like working on a jigsaw puzzle. This Laurel pot was found in several small pieces that archaeologists glued back together.

Making a Laurel pot

Figure 2.20 Laurel pots were made by rolling the clay into coils and piling the coils one on top of the other.

Figure 2.21 About every four layers, the coils were smoothed on both sides with a scraping tool.

Figure 2.22 When the pot was finished, it was left for a few hours to allow the clay to harden. It was then carefully smoothed on the inside. The pot was then decorated (above) with tools made from bone or wood and, finally, fired red-hot in an outdoor fire to bake the clay, so it was strong and waterproof.

Blackduck-style pottery

Beginning in about 700 CE, the potters in Manitoba began making lighter, larger vessels that could hold more food than Laurel pots. Known as "Blackduck" pottery, the vessels were round in shape. They were moulded in woven bags made of fibres from the inner bark of the basswood tree or inner strands of plants such as the nettle.

To make the pots, women first collected clay and tempering material. The tempering material, often crushed granite, helped prevent the pots from breaking when they were being fired.

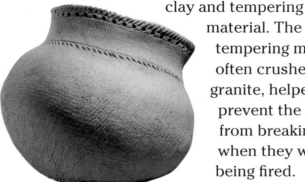

Figure 2.23 The pattern of the woven bag (see figure 2.24) can be seen on the body of this unfired Blackduck pot.

Making a Blackduck pot

Figure 2.24 The clay was formed into a conical shape, and placed inside the woven bag. The potter used the bag to support the clay, then scraped and thinned the clay from the inside until the pot was globe-like in shape.

Figure 2.25 The bag was peeled away from the clay pot, top to bottom, and the pot was decorated with a piece of bone or wood. It was then left to dry. After the pot was fired red-hot in an outdoor fire, it was ready to use.

The peace meeting at The Forks

When archaeologists were working at The Forks (located at the junction of the Red and Assiniboine rivers in Winnipeg), they found several campsites containing many different kinds of pottery mixed together. While there, they were approached by Elders from two different Aboriginal groups. The information the Elders shared, passed on through oral tradition, provided an explanation for what had been found. Both Elders told of a great peace meeting that had taken place at The Forks hundreds of years ago. Eight or nine Aboriginal nations had come together to talk about a peace settlement among nations of the northeast Plains and Parklands. Warfare was disrupting and destroying their economies.

The campsites at The Forks date to about 1000 CE –1200 CE. This mixture of pottery is believed to be evidence of several nations coming together.

Figure 2.26 This photograph shows pottery rims of many different styles of ceramic cooking pots that were found at The Forks in Winnipeg. It is unusual to find such a variety together. Each Aboriginal nation usually had its own way of decorating pots. Therefore, pieces of pottery found at an archaeological site usually look very similar.

Trade
on the Interior Plains

Aboriginal peoples often traded for items and materials that they did not have. In Manitoba, they traded food and hides for materials to make tools and jewellery. Stone included Knife River flint from western North Dakota, obsidian (volcanic glass) from Wyoming, and catlinite (red pipestone) from southwestern Minnesota. They also traded for conch shell from the southern United States, dentalium shell from the Pacific Ocean on the west side of Vancouver Island, marginella shell from the Atlantic Ocean, and copper from around Lake Superior.

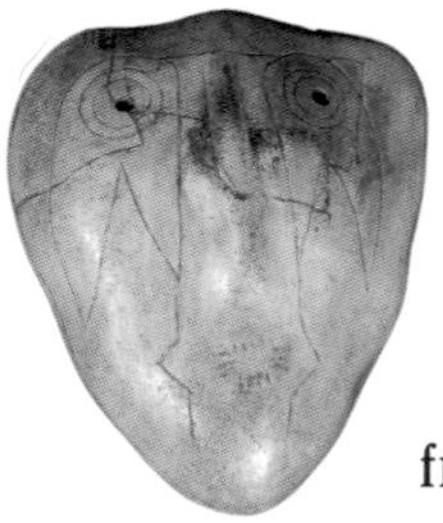

Figure 2.27 This mask, found in Sourisford, in southern Manitoba, is made from the shell of a huge snail known as conch or whelk. Conch shells were traded all the way up the Mississippi River and across country to southern Manitoba. This mask dates to about 850 CE to 1300 CE.

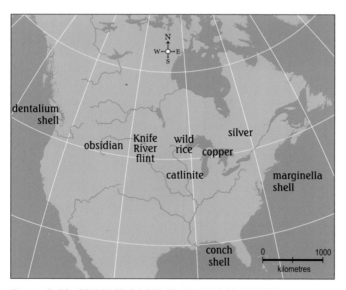

Figure 2.28 SOURCES OF SOME TRADE MATERIALS. Trade networks encouraged different groups to develop trading partnerships and **alliances**. Over centuries, nations came to know each other as allies or rivals, much like nations do today.

Longhouses
of the Great Lakes – St. Lawrence Lowlands

About 900 CE, Aboriginal peoples living in southern Ontario began to farm. They grew maize (corn), beans, and squash ("the three sisters"). These crops, introduced by peoples living to the south, had been domesticated over thousands of years. Maize, for example, was first domesticated from wild grasses in the highlands of Mexico starting about 7000 years ago.

Figure 2.29 Archaeologists look for, and find, more than just objects. They study the soil as they are digging and look for changes in colour and texture. Sometimes, they find evidence of a long-ago campfire or of a building. In this photograph, the holes are places where archaeologists found dark round stains in the soil. These once held wooden posts. The larger holes were fire pits.

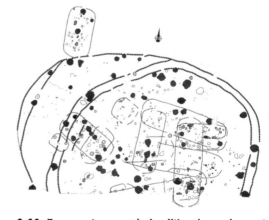

Figure 2.30 By mapping post holes (like those shown in figure 2.29), archaeologists were able to determine the locations of several longhouses. At the Calvert Village site, above, longhouses that overlap were built at different times.

These first farmers made a variety of stone tools. They had triangular arrow points, scrapers for working animal hides, and spokeshaves for scraping bark from wooden shafts and handles. They made bone and antler into awls for working hides. Trade items included shell beads and copper beads.

Early Iroquoians lived in **longhouses** inside **palisaded** villages for three seasons of the year: summer, fall, and winter. In the spring, they moved to fish camps near to where fish were **spawning**. Archaeologists have located many villages in southern Ontario.

Figure 2.31 Because the Iroquois farmed, they had time to do things other than hunt for food. This pottery and ceremonial pipe are from around the 1600s.

Farming
on the Interior Plains

The discovery by archaeologists of maize and storage pits on the Plains showed that not all Plains people were bison hunters. By about 1400 CE, at least one group, living along the Red River near Lockport, Manitoba, was also growing crops of maize and probably beans and squashes.

Figure 2.32 Women worked the fields with hoes made from the shoulder blades of bison. Plains farmers also fished in the Red River.

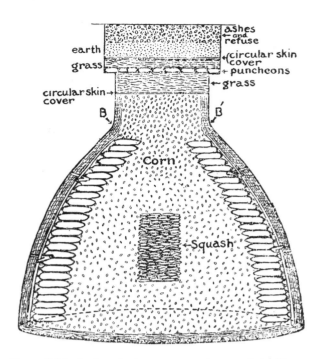

Figure 2.33 Archaeologists uncovered several pits like this one near the rapids at Lockport in southern Manitoba. The pits were up to 1.5 metres deep and contained pieces of maize. When scientists tested the maize, they discovered it was about 600 years old.

Plains farmers grew so much food that they had to dig deep storage pits to store the large surpluses of maize. The Plains farmers were the most northerly Aboriginal farmers in North America.

Conclusion

By the time Sara's week at archaeology camp ended, she had learned a great deal about how early people had survived on the land. As she looked at all the labelled artifacts in the temporary laboratory set up alongside the excavation area, she began to wonder what life could have been like so very long ago.

In chapter 3, join Sara and Ben as they find answers to some of Sara's questions.

3

Canada's First Peoples

Ben set his book down on the table. He was very confused. He had never really thought before about what the word *nation* meant.

Just then, Sara walked into the room. "How's it going?" she asked.

Ben sighed. "It's my social studies project. I'm reading about the Iroquois, and the writer keeps talking about the 'Iroquois nation.' I'm trying to figure out what that means."

The dictionary helped a little. It said a nation was a large group of people organized under a single government, or a group that shared customs, origins, history, and often language. Ben was curious to find out how the Iroquois governed themselves, and about the customs they shared. He wanted to learn more.

Today, when we think of nations, we think of countries. Each country has a main government, and its people have some sense of being a single group. Today, most nations have large numbers of people. Canada and the United States, for example, are each a nation.

Before Europeans began travelling to different parts of the world in the late 1400s, many small nations lived independently and self-sufficiently. In Canada, Aboriginal peoples lived that way. Many present-day Aboriginal groups have given their communities traditional names to remind people that they come from these early nations. For example, Nelson House Reserve in northern Manitoba is now Nisichawayasihk Cree Nation and The Pas Reserve is Opaskwayak Cree Nation.

Getting an education

In all **First Nations,** children and young people learned the skills and knowledge that they needed by working with older family members. Their classroom was the world around them. At a young age, girls and boys learned about herbal medicines. Both boys and girls were taught stories by their Elders. They learned that everything had life, all life was interconnected, and all life had to be respected. They learned to conserve resources and use only what they needed. Girls learned to work hides, sew and decorate clothing, make pottery and birchbark containers, collect edible plants and berries, make thread, snare small animals, and cook.

Boys learned to hunt and fish. They studied the behaviour of animals and learned respect for all the animals and their spirits. Boys also learned how to make stone tools, and how to carve hunting and fishing tools from wood and bone.

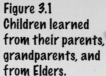

Figure 3.1
Children learned from their parents, grandparents, and from Elders.

When people first arrived in the land we know as Canada, they came in small groups and went to many different places. As with people everywhere, they had to find food, shelter, and clothing. They had to work together to survive. To do this, members of a group learned to speak the same language so that they understood one another. They also shared the same beliefs and values about the world. As people moved across the land, they learned how to get the things they needed from the places they travelled to. Different groups of people in different places adapted to the land they lived in. The tools they created, languages they spoke, clothing they wore, foods they ate,

As you read, think about

- **where Canada's Aboriginal peoples lived**
- **how they adapted to the places they went to**
- **how they governed themselves**

and spiritual beliefs they practised – all the things they learned to do to survive – are known as their culture. Over time, they became many nations, speaking many different languages.

In this chapter, you will read about how some of these nations lived before Europeans arrived in their region.

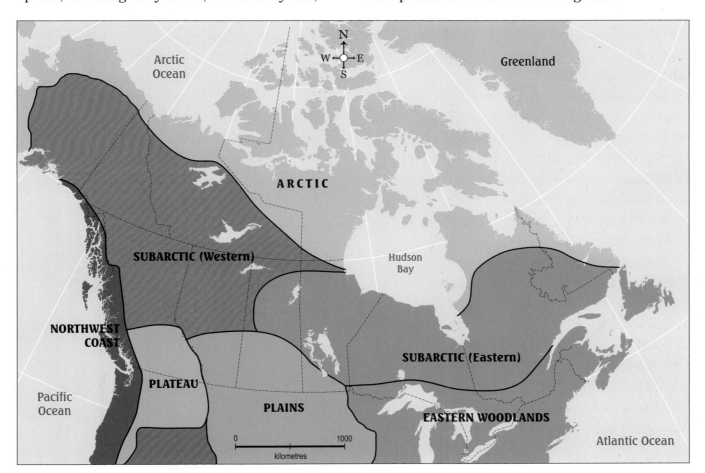

Figure 3.2 GEOGRAPHICAL ZONES. Canada's Aboriginal peoples lived in several different geographical zones. These zones are: the Eastern Woodlands, the Eastern Subarctic, the Western Subarctic, the Arctic, the Plains, the Plateau, and the Northwest Coast.

Peoples of the Eastern Woodlands

Who they were

The Mi'kmaq, Odawa (Ottawa), and Algonquin were Algonquian-speaking nations. Their people were fishermen, hunters, and gatherers. They lived in temporary dwellings called "wigwams," and they moved often in search of food. Most Aboriginal peoples who lived in the Eastern Woodlands were Iroquioan-speaking farmers. These included the nations of the Iroquois confederacy (Mohawk, Oneida, Onondaga, Cayuga, and Seneca), as well as the Wendat (Huron), Petun (Tobacco), Neutral, and Erie. On these two pages, you will read about the farming nations.

What they lived in

People lived in longhouses made of poles covered with flat sheets of bark. Each longhouse was about 11 metres wide and between 45 and 55 metres long. Inside, the longhouse was one large open building with a central corridor. Several fire pits burned along this corridor, and families lived in areas separated by partitions on each side of each fire. The longhouses were like small apartment blocks, where all of the relatives lived close to each other. In this way, members of a family could work together and help one another. Some longhouses were built specifically for religious ceremonies. Others were used as storage buildings.

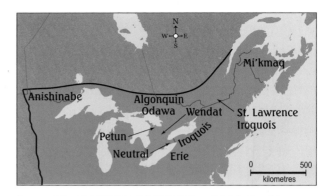

Figure 3.3 EASTERN WOODLANDS, c. 1600. The Algonquian-speaking nations lived on the east coast and along the northern edges of the Eastern Woodlands. The Iroquioan-speaking farmers lived around the Great Lakes. In 1535, Jacques Cartier reported they were also living in villages along the St. Lawrence River at Stadacona (now Quebec City) and Hochelaga (now Montreal).

What they ate

The women and children cultivated maize (corn), beans, and squash. Women also collected a variety of plant foods, such as seeds, nuts, and berries. They gathered milkweed, mustard grass, and skunk cabbage for salads and stews. They ate meat, particularly deer, but also bear, beaver, and elk that the men hunted. The men also trapped geese, ducks, and pigeons

Figure 3.4 Most villages were connected by pathways through the forests. Since only the most important villages were surrounded by palisades, these villages became safe havens during times of war.

Maize, beans, and squash were known as "the three sisters." After the men cleared and prepared the land, the women planted maize and beans on mounds of earth. The tall stalks of maize provided support for the climbing bean plants. The beans provided the nitrogen that the maize needed to grow well. Squash was planted in the space between the mounds. As the squash grew, its long vines and large leaves covered the ground and prevented weeds from growing there.

and fished for whitefish, trout, and sturgeon. In the spring, families tapped the maple trees to make maple syrup and maple sugar.

The main everyday meal was *sagamite*, a soup made of maize, with pieces of fish, meat, or squash added. Sagamite was boiled slowly in large clay pots. A favourite food was corn bread, made of cornmeal, deer fat, and sometimes dried berries.

What they made

Women made large clay cooking and storage pots. They wove baskets, nets, dolls, and ceremonial masks from plant fibres. Men made and decorated clay smoking pipes. They made light, efficient birchbark canoes for summer travel. For winter travel, they built wood or bark toboggans and snowshoes made from wood and sinew. Leather from the hides of animals, particularly deer, was made into clothing, quivers, drum covers, and containers. Wood was split and carved into many tools, such as shafts for arrows and spears. It was also used for food bowls, mortars and pestles for crushing seeds, and ceremonial masks. Some people became master carvers who added beautiful designs on the things they made.

How they governed

Several families, related through the mothers and grandmothers, lived in each longhouse. One of the older women was selected as leader of the longhouse. The families of two or more longhouses made up a clan. A clan was a group of about 15 or 20 families who were related through several generations to a female ancestor. A clan included grandparents, aunts and uncles, cousins, as well as the men who had married into the family. A matron, or clan mother, led each clan. Each clan mother chose male *sachems*, or chiefs, to sit on the **village council** to represent the clan interests. **Tribal councils** were made up of men from the various village councils.

Tribal councils met at least once a year to discuss general matters. A chief's decisions were often influenced by the clan mother.

Peoples of the Eastern Subarctic Forests

Who they were

These Algonquian-speaking nations included the Nehiyawak (Cree), Anishinabe (Ojibwa), Odawa, Beothuk, and Innu (Montagnais and Naskapi). Their peoples were fishermen, hunters, and gatherers. On these two pages, you will read about the Anishinabe.

Where they lived

These people lived in the boreal forests of the Eastern Subarctic. This vast forested land stretches today from the east coast to north and central Saskatchewan.

What they lived in

The people lived in wigwams covered with bark or rush mats.

What they ate

The Anishinabe travelled along carefully planned routes, so that they were always where the plants and animals were most plentiful. In the spring, they gathered along rivers where huge schools of fish swam upstream to spawn. Spring was also the time for tapping maple trees to make syrup and maple sugar. During the summer, the people gathered in villages and hunted and gathered the animals, birds, and plants that grew nearby. In the fall, Anishinabe families met around the shallow lakes to harvest wild rice. During the winter, they separated into small camps of a few extended families and hunted animals such as moose, deer, beaver, elk, and rabbits. They also ice fished on the frozen lakes and rivers.

Rite of passage

At puberty, boys began a Vision Quest. During the quest, a young boy spent up to four days alone in the forest without food or water. His mind, body, and spirit were thought to become connected, and his guardian spirit, usually an animal, was revealed to him. While he waited for his vision, he learned about the world by watching everything around him.

Figure 3.5 When the Anishinabe moved campsites, they brought the sheets of birchbark they used on their wigwams with them, but left the wooden frames behind.

What they made

The Anishinabe, like the other groups living in the eastern forests, used the natural materials around them to make everything they needed. In summer, they travelled by lightweight birchbark canoes. In winter, they travelled on the frozen rivers or across country with their rawhide-and-wood snowshoes and wooden toboggans. They made containers from birchbark. They made clay cooking and storage vessels and wooden hunting and fishing tools. Animal hides were made into clothing and drum covers, covers for *tikanagans* (baby backpacks, or cradle-boards). From plant fibres, they wove

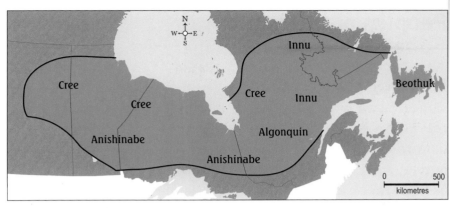

Figure 3.6 EASTERN SUBARCTIC REGION, c. 1800. These nations lived in the boreal forests of the Eastern Subarctic. This vast forested land stretches from the east coast of Newfoundland to the north-central area of Saskatchewan.

rush mats to sleep and sit on; cordage, for making string, rope, and netting; and woven baskets, such as winnowing baskets, for processing wild rice.

How they governed

The Anishinabe were made up of many nations. Each nation was made up of several small groups of closely related **extended families**. In the spring and summer, when there was a lot of food available, an entire nation (usually between 100 and 400 people) gathered together.

Members of a particular clan, called a *dodem*, were related through the same spirit ancestor, such as a bear, moose, sturgeon, or crane. Members of a clan thought of each other as brothers and sisters, and helped one another when needed.

Peoples of the Arctic

Who they were

These people called themselves Inuit. Although we often think of the Inuit as one group, there were many different nations. Some of the nations were the Inuvialuit, Copper Inuit, Caribou Inuit, and Labrador Inuit (see figure 3.8 for a more complete list). All spoke variations of the Inuktitut language.

What they lived in

The Inuit, particularly those who lived in the Central Arctic, built dome-shaped igloos made from snow blocks. In the summer, they built skin-covered tents. In the Eastern Arctic, they made large permanent sod-and-stone houses that were dug partially into the ground. In the western Mackenzie Delta, the Inuit made large permanent structures of driftwood and earth that were also dug partially into the ground.

For much of the year, the Inuit lived in small camps of several families. Larger groups of families came together when food was plentiful. In the Mackenzie Delta area of the Western Arctic, five groups, representing 2000 to 4000 people, lived in permanent villages. Here, food was plentiful.

What they ate

In winter, most Inuit groups hunted seals and caught fish through holes in the ice. They travelled and hunted by *komatik* (dogsled) and dog team. Groups of people who lived along the oceans and seas hunted beluga whales, walruses, narwhals, and giant bowhead whales from ice floes.

Sometimes they hunted from large whaling boats called *umiaks*.

In the summer, many Inuit groups, especially those in the Central Arctic, moved inland where they hunted herds of caribou and, sometimes, musk oxen and the massive, ferocious polar bears. They caught fish in the rivers by spearing them or building weirs across the rivers. They hunted ducks and geese, and they also collected eggs. In kayaks and umiaks, they hunted many of the same sea animals they caught in winter along the ocean coast.

What they made

The land and waters provided everything the Inuit needed to develop many **innovative** inventions. The Inuit found effective ways to live in the cold Arctic. They wore double-layered, tailored coats, pants, gloves, and mukluks, all made of animal skin. They carved bone and ivory sunglasses to prevent blindness from the bright snow. They built harpoons

with detachable heads and attached lines to catch the water animals.

The Inuit were also great artists who carved many items from bone and ivory. They carved containers, harpoon points, fishing gear, combs, and needle holders decorated with animals, birds, and camp scenes. The designs often had spiritual importance.

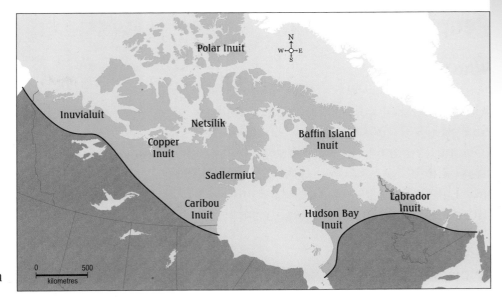

Figure 3.8 ARCTIC REGION, c. 1800. In northern Canada, small nations of Inuit learned to live in a cold, arid, treeless, and harsh land. There, the winters were long and cold. The lakes were frozen for nine or more months of the year, and darkness lingered for weeks in midwinter. During the brief summers, colourful plants came to life, the ice melted into bogs, and the sun never set.

How they governed

In each camp and community, decisions were made by **consensus**. When there was a problem, it was discussed until everyone, or at least most people, agreed. The Inuit did not have an elected leader. The group was **egalitarian**. That meant everyone was considered equal. Everybody's ideas were considered important.

Figure 3.9 This young Inuit boy in Arviat, Nunavut, is learning how to set up a harpoon for beluga hunting in the same way that his ancestors did.

Figure 3.7 Among the Inuit, men and boys were responsible for making tools, building water crafts, and getting food. Women and girls cleaned the fish and other animals and cut up the meat. They also prepared the animal hides to make clothing.

Peoples of the Plains

Who they were

Several nations lived on the Plains. There were the Nakota (also referred to as the Assiniboine), Stoney (Nakoda), Piikani (Peigan), Kainai (Blood), Siksika (Blackfoot), Tsuu T'ina (Sarcee), and Atsina. The Nakota were Siouan speaking. The other nations spoke Algonquian languages.

What they lived in

Since they had to move seasonally, the Plains nations built portable, conical teepees. The teepee cover was often made of eight to twenty bison hides that were stretched, scraped clean, softened, smoked, and sewn together. Teepees could be set up and taken down quickly.

What they ate

Plains nations were nomadic, because their main source of food – the bison – moved with the seasons. The people planned their movements carefully to track the movements of the bison. The people not

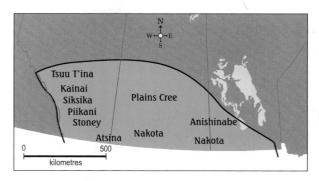

Figure 3.10 PLAINS REGION c.1800. In southwestern Manitoba, the Nakota (also known as the Assiniboine), from the Cree word for "stone people," were the main inhabitants. Certain place names used today, such as the Assiniboine River, recall their presence. In the east, the Plains Anishinabe and Plains Cree (Nehiyawak) were more common. The Dakota and Lakota did not move into the region until after 1863.

only ate the bison, they also used its bones, hides, and sinew to make many of the tools and utensils. The bison were like a shopping centre on the hoof.

Plains hunters developed several techniques to hunt the bison. They drove entire herds over cliffs or river valley edges. Sometimes they corralled herds into **pounds**. Sometimes hunters drove small herds into ponds of water or deep snowdrifts where the animals became trapped. Hunters could direct the movement of the herds by having someone imitate the sounds of a lost bison calf, while someone else moved slowly from behind like a prairie wolf. Hunts always began with prayers to the Creator and to the spirit of the great bison. Prayers of thanks were offered after the hunt.

Figure 3.11 In this illustration, the dog is pulling a **travois**. The openness and flatness of the Plains made the travois an ideal way to carry people's personal possessions. After Europeans brought horses to North America in the 1700s, Plains peoples usually used horses to pull travois.

The people of the Plains also hunted antelope and collected plants, such as the prairie turnip. The groups who lived along the northern edge of the Plains fished in the rivers and lakes. The bison hunters also traded any extra goods they had for produce, such as maize, beans, and squash. These came from village tribes, such as the Mandan and Hidatsa people who lived on the Missouri River to the south.

What they made

The bison was at the centre of Plains culture. Plains people used every part of the bison (see figure 3.12, below).

Plains people often decorated the items that they made. Teepee covers and shields had drawings of animals. These drawings represented an important event or spiritual vision or dream that the owner had. Containers called *parflêches* were often decorated with geometric designs. People painted their faces and upper bodies for special ceremonies. Women sometimes had lines tattooed on their faces.

How they governed

The large amounts of food provided by the bison made it possible for large groups of people to be together. Each nation or tribe was made up of several bands. Each band consisted of 400 to 800 people. Each band selected chiefs, based on wisdom, or skill in hunting or in warfare. The chiefs tried to reach agreement with others through discussion. All Plains nations were egalitarian, and decisions were made by consensus. During bison hunts, when the entire clan or nation came together, councils of chiefs met to discuss ideas. The chiefs then met with their bands to reach consensus on these ideas.

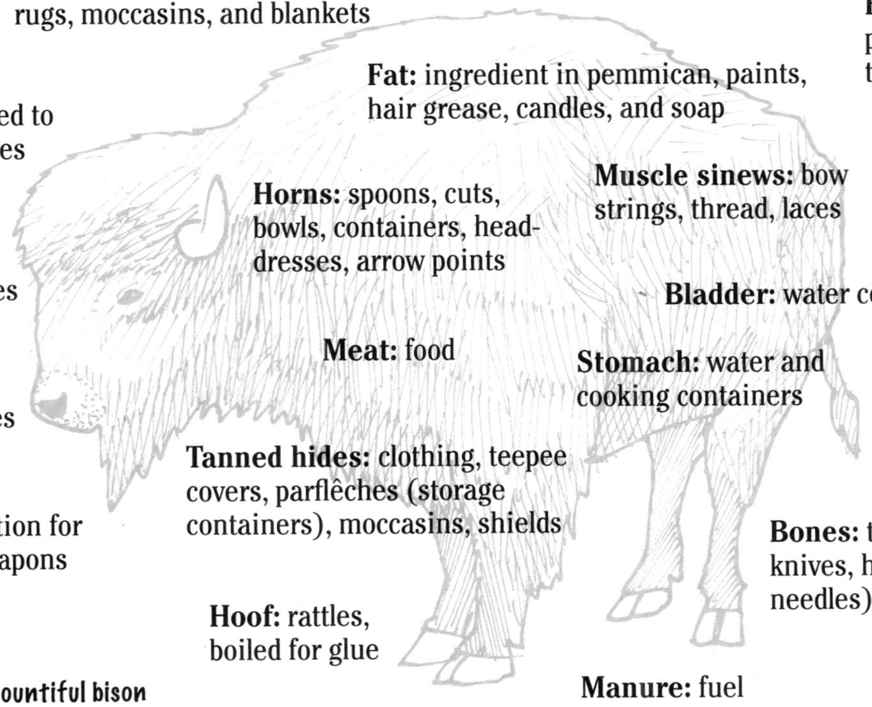

Hide with hair: winter clothes, rugs, moccasins, and blankets

Hair: stuffing for pillows and cradles, thread, and rope

Brain: used to soften hides

Fat: ingredient in pemmican, paints, hair grease, candles, and soap

Horns: spoons, cuts, bowls, containers, headdresses, arrow points

Muscle sinews: bow strings, thread, laces

Skull: used for ceremonies

Bladder: water containers, pouches

Meat: food

Stomach: water and cooking containers

Teeth: necklaces

Tanned hides: clothing, teepee covers, parflêches (storage containers), moccasins, shields

Tail: fly swatter

Beard: decoration for clothes and weapons

Bones: tools (scrapers, knives, hoes, and sewing needles) and sled runners

Hoof: rattles, boiled for glue

Manure: fuel

Figure 3.12 The bountiful bison

Peoples of the Western Subarctic

Who they were

The nations of this region included the Dene, Tlingit, Chilcotin, Beaver, Carrier, Slavey, Hare, and Yellowknife. All spoke the Athapaskan language. The Cree who lived in the east spoke the Algonquian language. On these two pages, you will read about the Dene.

What they lived in

Since the Dene had to move regularly from fishing stations to caribou crossings, they travelled lightly. They lived in small conical teepees covered by moose or caribou hide. Some people made solid structures, using poles with moss **chinking** filling the cracks and holes.

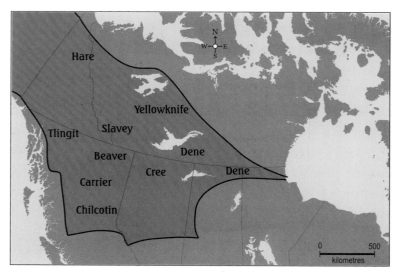

Figure 3.13 WESTERN SUBARCTIC REGION, c. 1800. This area included northern boreal forest, sparsely treed barren grounds, and tundra. Winters were long and cold. Summers were short and hot. The land varied from flat to gently rolling Canadian Shield to the high Cordilleran Mountains of British Columbia and the Yukon.

into large pounds or hunted them while the animals were swimming across rivers.

Other nations to the southwest also hunted moose and woodland caribou. The nations who lived in the mountains hunted mountain goats.

Teepee or wigwam?

A wigwam was a dwelling with a framework of poles. It was usually rounded, but sometimes cone shaped. It was covered with bark, reeds, or thatching, and was made by the people of the Eastern Woodlands region. The word *wigwam* comes from the Mi'kmaq word *wikuom*, meaning "dwelling."

The teepee was a dwelling first made by the Plains people. It was similar to the cone-shaped wigwam, but larger, and usually covered with hides rather than plant material. The word *teepee* comes from the Lakota phrase *ti pi* meaning "used for dwelling in."

What they ate

Most Dene ate caribou, moose, and fish. They were nomadic and used their knowledge of the animals' routes to meet the migrating herds. They drove the caribou

Figure 3.14 During the summer months, Dene women spent much of their time catching fish, which they smoked over fires in preparation for the long winter ahead.

What they made

The Dene travelled the rivers in canoes covered with spruce or birchbark and, rarely, moose hide. They travelled long distances across the land. In the winter, they used snowshoes. Women pulled toboggans. When travelling across land during the summers, they walked long distances. They had to carry their canoes with them, because they might not find the materials they needed to make new ones when they reached another river or lake.

How they governed

Throughout much of the Dene lands, the various nations lived as small, egalitarian groups of extended families. Many hundreds met each year for the traditional communal caribou hunt.

When there were problems, or plans needed to be made, representatives of the different families met to arrive at decisions by consensus.

Yamozha (also known as Yamoria) was an important character in Dene oral tradition. Yamozha lived long ago, and circled the north making the land safe for the people and animals who lived there. Also known as the "Great Law Giver," Yamozha set laws for the Dene people that are still practised today.

In one story, Yamozha chased a family of giant beavers – said to be the size of black bears – from the north shore of Great Bear Lake. The beavers were tipping canoes and kayaks, causing flooding, and creating all sorts of problems for people. Whenever the beavers built a dam, Yamozha chased them away. Finally, at a place called Bear Rock, Yamozha killed three of the beavers and stretched their hides on the face of the cliffs. The place where the hides were stretched can still be seen today.

Multi-purpose mammal

Herds of caribou provided most of the Dene needs. The animals' skins were cleaned and made into clothing, teepee covers, and robes. Hides were also cut into thin strips or thongs, which were twisted, like rope, into deer snares, bowstrings, net-lines, fishnets, and snowshoes. The tendons were split into small strands that the women used for sewing thread. The horns were carved into fish-spears, ice chisels, and other utensils. Unused animal bones were smashed into tiny pieces, then boiled to make grease and to get the nutritious marrow in the centres.

Peoples of the Northwest Coast

Who they were

Many different nations lived on the Northwest Coast. They included the Tlingit, Haida, Nisga'a, Gitskan, Tsimshian, Haisla, Heiltsuk, Kwagiulth, Nuu-chah-nulth, Nuxalk, and the Coastal Salish.

The nations spoke at least sixteen different languages from five different language families. Many who spoke the same language spoke a different **dialect**. According to one theory, the development of many languages on the Northwest Coast suggests that the nations separated thousands of years ago.

What they lived in

Because they did not have to travel to find food and other materials, people lived in permanent villages of large, multi-family houses. The houses were made of wooden planks split and chiseled from the tall red-cedar trees. People often had homes in both summer and winter villages. They moved their belongings from one home to the other in large wooden dugout canoes.

What they ate

Rivers such as the Nass, Skeena, and Fraser teemed with fish, particularly salmon and the oily eulachon. The sea provided a limitless supply of halibut and herring. It also yielded several species of whales, including killer whales, humpbacks, and California grays, and seals and sea lions. The shorelines yielded clams, mussels, and other kinds of shellfish, as well as seaweed. Elk, moose, deer, and bear were sometimes hunted in the forests and along the riverbanks.

What they made

Lush rainforests of fir, hemlock, spruce, and cedar provided the main building materials. Cedar was particularly important for making buildings. Men were carvers, and made everyday items like storage and cooking boxes, and dishes and spoons. Women wove baskets and made cloth from cedar fibres. The cedar tree was considered a sacred life form. People expressed their thanks with a prayer whenever the bark was stripped off.

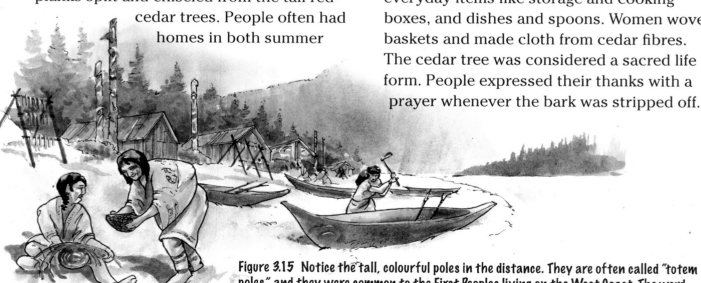

Figure 3.15 Notice the tall, colourful poles in the distance. They are often called "totem poles," and they were common to the First Peoples living on the West Coast. The word *totem* comes from the Algonquian word *dodem*, which means "clan." The figures and crests carved into the poles represented a family's or clan's ancestry, accomplishments, rights, and prestige. Traditionally, these poles were raised during potlatch ceremonies.

Because people in the Northwest had such an abundance of food and other resources, they had leisure time that many other First Nations did not have. With this extra time, individuals could focus on learning special skills, and many became excellent craftspeople and artists. Carvers of the Northwest created lavish ceremonial objects, such as **ornate** face masks and carved poles (that we call totem poles).

Making a dugout canoe

Canoe makers first cut down a tree, then hollowed out the trunk with stone adzes. The hollowed-out trunk was filled with water that had been heated enough to bend the wood. The boat makers then bent the wood into the desired shape. Dugout canoes varied in size from small two-person fishing and sealing canoes to large whaling, trading, and war canoes that held up to 50 people.

How they governed

First Peoples on the Northwest Coast were the only nations in the land we now call Canada where leadership was **hierarchal** (not egalitarian and consensus oriented). People were ranked or clustered into levels of social status – the high-ranking **elite**, the commoners, and the slaves. People were born into the elite or commoner group. Slaves were often people who had been purchased or captured during warfare. Slaves could be sold or even killed.

The highest level included all of the chiefs and nobles. Chiefs and nobles were consulted about matters concerning the land and major resources (such as salmon-fishing stations, sections of cedar forests, and hunting territories). These were considered private property that belonged to groups of relatives. The chiefs advised people on how to use the resources.

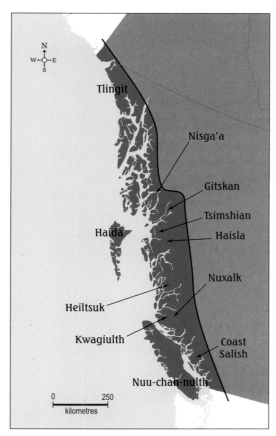

Figure 3.16 NORTHWEST COAST REGION, c. 1800. Northwest Coast nations lived in the rich rainforests beside the coastal waters of British Columbia. The land and ocean provided people with all the foods and building materials they needed.

The potlatch

Potlatches were great public feasts given by a chief or high-ranking member of the community to celebrate special events, such as a marriage, birth, naming, or the completion of a new house or totem pole. Potlatches included storytelling, singing, and dancing. Generous gift-giving and lavish feasting maintained the chief's status in the community. A chief's generosity was returned by another host in the next potlatch. Potlatches could last for days or even weeks.

Peoples of the Plateau

Who they were

These people included the Lillooet, Thompson (Nlaka'pamux), Okanagan, Lakes, Shuswap, Kutenai, Nicola, Chilcotin, and Carrier peoples. Peoples in this region spoke Salishan languages.

What they lived in

During the hot and dry summer, Plateau peoples travelled about in small bands made up of many families. They lived in teepees covered with mats or bark. In the winter, they lived in small villages of pit houses. These houses were round and dug about 1.2 metres into the ground. The roofs were earth-covered logs. People travelled the rivers by canoe and the forests by foot.

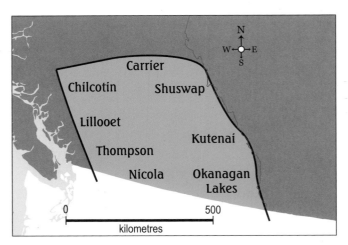

Figure 3.17 PLATEAU REGION, c. 1800. This area is between the Rocky Mountains and Coast Mountains of the southern interior of British Columbia. There are flat desert plateaus, valleys, and forested mountain slopes. The Fraser and Thompson rivers flow through to the Pacific Ocean.

What they ate

All of the Plateau nations relied upon fishing, collecting roots and berries, and hunting. The rivers provided fish such as salmon and sturgeon. Women gathered wild plants, including the balsamroot, bitterroot, wild onions, fireweed, and cow parsnip, as well as many kinds of berries. The men hunted deer, elk, mountain goat, bighorn sheep, and bear. People who lived in the eastern Plateau relied largely on the bison of the Plains for food. Surplus food was stored in bark-lined storage pits. Salmon was dried to make fish jerky or pounded into fish pemmican.

What they made

The Plateau nations traded with Plains nations to the east and Northwest Coast groups to the west. They had both eagle-feather Plains bonnets and the basketry hats of the Northwest Coast. They wore Plains-style leather clothing and winter fur caps. On their feet they wore moccasins of leather or salmon skins.

The people in the west of the area were fine artists and craftsmen. They wove blankets from mountain-goat hair, and made coiled cedar-root baskets in colourful geometric designs. Some baskets were woven so tightly that they could hold water. The eastern groups used birchbark for their baskets and made hide bags. They also produced wood carvings, but these were not as fancy as those made by the Northwest Coast nations (see p. 46).

(see p. 46)

How they governed

Each village of pit-houses had one or more chiefs. These positions were usually inherited, but the chiefs had to prove their leadership abilities through their wealth, their speaking abilities, or their skills in hunting, fishing, or warfare.

Conclusion

Ben learned a great deal about the many First Nations, and their influence on one another. He learned how Aboriginal customs and cultures developed, and how First Peoples governed themselves.

The Aboriginal peoples, over many thousands of years, had learned to live in the different regions of the land we now call Canada. Soon, however, they would find themselves sharing their knowledge with newcomers. The coming of Europeans would bring tremendous change for First Peoples.

Figure 3.18 The sturgeon-nosed canoe in this illustration was unique to the Kutenai people. The design gave the canoe stability in fast-moving water. These canoes were made from pine bark, which made them light enough to carry over portages.

PART 2

Early European Colonization

GIOVANNI CABO

1000
The Norse travel
to the east coast
of North America.

1497
John Cabot
lands in
Newfoundland.

1608
Samuel de
Champlain founds
a French settlement
at Quebec.

1617
Louis Hébert,
the first European
farmer in New France,
returns from France.

4. The Europeans Come to North America   5. The French in Canada, 1604–1759

1492
Christopher
Columbus arrives
in North America.

1535
Jacques Cartier
explores the
St. Lawrence River.

1610–1611
Henry Hudson
explores Hudson Bay,
then dies when his
crew sets him adrift.

1642
The French settlement
of Ville Marie
(Montreal)
is founded.

1611
The English settlement
of Cuper's Cove,
Newfoundland,
is established.

1665
Jean Talon
arrives as the
first intendant
of New France.

1749
The British
found Halifax.

1759
The British
defeat the French
in the Battle of the
Plains of Abraham.

1774
The Quebec Act
establishes
French civil law
in French Canada
and promises
religious freedom.

6. The British in North America

1713
The Treaty of Utrecht
gives former French
territory of Newfoundland
and Nova Scotia to
Britain. The French begin
building Louisbourg on
Cape Breton Island.

1756
The Seven
Years' War
between Britain
and France begins.

1763
Royal Proclamation
defines Aboriginal
Territories and colonies
of British North America.

4 The Europeans Come to North America

Ben squinted as he went below deck. He was touring the replica of a 17th-century sailing ship, and he was having a hard time seeing in the dim light. When his eyes adjusted to the lighting, he noticed how short the sleeping bunks were. My head would be touching my sailing mate's feet, he thought. As he looked around, he did not see where a sailor could find any space away from the other sailors on the ship. Ben also realized there was no running water on board. It was one thing to spend a summer weekend camping on an island with no showers and no toilets. It was quite another to spend weeks, and maybe even months, at sea with no showers and toilets.

He tried to imagine what it would have been like to sail across the Atlantic Ocean in this ship 400 years ago, without a sure destination. He felt the huge waves rolling the vessel back and forth, day after day. He imagined the crew trapped in the Arctic ice while looking for a Northwest Passage. He saw the hold at the beginning of the expedition – full of supplies and goods for trading, but also crawling with mice and rats.

He imagined how awful living conditions were near the end of a voyage, long after all the fresh fruits and vegetables were eaten. Without enough vitamin C, most

Figure 4.1 Countries such as Spain, Portugal, England, France, and the Netherlands had sailing ships similar to the one pictured here. For many European adventurers, the 16th and 17th centuries were exciting times of exploration to unfamiliar lands.

crew members suffered from **scurvy**. Their teeth fell out and their joints ached. Many died. Perhaps several weeks on a small ship in the middle of the ocean would not be as much fun as Ben first thought.

A Mi'kmaq story

A young Mi'kmaq woman had a strange dream. In it, she saw a small white island moving through the great waters. On this floating island were trees and living beings. One figure, a male, stood apart from the others. He was dressed in white rabbit skins and had hair on his face.

The next morning she told her dream to one of her Elders, who was unable to interpret its meaning. Not long afterward, the woman saw what looked like a small island moving through the water toward her village.

The Mi'kmaq warriors took up their weapons and prepared to kill what they thought were bears on the moving island. They were surprised when they realized that the bears were actually white-faced men, and the island was a large boat. One man, dressed in white, stood apart from the others and made signs of friendship.

When the boat landed, the Elder brought the young woman to the man in white. The Elder asked her if this was the man in her dream. "Yes," she replied.

Figure 4.2

For thousands of years, peoples of different backgrounds have worked, fought, and traded with each other. In this chapter, you will investigate some of the earliest meetings between the Aboriginal peoples of North America and the Europeans who explored and claimed these lands as their own. You will also find out why Europeans wanted to expand their **empires**, why this was a good time for them to expand, and why Europeans came to North America.

As you read, think about

- **what made the Renaissance so important to the people of Europe and the history of the world**
- **why Europeans were so keen on finding another route to Asia**
- **how it became possible for Europeans to sail far beyond Europe and the Middle East**

The Norse in North America

As early as 800 CE, the Norse were on the move. Overcrowding and political unrest in Scandinavia led some people to search for new lands. Others were sent away as punishment for crimes they had committed. In around 870, some of these emigrants landed in Iceland where they built a colony. They were a hardy and independent people.

Eric the Red

Around 982, a man named Eric the Red was **exiled** to Iceland for a crime he had committed in his homeland. Soon, he was in trouble with the law again, and took to the seas, looking for a place to build a new settlement. He landed in a place he named Greenland, even though it was treeless, cold, and wintry. He thought that more people would come to live there if the land sounded like it was a warm and fertile place.

Soon Eric the Red (so named because of his red hair and beard) was joined by more than 300 new settlers from Iceland. The settlement on Greenland would survive for nearly 500 years. From Greenland came the Norse settlers who would explore North America.

Leif the Lucky

Leif Ericsson (son of Eric the Red) set sail from Greenland. He was searching for a tree-covered island he had heard

about years earlier from a merchant named Bjarni Herjolfsson. He landed at a place he called Helluland (meaning "land of the flat stones"), believed to be Baffin Island. He also explored present-day Newfoundland and Labrador. He named the most fertile of these stopping points "Vinland." Leif took a shipment of lumber back to Greenland, made his fortune, and never returned.

Figure 4.3 Little is known of the Norse ships that sailed across the Atlantic Ocean a thousand years ago. Most historians believe Leif Ericsson and others travelled in a one-masted ship called a *knarr*. Knarrs were about 16–17 metres long and 4–5 metres wide.

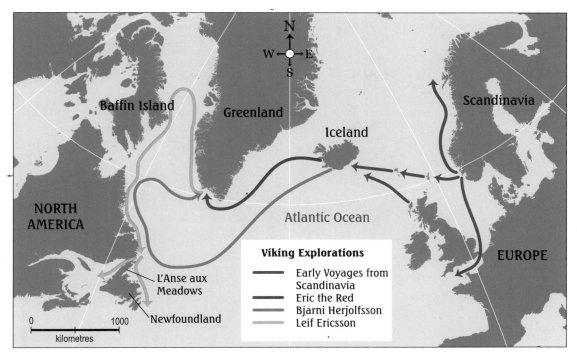

Figure 4.4 VIKING EXPLORATIONS. Vikings explored North America around 1000 CE.

Thorvald the Luckless

Thorvald, Leif's brother, did return to Vinland, however. Thorvald arrived with supplies and 30 men who were determined to build a **colony** there. They were impressed with the pastures, the trees, the fish, and the wild fruit.

The Sagas

Much of what we know about Norse exploration and settlement comes from the Sagas. These are stories that were passed on from generation to generation. At first, the stories were told orally. Later, the stories were written down. For many years, no one knew if the stories were true. However, archaeologists have found things that can be read about in the Sagas. Some of the Sagas are actually fun to read. In one, we learn that Leif's mother-in-law was named "Thorbjorg the ship-chested." We also find out that Leif's father and grandfather spent time in exile for murder.

They also found out that the land was already inhabited. In the first recorded encounter with Aboriginal peoples of Labrador, the Norse stumbled across nine men sleeping under boats. They killed eight of them, but one escaped and returned with others to fight the intruders. Thorvald was wounded and died as a result of this **skirmish**. Those who survived returned to Greenland.

The Vinland settlement

In about 1012, a group of approximately 160 Greenlanders sailed to Vinland to establish a permanent colony there. Although they traded with Aboriginal peoples, the two groups sometimes fought and even killed each other. After a while, the Norse decided to leave Vinland and return to their homeland.

L'Anse aux Meadows

For a long time, scholars believed that the Norse had built a settlement in the place we now call Newfoundland. Many other people, however, thought this was just a story. Then, in 1960, archaeologists uncovered an ancient Norse settlement in Newfoundland. This settlement is called L'Anse aux Meadows. It proved, for the first time, that Vikings had crossed the Atlantic Ocean and landed in North America around 1000 CE, 500 years before any other Europeans would try.

Is L'Anse aux Meadows the land that Leif named Vinland? No one knows for sure, although there are several theories.

Theory 1: The *vin* in Vinland refers to wine, or grapes. Since no one has ever grown grapes as far north as Newfoundland and Labrador, Vinland must be located in a yet-to-be-discovered place farther south.

Theory 2: L'Anse aux Meadows is Vinland. Vin refers to pastures, of which Newfoundland and Labrador have plenty.

Theory 3: *Vin* does refer to wine, or grapes. The Norse thought the wild berries growing in abundance in the area, such

Figure 4.5 Artifacts such as these brooches and cloak pin have allowed historians to identify where the Norse explorers landed in the New World.

as crowberries, partridgeberries, and blueberries, would make good wine.

Theory 4: Like father, like son? Greenland was named by Leif Ericsson's father, Eric the Red, even though it was treeless, cold, and wintry. He thought that more people would come to live there if the land sounded like it was a warm and fertile place. Perhaps Leif Ericsson named L'Anse aux Meadows "Vinland" because he thought people would settle there if they believed the place was warm enough to grow grapes.

Figure 4.6 Today, the historic site of L'Anse aux Meadows features buildings reconstructed to look like those from 1000 CE. Archaeologists have concluded that early Norse settlers lived in sod houses like those in the picture above.

The Basques

The Basques, who came from a small region between France and Spain, were good fishermen. Like most good fishermen, they probably kept their favourite fishing spots a secret. This may be why the Basques were never credited with being among the first Europeans to arrive in North America.

There is evidence that the Basques had been fishing for cod in the North Atlantic since 1511. Some historians believe they were there even earlier, in the late 1400s, before the arrival of other Europeans. The Basques became wealthy, because they had an endless supply of cod to sell to the rest of Europe. For years, fishermen from other countries wondered where the Basques caught their fish.

Figure 4.7 Cod stream: In the early 16th century, Portuguese fishermen heard about abundant supplies of cod off the coast of Newfoundland. This map was published in 1563, and the fishing grounds were no longer a secret. The double line on the map, called the "cod stream," showed fishermen where the fish could be found.

DID YOU KNOW?

Basque fishermen discovered a way to dry and salt cod so that the fish would last for many months. Not only did salt cod provide cheap and healthy food to Europeans, it also meant that Basque sailors could stay longer at sea because they had a regular food supply. They became excellent sailors. When Christopher Columbus went to search for a route to Asia (see p. 62), most of his crew were Basque.

The Renaissance

Between the 14th century and the 16th century, most of Europe emerged from the Middle Ages and with new inventions and ideas experienced a "rebirth."

The printing press changed the way people learned and communicated. For the first time, people, other than small groups of priests and scholars, could buy books. This resulted in new ideas spreading faster than ever before.

New inventions also affected the economy of Europe, which, in turn, changed the way people lived. The invention of the telescope helped people discover new things about science and astronomy. They began to question long-standing beliefs, including the idea that the sun revolved around the earth.

Ship designs improved. People were able to explore and sail farther than they ever had before. New instruments like the quadrant, sextant, and compass helped sailors determine direction easily, ensuring quicker and safer ocean voyages. Even the Basques' method of keeping cod from going bad had an impact. Fish, which provided sailors with a good source of protein, did not spoil quickly when it was salted.

Spices like cinnamon, ginger, and pepper were no longer just for the rich. The growing middle class could now afford to buy them. However, the overland trip to obtain spices took years to complete, and many of the routes were dangerous because of bandits. Europeans wanted to find a safe route by sea to the spice-growing countries in Asia and Indonesia. They thought that if they found a western sea passage to Asia, they could easily get the things they wanted from the East. It was like a great big treasure hunt. Whoever found the sea route to the East (called the Northwest Passage) would be rewarded by his king and queen.

This period of time is called the Renaissance.

Figure 4.8 Spices from Asia

DID YOU KNOW?

Pepper was especially prized and, literally, worth its weight in gold. When Columbus returned from his voyage to the New World, he brought chilis, which were grown by the Aboriginal peoples. In an effort to convince his **benefactors** that his trip had been worth it, he called the chilis "red peppers."

Travel to the western world ... is a consequence of the long struggle of the nations of Europe vying for supremacy and control of trade with the East .... For all those who pushed back the limits of the unknown world, there is always the glitter of gold and the odour of far fetched spices.

— *Sir Walter Raleigh, 1605*

Figure 4.9 This painting, *The Ambassadors*, was painted in 1533 by Hans Holbein the Younger (1497-1543). The objects in the painting show some of the advances made during the Renaissance. Inventions include a sextant and astrolabe, navigation instruments that allowed sailors to travel the world's oceans. Books show how new ideas could be spread to everyone. The globes show how knowledge of the world was growing. The carpets on the floor and table reflect the ongoing trade between Europe and East Asia.

The power of the Church

In the mid-1500s, most Europeans followed one of two Christian traditions. Roman Catholics followed the traditional teachings of the Roman Catholic Church. In the early 1500s, some people had disagreed with the Catholic Church and formed their own group, known as the **Protestants** (because they had protested some of the Catholic Church's main teachings). This was important to exploration, because the Catholic popes made decisions about who could claim what lands in the New World.

Throughout Europe, countries such as France, Spain, and Portugal remained Catholic. Other countries such as England and the Netherlands followed the Protestant faith.

The Empires

During the Renaissance, kings and queens hired explorers and crews to expand their empires, or the lands they controlled all over the world. They competed for new lands, slaves, trade routes, and precious goods like spices and gold. They also wanted to spread their religions to people in new lands. The public loved to hear about exotic places, and many explorers wrote stories based on their experiences. Because sensational stories sold, some explorers even altered their adventures to include stories of fantastical people.

Sometimes, explorers made their trips sound more successful than they were. By doing this, many got sponsors to fund their expeditions. One explorer, for example, reported that the Aboriginal peoples of North America were Chinese. Others wrote that they had found a river in North America that would take them to the Pacific and across Asia. In truth, no one had any idea how wide North America was, and the earliest maps often show coastline with a rather skinny strip of land (see p. 64).

Figure 4.10 Christopher Columbus travelled to Spain to find backing for his travels. King Ferdinand and Queen Isabella were eager to find a way to the riches of Asia and so funded Columbus's expeditions to search for a passage to Asia.

At first, the search for a Northwest Passage was the reason for much of early North American exploration. Soon, however, explorers began to realize the enormous size of North America. They knew it would be both costly and difficult to find a way around or through the continent. At about the same time, they also discovered new riches on the lands that they were exploring. Gold and silver from South and Central America, and luxurious furs from North America would be valuable goods in Europe.

Explorers began claiming more and more land for the rulers of the countries sponsoring their expeditions. In turn, the rulers started to plan **colonies** in these newly claimed lands. They wanted to make sure they could control both the people and the riches they found there.

Some of the countries that explored during this period of exploration are discussed below.

Portugal

One of the first people to finance explorations during this time was Henry the Navigator, the king of Portugal. During the 1430s, he founded a court to which he invited Europe's best cartographers (mapmakers), shipbuilders, astronomers, instrument makers, and sailors. Portugal, located on the Atlantic Ocean, was active in exploration during the 1400s and 1500s.

Spain

Eager to find a way to the riches of Asia, the royal court of Spain sponsored many expeditions to search for a passage to the East. When the Spaniards found gold and silver in South America and Central America, they gave up on their search for the Northwest Passage and put their energy into mining these riches. Spain became very wealthy.

The Aztec and Maya **civilizations** of Mexico and Central America and the Inca of South America had flourished before the Spaniards arrived. But European illnesses and sophisticated weapons would destroy the civilizations.

England and France

Both England and France began exploration later than Spain and Portugal. They sponsored explorations after hearing reports of gold in South America. By this time, however, Spain and Portugal had laid claim to South America and Central America. England and France decided to focus on finding the Northwest Passage to Asia. They had different ways of pursuing their interests in North America. Their activities are outlined in chapters 5 and 6.

Figure 4.12 Europeans expected that people in the New World would look very different from themselves. The artist of this painting imagined people's heads were in the middle of their chests.

The Netherlands

The Netherlands entered the race for spices and wealth during the 1600s. The Dutch were involved in the North American fur trade, but when Spain and Portugal left Asia to explore the Americas, the Netherlands took their place. The Netherlands traded all over Asia, largely through the activities of the powerful Dutch East Indies Company.

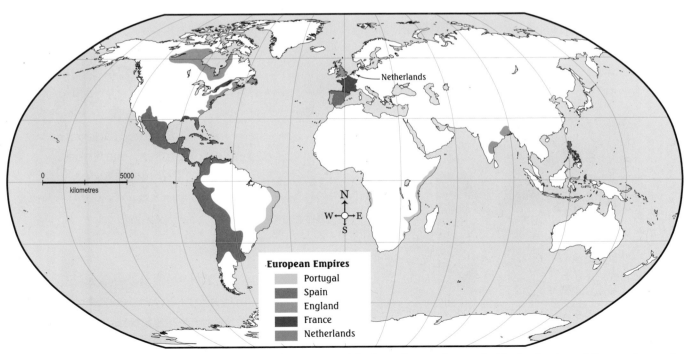

European Empires
- Portugal
- Spain
- England
- France
- Netherlands

Figure. 4.11 EUROPEAN EMPIRES. This map shows the empires of England, France, Spain, the Netherlands, and Portugal around the mid 17th century.

The Explorers

During the Renaissance, hundreds of explorers set out on uncharted waters to find fame and riches. They were fearless adventure seekers. Many died from disease or were killed in battle. Some, such as Henry Hudson, were left at sea. Others, such as John Cabot, simply never returned. The following men are just a few of the many who had an impact on the history of our world.

JOHN CABOT

John Cabot (1450–1498) is also known by his Italian name, Giovanni Caboto. Like Columbus, Cabot believed he could reach Asia by a westerly route. He had determined that the voyage would be shorter if he sailed as far north as possible. Sailing under England's flag, Cabot landed in Newfoundland in 1497. He was likely the first European since the Vikings to arrive on the continent of North America. Cabot disappeared under mysterious circumstances in 1498 and was never seen again.

BARTOLOMEU DIAZ

In 1488, Diaz (1450–1500), who sailed for Portugal, was the first to round the southern point of Africa. He named it the Cape of Storms. It was renamed the Cape of Good Hope by the king soon afterward so that it would sound less dangerous. This is the name that remains today. In 1498, Diaz sailed with another Portuguese explorer, Vasco da Gama (1469–1524) to India around the Cape of Good Hope.

CHRISTOPHER COLUMBUS

Columbus (1451–1506) was an Italian who sailed for Spain after he failed to secure sponsorships from the kings of both Portugal and England. He was sure he could reach Asia by sailing west rather than by going around Africa. He was the first European to travel west in the ongoing search for a passage to the East. Columbus made four voyages between 1492 and 1502, landing on islands in the Caribbean Sea and in Central America. He believed he had reached Asia on each of his voyages. As a result, he mistakenly identified the Aboriginal peoples of the Americas as "Indians."

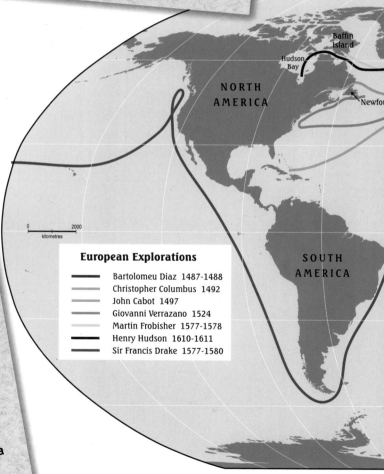

European Explorations

———	Bartolomeu Diaz 1487-1488
———	Christopher Columbus 1492
———	John Cabot 1497
———	Giovanni Verrazano 1524
———	Martin Frobisher 1577-1578
———	Henry Hudson 1610-1611
———	Sir Francis Drake 1577-1580

Figure 4.13 EUROPEAN EXPLORATIONS OF THE RENAISSANCE. Some important voyages of the 15th, 16th, and 17th centuries

GIOVANNI DA VERRAZANO

Verrazano (1485–1528) was an Italian who sailed for France in search of the Northwest Passage. He explored much of the eastern coast of North America, all the way up to Newfoundland, which he claimed for France. He noted in a letter to his king that colonization would be difficult because of the Aboriginal peoples living along the coast. He died at the hands of the Spaniards, who hanged him for piracy. Some historians think Jacques Cartier travelled with him to Newfoundland. We know that Cartier followed up Verrazano's explorations with his own ship in 1534.

MARTIN FROBISHER

Frobisher (1535–1594), who first went to sea at the age of nine, sailed for England. He travelled to North America in search of the Northwest Passage, but he was sidetracked in the Arctic at Baffin Island by what he thought was gold. He filled his ships with tons of gold-speckled rock and headed back to England. There, he found out that what he thought was gold was actually iron pyrite, a worthless rock also known as "fool's gold." Many of his backers were financially ruined, and the rock was eventually used for gravel.

Frobisher died after being wounded in a battle against Spain, and his internal organs were buried separately from the rest of his body. No one knows the reason for this.

HENRY HUDSON

Hudson (1565–1611) sailed under both Netherlands' and England's flags. He explored a large body of water, now called Hudson Bay, thinking that he had found the Northwest Passage. He and his crew spent the winter in Hudson Bay. When spring arrived and the ice melted, his crew wanted to return to Europe. Hudson, however, was determined to explore more of the large bay. His crew, tired of searching for the passage to the East, mutinied. Hudson, his son, and a few loyal crewmen were last seen alive in a small boat drifting on the bay. The mutineers returned to England. Several of them later returned for further explorations.

SIR FRANCIS DRAKE

Drake (1540–1596) sailed for England. In England he was regarded as a hero for his explorations, but the Spaniards saw him as a pirate and despised him. Drake first went to sea as a cabin boy when he was about 13 years old. Although the explorer Ferdinand Magellan is credited with being the first person to sail all the way around the world, Sir Francis Drake was the first to complete the trip and live. (Magellan died en route.) In 1580, he was knighted by Queen Elizabeth I.

Figure 4.14 Look at a map of present-day North America, and compare it with this map. In 1550, mapmakers did not have instruments (such as satellite images) that present-day mapmakers have to help them draw maps. The person who made this map believed North America was very narrow. Like many people of the day, the mapmaker probably thought North America would be easy to cross to reach the riches of the Orient.

Cartier and Donnacona— Friends and Enemies?

In 1534, Jacques Cartier (1493–1557) set sail from St. Malo, France. His voyage, paid for by the king of France, was "to discover certain islands and lands where it is said that a great quantity of gold, and other precious things, are to be found." He was also determined to find a Northwest Passage to Asia. Jacques Cartier gets credit as the first European to enter (and name) the St. Lawrence River.

Cartier made three voyages to North America. He explored the northeast coast of North America, sailed up the St. Lawrence River to Hochelaga (called Montreal today), and tried to establish a colony, which he called Charlesbourg-Royal, between Stadacona (today's Quebec City) and Hochelaga.

On his first voyage in 1534, Cartier sailed into Gaspé Bay. There, he met several hundred Aboriginal people. Relations started out well. However, when Cartier erected a nine-metre-high cross (a symbol of Christianity) and claimed the area for France, Donnacona, leader of the Wendat, became suspicious. As Cartier prepared his return voyage, he kidnapped Donnacona's sons Domagaya and Taignoagny and brought them back to France for the winter. Cartier wanted to prove to people in France that he had found new lands and peoples. He also wanted his captives to learn to speak French, so they could act as interpreters. He promised Donnacona he would bring his sons back the following year.

On Cartier's second trip, in 1535, he entered the St. Lawrence River for the first time. He then sailed to the village of Stadacona, where Donnacona and his sons were reunited. Cartier also went farther upriver to Hochelaga.

As it was getting late in the season, Cartier decided to stay the winter. He and his men were ill-prepared for the long, cold

Figure 4.15 When Cartier and Donnacona first met, they became friends. In the end, however, Cartier betrayed both Donnacona and the Wendat.

winter. Soon, many of the French became very sick. Not wanting to appear weak, the French tried to hide their illness from the Wendat (Hurons). However, one of Donnacona's sons immediately recognized the illness as scurvy. He taught Cartier and his men how to make the cedar bark tea used to cure the illness. Within a few days, most of the men were well again.

Before returning to France in the spring of 1536, Cartier kidnapped Donnacona and took him and his sons back to France. He wanted Donnacona to tell the king of France about the "Kingdom of Saguenay," a mythical place said to be full of gold and diamonds.

Cartier was sure this would convince the king to develop a permanent settlement along the St. Lawrence River. However, war broke out between France and England, and it was another five years before Cartier went back to North America. During those five years, Donnacona and his sons died in France.

When Cartier finally arrived back in Stadacona in 1541, he told the Wendat that their great chief, Donnacona, had died. The others, he explained, were living like lords in France and had not wanted to return. The Wendat suspected the truth, and they never trusted Cartier again.

Cartier and the settlers who travelled to North America with him on his third voyage were not welcome in Stadacona. Instead, they settled 14 kilometres away in Charlesbourg Royal. There, they planted a garden and built a fortified settlement. However, scurvy, distrust between the French and Aboriginal peoples and not enough support from France made the winter very difficult. By 1543, the colony broke up, and the settlers returned to France.

Jacques Cartier never returned to Canada. Nonetheless, he set the stage for later settlements under Samuel de Champlain, who would return in about 60 years to start a colony for France.

Figure 4.16 The Stadacona people showed the French how to make tea from the bark of the white cedar to cure scurvy.

We had a cross made 30 feet high [10 metres], which was put together in the presence of a number of the [Stadacona] Indians on the point [opposite Sandy Beach] at the entrance to this harbour, under the cross-bar of which we fixed a shield with three fleurs-de-lys in relief, and above it a wooden board, engraved in large Gothic characters, where was written, "Long live the king of France." We erected this cross on the point in their presence and they watched it being put together and set up. And when it had been raised in the air, we all knelt down with our hands joined, worshipping it before them....

When we had returned to our ships, the chief, dressed in an old black bearskin, arrived in a canoe with three of his sons and his brother... And pointing to the cross he made us a long harangue, making the sign of the cross with two of his fingers; and then he pointed to the land all around about, as if he wished to say that all this region belonged to him, and that we ought not to have set up this cross without his permission....

— *From the journals of Jacques Cartier*

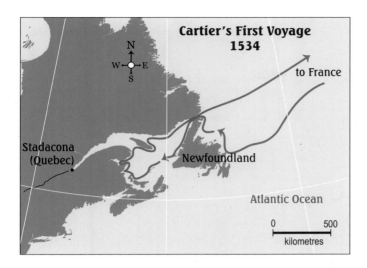

Cartier's First Voyage 1534

to France

Stadacona (Quebec)

Newfoundland

Atlantic Ocean

0 — 500
kilometres

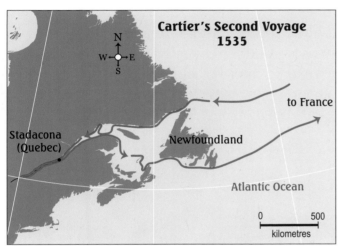

Cartier's Second Voyage 1535

to France

Stadacona (Quebec)

Newfoundland

Atlantic Ocean

0 — 500
kilometres

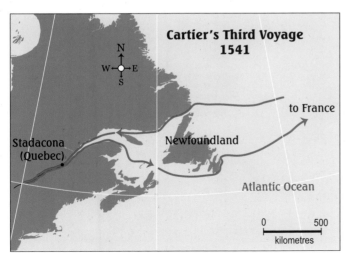

Cartier's Third Voyage 1541

Stadacona (Quebec)

Newfoundland

to France

Atlantic Ocean

0 — 500
kilometres

Figure 4.17 CARTIER'S THREE VOYAGES

DID YOU KNOW?

Jacques Cartier was the first person to refer to the land at the mouth of and along the St. Lawrence River as "Canada." Canada comes from the Algonquian word *Kanata*, which means "village."

Conclusion

Most of the explorers discussed in this chapter, and many others we have not named, led the European expansion into new areas. The leaders of the empires they represented thought this would be a good way to (1) find the Northwest Passage to Asia, (2) find gold and other precious metals, (3) convert Aboriginal peoples to European faiths, and (4) claim land for their empires.

Jacques Cartier did not find gold like the Spaniards did in South America and Central America. He did not find the mythical kingdom of Saguenay. Cartier did, however, open the way for explorers of the next century.

In the next chapter, join Sara and Ben as they explore the French presence in North America and learn about the role France played in colonizing the land that would come to be called "Canada."

5

The French in Canada, 1604–1759

Sara was confused. She had been watching a show on TV about the city of New Orleans. People kept talking about the "French Quarter." Wasn't New Orleans in the United States?

"Mom," she asked, "if New Orleans is in the United States, how can it have a French Quarter? There aren't any French people in the United States like there are in Canada, are there? They don't even learn to speak French in school the way we do."

"Yes, that does seem a bit confusing, doesn't it?" her mom answered. "But years ago, France was trying to take over many parts of North America and South America. New Orleans is one place they settled. They called it 'La Nouvelle-Orléans.' Another name that might surprise you is 'Ville d'étroit.'"

"Ville d'étroit," Sara said. "Detroit?!"

Figure 5.1 Daily life in New France

What's in a name?

Remembering all the different place names in New France can be confusing! Some places had an Aboriginal name and a French name. In addition, the names of most places changed over time. Below are some of the places mentioned in this chapter that were important to the early explorers and settlers.

ABORIGINAL NAME	NAME IN NEW FRANCE ERA	NAME TODAY
Hochelaga	Mont Royal, Ville Marie	Montreal
Stadacona	Quebec	Quebec City

As you read, think about

- why France decided to colonize North America
- what life was like for the early inhabitants of New France
- who was responsible for colonizing New France
- who lived and worked in New France
- how the Aboriginal peoples responded to the newcomers

Figure 5.2 NORTH AMERICA, 1700. This map shows the areas of North America claimed by European countries.

"That's right. Can you guess the name of the Frenchman who founded Detroit?"

"Dunno. What was it?"

"His last name was Cadillac."

"You mean like the car? That doesn't even sound French to me."

Sara discovered that much of North America had, at one time, been under French rule. She also learned that the area claimed by France in North America was known as "New France." She was surprised to find out how many cities, towns, lakes, and rivers were renamed by the French.

By the early 1600s, France was ready to establish a colony in the area of North America visited by Jacques Cartier over 50 years earlier. In this chapter, you will learn more about the French presence in North America. You will also learn about the role France played in the colonies that would eventually become Canada.

Early Settlements: Acadia

Samuel de Champlain explored and mapped territory all the way to Lake Superior, and he was determined to settle Quebec. He crossed the Atlantic Ocean about 20 times and never lost a sailor at sea. On land, his crew members were not as lucky, as you will find out.

Another European explorer was Pierre de Monts. Although Champlain is often called the "Father of New France," de Monts was the one who hired Champlain in 1604 to join him on his first expedition to New France to establish the French settlement that would become known as Acadia.

An interview with Pierre de Monts

Imagine you are listening to the following interview with Pierre de Monts on the radio!

Interviewer: You were given exclusive trading rights for furs in New France in 1604, were you not?

de Monts: Yes. I was given a 10-year monopoly on furs. In return, I was supposed to bring 60 colonists a year to New France.

Interviewer: Why did King Henry IV make this arrangement with you?

de Monts: It was an inexpensive way for the king to settle this new land. Instead of investing gold in a colony and paying for new colonists, he simply gave me the monopoly. Since I was expected to make money off the fur trade, it was my responsibility to pay for the colonists. However, things didn't work out the way they were supposed to. The Basques did not respect my monopoly. They obtained furs directly from the Aboriginal peoples instead of buying them from me. There was nothing I could do about it.

Interviewer: The colony itself, how was that?

de Monts: Samuel will tell you how difficult the winter of 1604–1605 was. Things got better when we moved to Port Royal, on the mainland, the next winter. It was milder for one thing. Also, Samuel and my lawyer, Marc Lescarbot, started a dinner club called "The Order of Good Cheer." We all took turns providing the best meal we could for everyone else in the club. Many Mi'kmaq people joined us. Everyone ate well, and we entertained each other. Marc even wrote a play, which some of the men performed. Hardly anyone died.

Interviewer: And then the disappointment....

de Monts: The king cancelled my monopoly because I wasn't building up the colony quickly enough. In 1607, I returned to France. After that, my friend Chief Membertou looked after the settlement as if it were his own.

Figure 5.3 Pierre de Monts travelled to North America only once. He founded Port Royal, the first French colony in North America.

An interview with Samuel de Champlain

Imagine you are listening to the following interview with Samuel de Champlain on the radio!

Interviewer: Mr. Champlain, although you were a passenger on a ship that sailed to Hochelaga in the spring of 1603, you returned to France before winter set in. What can you tell us about your first winter in North America, in 1604?

Champlain: Mostly, I remember the cold. As you know, we stayed in Acadia. Acadia is no farther north than France, so we thought winter would be the same. When snow started falling in October, we started to worry.

Interviewer: You set up camp on Île de St. Croix, did you not? Why did you choose to stay on an island?

Champlain: We felt that on an island we would be able to defend ourselves easily if we were attacked. Unfortunately, we had no idea that the ice would build up in the Baie Française to the point where, for long periods of time, we could not safely cross. It is so frustrating to see a moose that will feed your whole group for several days come within firing distance, but because you are on the island and it is on the mainland, you have no

Figure 5.4 This portrait of Champlain is based on written accounts of the explorer. Historians do not believe Champlain ever had a portrait painted of himself.

Figure 5.5 Champlain drew this map of Port Royal.

way of getting to the animal. Then we ran out of firewood. Then the freshwater spring froze over.

Interviewer: It must have been a very difficult several months.

Champlain: It was. Of our 79 men, we lost 35 to scurvy, malnutrition, or the cold. Only two others and I stayed on in the New World after that winter. It became harder and harder to get people to come from France. All they heard about was how cold the winters are here.

Interviewer: Is there anything else you would like to add?

Champlain: I would like them to know that even though we have had some difficult times, I remain optimistic about the future here. The Mi'kmaq have helped us to overcome scurvy. I believe in the tremendous riches of this new land. Someone once said that even the moon shines brighter here. And that's true – this is a glorious land.

Chief Membertou

Membertou was a Mi'kmaq chief who, during the early years of the Acadian settlements, worked and traded with the French. He was a good friend to the French. Membertou looked after the settlement at Port Royal for three years (1607–1610). He even kept up the gardens. In 1610, Jean de Poutrincourt, one of the original colonists, returned to New France to help resettle the colony. In 1613, the British destroyed Port Royal, which

Membertou had carefully tended. The British attack set the stage for many years of fighting over who would control the colony, the French or the British.

Figure 5.6 In 1605, Champlain and de Monts established a colony at Port Royal. The French and the Mi'kmaq began to trade furs at the settlement.

Different points of view

The settlements in Acadia were the first European settlements in Canada. In the beginning, the Mi'kmaq people welcomed the French settlers. They traded with them and showed them how to live on the land. Soon, however, the Mi'kmaq people became concerned. They realized that their view about the land was different from the view of the French. To the Mi'kmaq, land was not owned, or possessed, by one person or group. Land was shared. The Mi'kmaq had rules about who could use the different territories to hunt and fish. These rules were decided by consensus. The Europeans did not want to follow these rules when they arrived in New France.

At one time, Europeans had recognized that land could not be claimed if people already lived

there. That all changed during the Renaissance. In 1493, the pope of the Roman Catholic Church said that inhabited lands could be claimed in the name of God. In 1763, the British passed the Royal Proclamation that gave the British the right to purchase land from Aboriginal peoples. No one ever thought to ask First Peoples what they thought about newcomers owning land that they had lived on for years.

When Aboriginal peoples allowed Europeans to use the land, they did not mean for the Europeans to own it and do whatever they wanted with it. The Europeans, however, believed the land was theirs to buy and sell, and that they could use it in whatever way they wanted. These two different ideas about possessing and using land became the root of many disagreements over the centuries.

An interview with Chief Membertou

Imagine you are listening to an interview with the Mi'kmaq chief Membertou on the radio!

Interviewer: Chief Membertou, please tell us what you thought when the French first came to trade with you.

Membertou: I thought that we could make an **alliance**. We would supply the French with furs – all those Europeans are crazy for fur, even old robes! – and they would supply us with other trade goods, such as cloth and metal objects.

Interviewer: Why are you so interested in metal things?

Membertou: Cooking pots made from metal are much lighter to carry than our clay pots, and they don't break. The women also like the sewing needles, which go through the animal hides much easier than bone needles do. Until we began trading with the French, we made everything from clay, bone, stone, or wood. Men like metal arrowheads, spearheads, fishhooks, traps. Metal tools last longer, and we don't have to spend as much time carving, sharpening, and repairing the tools. This gives us more time to hunt and fish, and more time to pick berries and other wild plants. Some of our relatives farther inland farm. But here on the coast we have plenty of food, so farming is not necessary. The French are very fond of farming, however.

Interviewer: What has been your greatest challenge in dealing with the Europeans?

Membertou: There have been many, but the greatest challenge has been dealing with the diseases the Europeans have brought with them. Although some of our people were in contact with Europeans long before the arrival of Champlain and de Monts, we have never before lived in such close quarters with Europeans.

Now we are spending more time with the explorers – as river guides and as trading partners. None of our medicines seem to cure the new diseases. Often, our Elders are the first to get sick and die. We are losing their wisdom. Our children are also dying, so we are losing our future. It is terrible.

Figure 5.7 Chief Membertou was a good friend of the French.

The Beginnings of Quebec

In 1608, Champlain returned to New France. There, he turned his attention to building his l'**Habitation** at Stadacona, which was farther inland than Port Royal. He called the settlement Quebec. The new village became the centre of the colony of New France. Whenever Champlain was in France, he encouraged immigration to New France. He convinced Louis Hébert and his wife to move to New France and farm. He asked Catholic priests to go over to look after the spiritual and social needs of the settlers and to convert the Aboriginal peoples. Still, in 1627, the colony had only 100 inhabitants.

In 1627, the Company of One Hundred Associates was created in France. Led by the powerful Cardinal Richelieu, the company was granted trading rights in return for building up the colony. That summer, a supply ship and 400 colonists set sail from France. By the time the ships reached New France, war with England had broken out, and the colonists were prevented from landing. The Kirke brothers, hired by the British to capture French land, blockaded Quebec and sent the ships back to France.

With no new supplies, Champlain and his men were facing starvation. In 1629, he was forced to surrender his beloved l'Habitation, and the Kirke brothers took him back to Europe. In 1632, after much

DID YOU KNOW?

The former village of Lachine is now part of the city of Montreal. It got its name from the French word for "China" (*la Chine*). Robert Cavelier de La Salle, who was exploring the interior of North America in search of a passageway to Asia, thought that the canal in the village would lead him to China.

negotiation, Quebec was returned to France. Champlain returned to New France the following year. He died in Quebec in 1635. At that time, the colony had a population of 200 people. It would be up to others to fulfill Champlain's dream of a French settlement in North America.

Figure 5.8 When Champlain arrived in Quebec, he built a wooden fort that he called "l'Habitation." It was surrounded by a tall wooden fence made of logs. The Aboriginal peoples came to the fort to trade furs for goods such as blankets, kettles, and tools.

People of the Colony

Following Champlain's death in 1635, the French colony continued to grow, but slowly. Compared to the populations of the English and Dutch settlements farther south, the French colony was small. Stories about the cold winters and the threat of the Iroquois attacks convinced most would-be settlers to stay in France.

In 1642, the French founded a **missionary** colony for the Roman Catholic Church at Mont Royal and called it Ville Marie. However, attempts to convert Aboriginal peoples to Catholicism were not very successful.

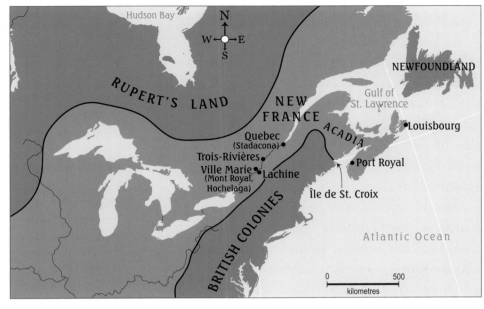

Figure 5.9 SETTLEMENT IN NEW FRANCE

In 1663, King Louis XIV cancelled the contract of the One Hundred Associates and put the French colony under direct royal control. He decided to send someone to run the colony as his own representative. This person was called an **intendant**. The first intendant of New France was Jean Talon. He arrived in 1665, and, during his years of rule, he helped the colony prosper. One of the first things Jean Talon did when he arrived in New France was take a **census**.

Figure 5.10 At census time, Jean Talon met with each family and discussed the settlers' needs and their goals for the future.

Governing New France

By 1665, New France was governed by a **sovereign council**. The council, **appointed** by the king and his representatives, was made up of three people: the governor, the intendant, and the bishop. The governor took care of military matters, such as dealing with the English and the Aboriginal peoples. The intendant looked after matters like business and industry within the colony. The bishop took care of health, education, and religion.

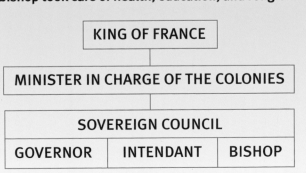

```
                    KING OF FRANCE

        MINISTER IN CHARGE OF THE COLONIES

                 SOVEREIGN COUNCIL
     GOVERNOR  |  INTENDANT  |  BISHOP
```

The *filles du roi* (daughters of the king)

From the census, Jean Talon learned that there were twice as many men as women living in the colony. He realized that if New France was to grow, more women were needed. He persuaded the king to send the *filles du roi* (daughters of the king), who would marry settlers and produce many children for the colony.

Between 1665 and 1673, 900 of these young women came from France to New France. Some were orphans. Others were simply looking for new adventures and opportunities. Young, strong country girls seemed to fare best in New France – they were used to working hard, gardening, and caring for animals. They ranged in age from young teenagers to women in their twenties. Most were married within two weeks of their arrival in New France. Each woman was given a **dowry** by the king. A dowry was money or property given by a wife to her husband when they married. In New France, it consisted of clothing and household items.

All people crossing the ocean faced many dangers. Shipwrecks were common, and ocean voyages could take anywhere from four weeks to several months, making it difficult to know how much food to bring for the crossing. For the filles du roi, however, the challenges were even greater. Sometimes ship captains stole the few possessions the women brought with them. Once they arrived in New France, though, the leaders of the colony did their best to help out the young women. Talon also used other methods to encourage population growth. Unmarried men were not granted fishing and fur-

Figure 5.11 Filles du roi arrive in New France.

trading rights. If a father had a son or daughter who was old enough to be married but was not, the father had to provide a good reason why his son or daughter was still single. Talon offered families money for having children – the larger the family, the more money it was given. For these reasons, after 1673, the population of New France grew quickly. While Talon was intendant, the population of New France grew from 3200 to 7600 people. Talon himself never took advantage of his own programs; he did not marry or have children.

Habitants

Jean Talon inherited the **seigneurial system** from previous leaders of the colony. Used as a means to divide the land, it was similar to the system used in France. Land was granted to **seigneurs**, or lords, who then rented the land to **habitants**. The seigneur was responsible for developing the land by building a mill or fort.

A habitant was responsible for cultivating the land. The land, which ran along both banks of the St. Lawrence River, was divided into long, thin strips so that each farm had access to the river. Jean Talon made sure to fill in vacant land and allot it, and, generally, brought organization to the plan.

Talon encouraged the habitants to grow a variety of crops. Before he arrived in New France, habitants had grown mostly wheat. Talon had them plant peas and beans, hemp and flax for cloth, and barley and hops for beer. Under his guidance, the habitants started exporting some of their surplus crops. Some habitants imported fruit trees from Europe. Many of the trees grew well in New France.

Figure 5.12 In New France, women usually wore separate tops and skirts (as seen here). The handwoven cloth came in stripes as well as plain or checkered patterns. Long-sleeved jackets helped to keep them warm. Men wore handspun breeches and short jackets. Hats were often similar to those worn in France, before the settlers started making hats that were warmer for the climate in New France.

Talon also increased the amount of livestock and other animals in the colony. In a very short time, the colonists were able to fulfill all of their own needs for meat and leather, eggs and milk, as well as wool.

Many habitants had their own horses, which they used for ploughing and for transportation. This bothered some of the newly arrived elite from Europe. They felt that the habitants were becoming too independent. In France, few farmers could afford a horse.

The Church and Its Role in New France

During this time in history, the Catholic Church had great power. Church leaders influenced governments throughout Europe. The power of the church was lessened somewhat, however, in New France. Although the people of New France were required to build a church and a home for the priest, some priests thought that colonists did not show enough respect. Priests complained of "parishioners chatting in the pews, wandering outside for a smoke during the sermon, bringing their dogs along to Mass, generally making themselves too comfortable."

It was very important to all the church leaders that those in their care learn to follow God from a Catholic, European **point of view**. These leaders believed that they were the only people who really understood what God wanted. As a result, they tried to make everyone believe exactly what they did. Some priests worked solely as missionaries among the Aboriginal peoples.

The two main **orders** of priests were the Récollets and the Jesuits. The priests, especially the Jesuits, travelled to the villages of different Aboriginal peoples, and learned their language and observed their ways. Once trust had been established, the Jesuits set about to convert them.

The missionaries were well educated. They often wrote about their travels in and observations of the country and the Aboriginal peoples whom they met there. Much of what historians know about New France comes from the writings of these priests.

Figure 5.13 Arrival of Madame Champlain, at Quebec in 1620. Champlain's wife, Hélène Boullé was only 14 years old when she arrived in New France. She rarely saw her busy husband and became very lonely, except for the Wendat children she grew close to. After four years, she returned to France. She became an Ursuline nun following her husband's death in 1635.

The church was involved in many other areas of peoples' lives. Priests and nuns, for example, ran all of the schools and hospitals in New France.

Schools

The Ursuline Nuns arrived in New France in 1639. They focused on educating young women and girls. They taught both Aboriginal and French girls religion, as well as reading, writing, and needlework. Marie de l'Incarnation was a widow and the first Ursuline Nun to come to New France. She learned Algonquian and

Figure 5.14 This is an original portrait of Marguerite Bourgeoys painted immediately after her death on January 12, 1700. A second portrait of Marguerite was painted over this one. In 1963, art restorer Edward Korany found this original under many layers of paint.

Iroquoian languages, and wrote dictionaries of both languages.

When Marguerite Bourgeoys arrived in 1663, she began several schools for girls in Ville Marie. She taught religion, reading, writing, and "domestic arts" like sewing and needlepoint. Some girls in her care became nuns. She also took charge of the filles du roi when they arrived. She interviewed them and housed them until they were ready to be married. For many years, her order, Congrégation de Notre-Dame de Montréal, was not officially recognized by the church, because she refused to become **cloistered**. Instead, she left her **convent** and travelled to where the people were. She is often referred to as "the mother of the colony."

Jesuit priests taught the boys religion, arithmetic, reading, writing, and a **trade**.

Some boys learned how to be carpenters. Others became sculptors. Some were trained to be navigators, others to be priests.

Hospitals

Jeanne Mance was the first nurse in North America. She arrived in 1642, and she started the first hospital, called the Hôtel-Dieu, in Ville Marie.

Nuns grew fruits and vegetables and raised animals so that the patients could be fed. Nuns also did housekeeping chores at the hospital.

The nuns received money from the French government to look after soldiers and officers of the king. They also used the money to help the poor when they were sick, and any orphans who came into their care.

Figure 5.15 Nuns and priests in the colony taught children and tended to the sick.

The Fur Trade

The intendant and other leaders wanted people to farm and settle the colony. Many habitants, however, were drawn to the money that could be made in the fur trade. While the church and the king wanted the Aboriginal peoples to live like the French, often it was the French fur traders who adapted to Aboriginal ways of life.

Many young men of the colony became *coureurs de bois*, or "runners of the woods." You will read more about the French fur trade in chapter 7.

> Though many nations imitate French customs, I observed, on the contrary, that the French in Canada in many respects follow the customs of the Indians, with whom they have constant relations. They use tobacco pipes, shoes, garters and belts of the Indians. They follow the Indian way of waging war; they mix the same things with tobacco; they make use of the Indian bark boats and row them in the Indian way… they have adopted many other Indian fashions.
>
> —*Swedish botanist and writer Pehr Kalm, 1749*

Frontenac

Louis de Buade, Comte de Frontenac, became governor of New France in 1672, after Jean Talon had left. Frontenac was vain, extravagant, and always in debt.

During Frontenac's second term as governor of New France (1689–1698), the French were constantly being harassed by the Iroquois. The Iroquois were being supplied and encouraged by the English, so the French raided British and Iroquois territory to the south. This made the English angry. In 1689, the English raided Quebec with over 2300 men, hoping to take over the colony. When the British asked Frontenac to surrender, he replied: "Tell your leader that I shall reply to him through the mouths of my cannon." The English, afflicted by smallpox and the onset of winter, had to withdraw.

Frontenac continued Talon's work of encouraging the growth of the colony, its agriculture, and economy. He worked to make peace with the Iroquois. He also built forts on the Great Lakes and along the Mississippi River. He built Fort Cataraqui on the eastern shores of Lake Ontario. From there, the explorer La Salle used it as a base from which to explore and trade fur. The fort was later named Fort Frontenac.

King Louis XIV of France was not happy with Frontenac. He thought he was too ambitious. He wanted Frontenac to protect New France, not find new lands. Although Frontenac made money from the fur trade he helped to build up, he also expanded French territory and influence in North America.

Figure 5.16 Louis de Buade, Comte de Frontenac

Louisbourg

In the early 1700s, Acadia changed between French and English rule many times. When Britain gained control of Newfoundland and Acadia in 1713, France wanted to guard its lands in the Gulf of St. Lawrence. It started to build the Fortress of Louisbourg on Île Royale, present-day Cape Breton Island.

It took 25 years to build the great stone walls of the fortress surrounding Louisbourg, the new capital of Île Royale. Louisbourg became a busy centre for the French colony. Its main industry was the cod fishery. Fishermen caught and dried their net loads of cod. The colony's merchants traded the fish in Europe and the Caribbean. The harbour bustled with merchant ships.

Between 1713 and 1758, several thousand people lived in Louisbourg. With soldiers protecting the town, government officials lived in beautiful homes, furnished with finery from France. In 1758, Louisbourg was attacked and destroyed by the British.

In 1961, the government of Canada decided to reconstruct much of the Fortress of Louisbourg. That way, visitors could experience what it was like to live there in the 18th century. Louisbourg is the largest historical reconstruction in the country.

Figure 5.17 Modern-day visitors at Louisbourg

Figure 5.18 The reconstructed fortress of Louisbourg is a national historic site.

Conclusion

Many French people settled on farms in present-day Canada in the early days of European expansion into North America. Others, especially the couriers de bois, travelled great distances in search of furs. The Jesuits ventured into unknown territory looking for Aboriginal peoples to convert to Catholicism. All contributed to the French presence in North America.

Although France lost its colonies to Britain from time to time, New France was always returned to the French. By the late 1600s, however, even Frontenac's daring defiance only helped to hold off the powerful English for a while longer.

In the next chapter, join Ben and Sara as they explore some reasons why France would eventually lose its North American colonies to the British.

6

The British in North America

While you and your classmates are at the gym, the students in grade 7 come into your classroom. They sit at your desks and begin to use your school supplies. Soon, some grade 8 students barge into your classroom. Their room is overcrowded, and they are looking for more space. Your classroom is perfect for them. When they try to kick the grade 7 students out of your classroom, fighting breaks out between the two groups of students.

It is at this moment that you and your classmates arrive back from the gym. You try to reclaim your desks, but the grade 7 and grade 8 students refuse to give them up. Eventually, you and your classmates are allowed to stay – not at your desks but on the floor at the back of the room.

The above scenario is not too different from what happened when Europeans began expanding into Asia, Africa, the Americas, and elsewhere. In North America, both the French and the English believed they had the

Figure 6.1 The construction of Halifax

right to claim the land as their own, and they gave little thought to Aboriginal ways of life.

As you saw in earlier chapters, France and England had been enemies, on and off, for hundreds of years. Not surprisingly, the wars they fought elsewhere in the world during the 17th and 18th centuries carried over to North America. At first, the French and the English military were fairly equal. Gradually, however, England became the more powerful country.

In this chapter, you will learn about the early years of the English presence in North America and find out how England was eventually able to take over New France.

Many portraits in this chapter show men with a lot of hair. Most men did not really have long, curly hair. They wore wigs. In 1620, King Louis XIII of France began wearing a wig, because he was going bald. Soon, men all over the western world were wearing wigs. Some wigs were made of human hair, others of yak or horsehair. Those made of human hair were the most expensive. Wearers had to be careful their wigs were not full of lice, or worse, that the hair came from the head of someone who had died of the **bubonic plague**.

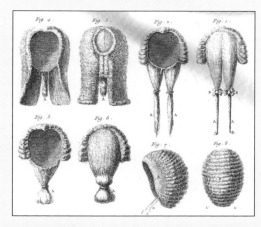

Figure 6.2 Hairdressers constantly cleaned, curled, and powdered wigs such as these for their clients.

As you read, think about

- **why the English decided to colonize in North America**
- **where the British colonies were located**
- **how the British colonies were different from the French colonies**
- **who lived and worked in the colonies**
- **how the British presence affected Aboriginal peoples**

Newfoundland

First settlements

In the mid-1500s, the English began to fish for cod off Newfoundland's coast. They were not interested in staying in Newfoundland year-round. However, they had to go ashore to set up seasonal fishing camps. There, they salted and dried the fish before they returned to England. Over the next one hundred years, they built more and more camps until they controlled most of the southeast coast of Newfoundland. This area became known as "The English Shore."

In 1611, John Guy, a merchant from Bristol, England, along with about 40 other colonists, formed Newfoundland's first permanent settlement at Cuper's Cove. Although Guy returned to England after a few years, approximately 60 people remained on the island.

In 1621, George Calvert (later Lord Baltimore) started a colony on the Avalon Peninsula. That year, he sent 12 settlers to Newfoundland. In 1628, Lord Baltimore, with 40 members of his family and house-hold, joined the settlers. However, he found the winter too harsh, he argued with the French, and he was unhappy that people within the colony fought over religious differences. Lord Baltimore moved to Maryland (see map, p. 86), but some of his colonists decided to stay in Newfound-land. Soon, the Newfoundland colony had grown to 100 people.

The Beothuk

The Beothuk people lived in Newfoundland before and during the time that Europeans began fishing in its coastal waters. In the

Figure 6.3 This picture from the early 1700s shows cod being processed. After the fish were caught, the fishermen went ashore to clean and wash the cod. Cod liver oil was collected, then the fish were salted and laid out to dry on platforms.

summer, the Beothuk fished for cod and harp seals along the shore. In the winter, they moved inland and hunted caribou, beaver, and other small fur-bearing animals. While most Aboriginal peoples traded with the Europeans, the Beothuk kept to themselves as much as possible.

For centuries, the Beothuk people had made yearly journeys between the coast and the Newfoundland interior. By the mid-1700s, however, the Beothuk no longer had access to the sea. European fishermen had taken over most of the coast, and the Beothuk were forced to remain in the interior. There, they could not find enough food, and many died from starvation. Diseases brought over by Europeans killed many others. Other Beothuk were killed by settlers.

In 1823, the last remaining Beothuk, a woman named Shanawdithit, was captured. She was taken to the home of William Cormack, an English explorer who was very interested in the Beothuk. Shanawdithit spent a great deal of time talking to Cormack about her people. She drew pictures and described the Beothuk ways of life. Most of what we know about the Beothuk is because Shanawdithit was willing to tell her story.

Shanawdithit's death from tuberculosis in 1829 was a terrible tragedy, signifying the death of an entire people. The Beothuk culture, which had flourished for hundreds of years, had been driven to extinction.

Henry Crout, an associate of John Guy, wrote about a meeting between the Beothuk and the English.

Then the governor sent the boat to go ashore and there landed one man called Master Whittington with our flag of truce. Then there landed one of theirs out of the canoe and so came to parlay by signs one to the other with handing and dancing together, they laughing much with very great voices. Then there came another of their men ashore [and] presently there landed another of ours.

Then afterward the governor landed and some 4 more of us. The governor made them a banquet with raisins, bread and butter and beer and aquavitae which they like well. But first they gave us at our coming ashore chains of shells and put [them] about our necks for great presents. The governor bestowed [on] them a shirt, napkin, handkerchiefs and points and our flag of truce. They gave us some of their dry venison. They were very Joyful of our flag of truce.

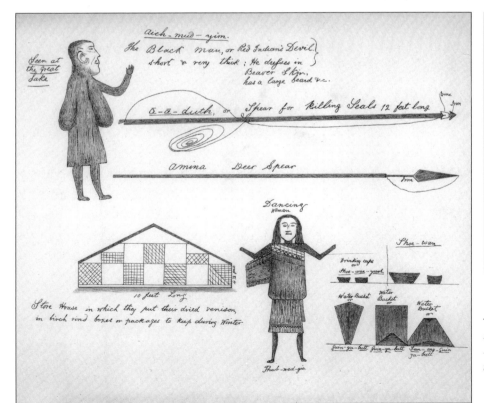

Diseases

Before Europeans came to North America, Aboriginal peoples had not been exposed to diseases such as smallpox, measles, and tuberculosis. Therefore, they were not immune to (had no way to fight off) these diseases. Many Aboriginal peoples died from illnesses brought over by Europeans; some Aboriginal nations died out completely.

Figure 6.4 This is one of 12 drawings that Shanawdithit drew while she stayed with William Cormack. She described what she was drawing, and Cormack made detailed notes.

The Thirteen Colonies

England was interested in New France for two main reasons. The first was the fishing industry. The coast surrounding Newfoundland had some of the best fishing grounds in the world. For many European countries on the Atlantic Ocean, fish was an important source of food. The second reason was defence. England did not want France to threaten its territory in North America.

As a place to set up colonies, England was much more interested in lands to the south of Quebec. There, the weather was warmer, the soil was more fertile, and the settlements were easier to reach. The first colony was settled in present-day Virginia in 1607. The land was excellent for crops, and tobacco soon became a wealth-producing export.

Throughout the 1600s, people from England crossed the Atlantic and established colonies along the east coast of present-day United States. Some groups of people, such as the **Puritans**, came to escape religious **persecution**. They were the founders of Massachusetts. New Hampshire was founded as a fishing village. Georgia, settled with people from "debtor's prison," acted as a barrier between the English colonies and Spanish-owned Florida. England's settlements became known as the Thirteen Colonies and, later, the United States of America.

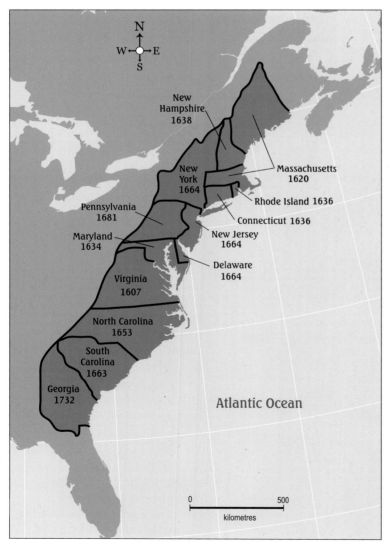

Figure 6.5 THIRTEEN COLONIES. This map shows the Thirteen Colonies in 1776. The dates show when each became a British colony.

War Between France and Britain

European countries were often at war with one another during the 17th and 18th centuries. Wars that involved France and Britain (see box, right) spread to their colonies in North America.

What is a peace treaty?

A peace treaty is a written agreement that is made and signed between two nations (sometimes more) or sides. Treaties set up the terms of peace after a war. They also set out the rules nations must follow in their dealings with each other.

Figure 6.6 In this battle scene from the Seven Years' War, British troops are attacking the French fort on the shores of the east coast of North America.

Four wars

NAME OF WAR	DATES	TREATY THAT ENDED WAR
King William's War	1689–1697	Treaty of Ryswick
Queen Anne's War	1702–1713	Treaty of Utrecht
King George's War	1744–1748	Treaty of Aix-la-Chapelle
Seven Years' War	1756–1763	Treaty of Paris

To keep the wars in order of when they happened, think: William, Anne, George, Seven Years: WAGS.

You will read more about the Seven Years' War on page 92.

The Founding of Halifax, 1749

Following King George's War, England decided to build its own fortified base to protect the country's interests in North America. In 1749, General Edward Cornwallis arrived in North America with 2500 settlers. Most were poor Londoners who had answered an advertisement that promised free land, transportation, food, and other supplies, as well as military protection. Others came from countries such as Switzerland and Germany.

Cornwallis, appointed as the new governor of Nova Scotia, chose a site

> *The grass on which you sleep is mine. I sprung out of it, as grass does, I was born from it from sire to son – it is mine forever.*
>
> *— Mi'kmaq chief to Cornwallis when asked for his loyalty to Britain*

for the base on Chebucto Bay. The base was called Halifax, in honour of George Montague-Dunk, Lord Halifax, who sponsored the expedition. By August, all the settlers had been assigned a piece of land. However, many were unable to build before winter set in. With the coming of spring, nearly 1000 of the settlers decided

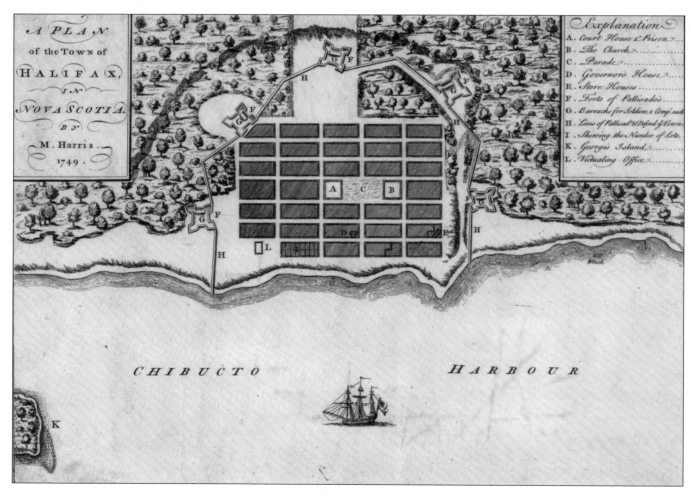

Figure 6.7 This plan for the town of Halifax, Nova Scotia, was made in 1749. The town was laid out in rectangular lots.

Figure 6.8 To protect their colonies, the British built a fort on top of the hill that overlooked Halifax's harbour. From this location, now called Citadel Hill, the British were able to guard against enemy attacks.

Figure 6.9 General Edward Cornwallis

to travel south. The Thirteen Colonies offered warmer weather and few problems with the French and Aboriginal populations. The French and Mi'kmaq in Acadia did not want British settlers, and joined together to fight them. Even so, the population of Halifax began to grow, and a strong British community sprang up.

Cornwallis was not happy with several of the English settlers. He found them to be lazy and unambitious. However, Cornwallis thought that the Swiss and Germans were "easily governed and work heartily." Cornwallis and his board of governors sought out more settlers from Switzerland and Germany. In 1753, because they were getting crowded in Halifax, the Swiss and German settlers began their own town, Lunenburg.

When Cornwallis first arrived in North America, he was on friendly terms with the Mi'kmaq. However, as he took over more

and more land for the colony, the Mi'kmaq declared war on the English. Rather than try to make peace with them, Cornwallis declared them enemies. He offered the settlers of Halifax money for proof that they had killed a Mi'kmaq man, woman, or child.

Halifax firsts

- The *Halifax Gazette* was the first newspaper in British North America, published on March 23, 1752. It was two pages long.

- In 1755, the first post office in what is now Canada opened its doors in Halifax.

- In 1758, Canada's first elected representative assembly met in Halifax.

Figure 6.10 This is the first page of the first edition of the *Halifax Gazette*.

Expulsion of Acadians, 1755–1763

The British in North America were nervous. It looked as if there might be another war. Thousands of French inhabitants lived in Acadia, land that England had won from France in Queen Anne's War. The Acadians had remained neutral in the earlier wars, but if they ever decided to fight for the French, England knew it would be in a lot of trouble.

A few years earlier, when Cornwallis founded Halifax, he had asked the Acadians to swear an **oath of allegiance** to Britain. They refused. However, they agreed to take a **modified** oath. They swore their loyalty to England in return for permission to keep their French language and Roman Catholic religion, and, in case of war, to remain neutral.

When Edward Lawrence became governor of Nova Scotia, the Acadians were again ordered to take an oath of allegiance to England. Once more, the Acadians refused. They thought that Lawrence would back down much the same way Cornwallis had. They were wrong.

Lawrence ordered the immediate deportation of Acadians. Their homes and barns were burned down, and their livestock killed or taken by the British. The Acadians were herded onto ships that were filled beyond what the ships could safely hold. Families were separated, and many people became sick and died. Acadia ceased to exist.

To prevent the Acadians from moving to French communities in Quebec or on Cape Breton Island, the British sent them to the Thirteen Colonies and to internment camps in Britain. Some fled to Quebec. About 2000 people escaped to Prince Edward Island, but they were rounded up and expelled again. Historians estimate almost 10 000 of Acadia's population of 13 000 were deported. Of the 10 000, almost 7000 were deported in 1755.

Some Acadians ended up in France, but they could not get used to life there. In Acadia, they had had many freedoms and everything that they needed. In France, the way of life for peasants seemed harsh and unforgiving. In 1785, almost 1600 Acadians sailed from France to Louisiana to join the Acadians who were already living there. The land around the mouth of the Mississippi River was similar to the land around the Bay of Fundy. Although Louisiana was a possession of Spain, people spoke French and the official religion of the colony was Roman Catholic. Their name "Acadian" was shorted to "Cajun," and today over 1 million Acadian descendants live in Louisiana.

Figure 6.11 The deportation of the Acadians

John Winslow was a British colonel. He was assigned the task of expelling the Acadians, on the order of King George II. Winslow wrote the following speech, which was read to the inhabitants of the Acadian village of Cobequid on September 4, 1755:

Gentlemen:

... The part of duty I am now upon, though necessary, is very disagreeable to my natural make and temper, as I know it must be grievous to you. But it is my business to obey such orders as I receive, and therefore without hesitation shall deliver to you his Majesty's orders and instructions, namely: That your lands and tenements, cattle of all kinds, and livestock of all sorts are forfeited to the Crown, with all your other effects, saving your money and your household goods, and you yourselves to be removed from the Province.

Thus it is, that the whole French inhabitants of these districts be removed, and I am through his Majesty's goodness directed to allow you liberty to carry off your money and household goods, as many as you can, without discommoding the vessels you go in. I hope that in whatever part of the world you may fall, you may be faithful subjects, a peaceable and happy people. I must also inform you that it is His majesty's pleasure that you remain in security under the inspection and direction of the troops that I have the honour to command; I therefore, in the King's name, declare you all prisoners.

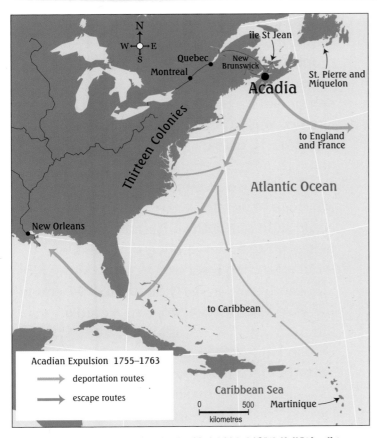

Figure 6.12 **ACADIAN DESTINATIONS AFTER DEPORTATION.** This map shows the places that Acadians went to after deportation.

Figure 6.13 In 1764, the Acadians were allowed to return to their former homeland, provided they took an oath of allegiance to Britain. Many families came back. Their farms had been taken over by others, so they settled on new land in present-day New Brunswick, Nova Scotia, and Quebec. Today, their descendants celebrate their Acadian heritage at festivals such as the one shown here.

The Seven Years' War, 1756–1763

In the Thirteen Colonies, settlers were running out of space. Their population had greatly increased, and settlements were crowded along the coast. English settlers wanted to move west to the Ohio River Valley, but the French had already claimed the land. When the French realized the British had their eyes on the Ohio River Valley, they began to build forts so that they could defend the area. This action led to the first official North American battle in the Seven Years' War between the French and the English.

France had many more Aboriginal **allies** than the English. They also had more land. Britain, however, kept sending more soldiers and supplies to North America, and grew stronger and stronger. The Battle of the Plains of Abraham was a turning point.

Battle of the Plains of Abraham, September 1759

The commanders
James Wolfe joined the British army at the age of 14. He fought his first battle three years later. He was sent to North America during the Seven Years' War. British forces had captured and destroyed French settlements in St. John Valley and Prince Edward Island, and they had control of the St. Lawrence River. In 1759, Wolfe was appointed commander-in-chief to capture Quebec. Wolfe arrived in June and spent the summer pounding the city with cannons, but he was unable to break Quebec's defences.

Figure 6.14
General Montcalm

Louis Joseph de Montcalm joined the French army at the age of 12. Described as opinionated and stubborn, he fought in many wars, including King George's War, before coming to Canada. In 1756, he was sent to New France to lead French troops against the British. In 1758, with only 3000 men, he won a huge victory at Fort Carillon against 15 000 British troops. He was then sent to defend Quebec.

The battle
The Battle of the Plains of Abraham began after months of British **siege** and attacks on nearby settlements. The city of Quebec was built on cliffs that rose 70 metres above the St. Lawrence and St. Charles rivers. Montcalm knew that if he could hold out until winter, the British would be forced to leave Quebec. All summer, Wolfe searched for a way to force Montcalm into battle, and in early September he found the way. The British had discovered an old pathway up the cliffs. Very quietly, the British landed their ships and climbed the path that led them to the Plains of Abraham.

Figure 6.15
General Wolfe

When Montcalm realized the British had landed, he opened the gates of Quebec and went out to fight. The French forces were surprised and disorganized, and the British troops were able to defeat them quickly. The French forces turned and ran, and the British took Quebec. It might have been one of the shortest battles of the war. It was over in about 20 minutes.

Each side lost about the same number of men, and both Wolfe and Montcalm died from injuries they received in the battle.

The British won the battle for Quebec, but they barely survived a difficult winter. With Quebec in ruins, there was not enough food or shelter. Almost 1000 people died, more than had died in the battle to take Quebec.

The following spring, the French recaptured Quebec, but they needed reinforcements to keep it. The French navy

Montcalm's note of surrender, written after he had been told that he had only hours to live, was sent to the British commander:

"Sir, being obliged to surrender Quebec to your arms I have the honour to recommend our sick and wounded to Your Excellency's kindness, and to ask you to carry out the exchange of prisoners, as agreed upon between His Most Christian Majesty and His Britannic Majesty. I beg Your Excellency to rest assured of the high esteem and great respect with which I have the honour to be your most humble and obedient servant, MONTCALM."

had been defeated by the British in Europe, and French reinforcements never arrived. British reinforcements did arrive, however, and England retook Quebec.

Figure 6.16 Wolfe's aide-de-camp, Hervey Smyth (1734–1811), made this painting. The British forces are seen moving up the river and using the path that leads to the Plains of Abraham. On September 13, 1759, Wolfe led a surprise landing from the St. Lawrence River at the base of the cliffs near Quebec. The French sentries thought that the boats were French supply boats from downstream, and were fooled into letting the soldiers land. Montcalm's forces were defeated quickly.

The Drummer Boy

Papa said that if we were to enlist, I should have a proper uniform, just like his. Now that I am signed up, I look like a real soldier, although a short one! I am only 12, after all. Yesterday, Papa gave me a sword. It's smaller than his, but also just like a real one.

"If the enemy comes after you, you must have a way to protect yourself," he said.

I felt as if I were being knighted. Too bad I don't feel like a knight. I feel very frightened. Still, I am tired of the waiting we have done for the last several months. Being part of a siege is boring. I've been able to play

Figure 6.17

games and explore with the other boys in the corps, but we've had to find ways to pass the time. Thankfully, we have not had to face the winter months here. That could be worse than any battles!

Tomorrow, the waiting will be over. I wonder if I will live to see the evening. Papa said that dying for one's country is the noblest way to die, but I don't think I want to be that noble. I know that I must do my job, and do it well. The commander will use me to make the troops aware of what they must do. Of course, no one will hear his shouts over the sounds of the battle, and so the bugle and the drum will help the troops respond as they should. I like setting the beat while marching, as well, although the

drum is so heavy that sometimes my shoulders ache at the end of the day. Tomorrow, however, we will not use my drum to march. It is to be a surprise attack.

The other boys don't seem frightened: they are thrilled with the idea of glory and honour. They are eager to see the enemy fall. I don't think they've considered that they are the ones who might fall.

Tomorrow. It feels like it will never come, and then it feels like it is coming much too quickly. I know that when it comes, I must do my duty. It is what I pledged when I became a drummer boy, and it is what I intend to do. May God grant me the courage to fulfill my role.

The Treaty of Paris, February 1763

The final North American battle of the Seven Years' War was fought at Fort William, in St. John's, Newfoundland. After losing that battle, France signed away all of its holdings in North America under the terms of the Treaty of Paris, except St. Pierre and Miquelon. Quebec no longer controlled the land around the St. Lawrence, or Acadia, and gave up any claim to the Ohio Valley and Louisiana.

Aftermath of War

The Royal Proclamation, 1763

The Royal Proclamation replaced French law with British laws and practices. England assumed that the people living in Quebec would want to become British subjects. England also thought that British colonists from the south would want to move to Quebec. Aboriginal peoples were also greatly affected (see next page).

The Royal Proclamation would have been hard for the French to accept, but they were lucky. James Murray, the governor assigned to oversee them, was Scottish and Catholic. Scotland had long been friends with France. Murray understood Catholics. He was comfortable with the seigneurial system, and felt that being too harsh with the French would cause them to rebel. He worked at making things fair for the French in Quebec without angering the incoming British merchants too much.

Figure 6.19 Signal Hill, in St. John's, Newfoundland, was the site of the last battle of the Seven Years' War. Today, it is a national historic site.

Figure 6.18 The British merchants were not happy that James Murray favoured the French-Canadian inhabitants. The merchants asked for him to be recalled. He was sent back to Britain, but he was cleared of any blame for his actions while governor of Quebec. He never returned to Quebec, but he had recommended the first two items of the Quebec Act of 1774: keep French civil law, and allow French Catholics to hold government positions.

[The Canadians are] perhaps, the best and bravest Race on the Globe, a Race, that have already got the better of every National Antipathy to their Conquerors, and could they be indulged with a very few Privileges, which the Laws of England do not allow to Catholics at home, must in a very short Time become the most faithful & useful Set of Men in this American Empire.

— *James Murray*

Effects on Aboriginal peoples

France's Aboriginal allies were not happy with France's loss of the Seven Years' War. They became concerned when the British started to build forts and allow white settlement on their traditional lands. They did not think the British respected Aboriginal ways. They also thought the British were unfair in their trade dealings.

The Royal Proclamation promised Aboriginal peoples that their land and ways of life would be preserved, and it limited western expansion into the Ohio Valley. This promise came a little late, however, and the Pontiac Uprising was already underway.

Pontiac's Uprising, in 1763, is the name given to a war between an alliance of Aboriginal peoples and the British. The Aboriginal peoples were led by Pontiac, a chief of the Odawa. Chief Pontiac was an influential warrior and peace negotiator. The uprising lasted about two years. In that time, many people from both sides died in battle. When the two sides finally agreed to stop fighting, England promised only to develop trading posts and not settle the land. The British did not keep their word, though. Soon, the Aboriginal peoples, further weakened by disease and war, could no longer fight.

Figure 6.20 Pontiac supported the French during the Seven Years' War. During Pontiac's Uprising, the British increased their forces, and soon Pontiac found that peace treaties were necessary if he and the Odawa people were to survive. Pontiac became loyal to the British. Many of his former allies were not happy with this change, so they murdered him in 1769.

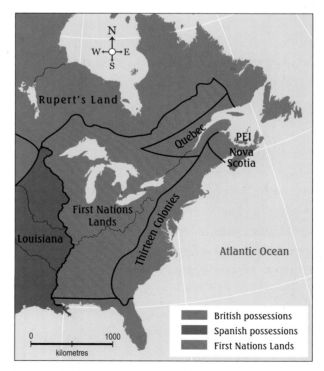

Figure 6.21 BRITISH TERRITORY, AFTER 1763

Future trouble

The new governor of Quebec, Guy Carleton, wanted to keep the French happy. He knew that the French living in Quebec would probably turn against Britain if the Thirteen Colonies did. Carleton told the king some things he could do to please the French, and Britain passed the Quebec Act in 1774. It included the right to practise the Roman Catholic faith and use French law in "civil matters" such as marriage and property rights. The ruling council of the colony, appointed by the king, could include French Catholics, instead of only English Protestants.

Figure 6.22 Guy Carleton, who replaced Murray as governor in 1768, passed the Quebec Act in 1774. He did not believe in Anglicizing the French inhabitants. He allowed the Catholic Church full powers.

> Although you have conquered the French, you have not conquered us. We are not your slaves. These lakes, these woods and mountains were left us by our ancestors. They are our inheritance, and we will not part with them. Englishmen, your king has never sent us any presents nor entered into any treaty with us, wherefore he and we are still at war; and until he does these things we must consider that we have no father nor friend amongst the white men than the King of France.
>
> —*Ojibwa chief Minweweh, speaking to the British in 1761*

The act made larger the "Province of Quebec" (as it had been named after the war). The province now included the land in the Ohio River Valley.

While the Quebec Act was planned to satisfy the French in Quebec, it just made the settlers in the Thirteen Colonies angrier. They could not move westward, and they did not want to move to Quebec. Britain had increased **taxes** to pay for the Seven Years' War, and the colonists did not want to pay them. With France no longer in North America and the Pontiac uprising over, the colonists decided they no longer needed the protection of Britain. Within two years, the Thirteen Colonies would turn against the British and declare their independence.

Conclusion

In this chapter, you learned about the early years of the English presence in North America. You also found out how England was able to take over New France, and how they tried to keep the French happy in an English-run colony.

In the next section, Sara and Ben learn about the start of the fur trade and how it helped to shape the country that would become Canada.

PART 3

The Fur Trade

1618
Étienne Brûlé
travels west toward
Lake Superior, trading
fur and looking for the
Northwest Passage.

1690
Henry Kelsey
explores inland
to the Canadian
prairies, the first
European to see
the bison.

1739
Pierre de
La Vérendrye
reaches
Lake Winnipeg.

1778
James Cook
arrives at
Nootka Sound,
Vancouver Island.

7. The Early Days of the Fur Trade, 1604–1760   **8. Into the Great Northwest**

1670
The Hudson's Bay
Company is formed
by royal charter. It is given
rights over all territory
whose waters drain into
Hudson Bay.

1701
Forty First Nations
sign a peace treaty
at Montreal.

1771
Samuel Hearne
and Matonabbee
explore the
Coppermine River.

1779
The North West
Company is
established in
Montreal.

1793
George Vancouver
maps the Pacific Coast.

1793
Alexander Mackenzie
reaches the
Pacific Ocean by land.

1812
David Thompson
completes his survey
of 3 million square
kilometres of land
west of Lake Superior
to the Pacific, and begins
work on his Great Map.

1816
Twenty-one
settlers are
killed in the
Battle of Seven Oaks.

1848
The Guillaume Sayer
trial breaks the
monopoly of the
Hudson's Bay
Company.

9. A New Nation: The Métis

1808
Simon Fraser
explores the
river that later
bears his name.

1812
Lord Selkirk
founds the
Red River Colony.

1821
The North West
Company and
Hudson's Bay
Company merge.

The Early Days of the Fur Trade, 1604–1760

7

ara and Ben were hot, dusty, and tired. They were helping their great aunt Lettie clean out her basement. She was going to move to a condo soon, and she wanted to start packing up.

"I'm moving because my children want me to," she said, "but I'd rather just stay here. This is where my father was born. My grandfather lived in an old cabin back there." She pointed out the window. The cabin had fallen down and rotted away long before Ben and Sara were born. All they saw was a place where the grass seemed to grow a little higher.

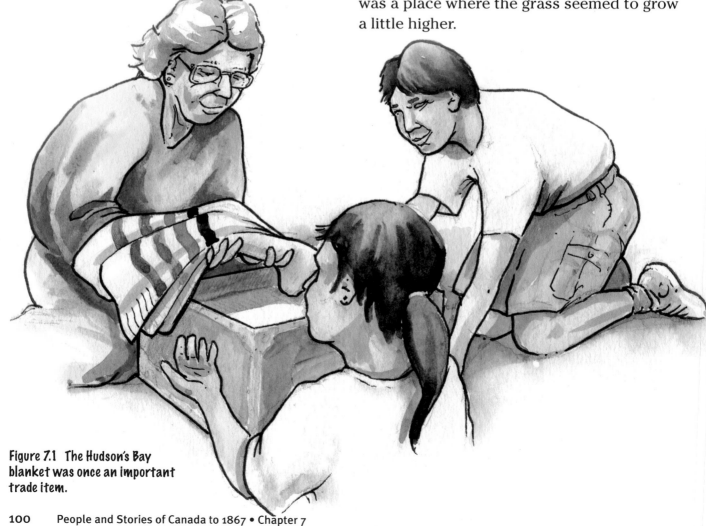

Figure 7.1 The Hudson's Bay blanket was once an important trade item.

"I remember my father telling me about the way things used to be, and about how life was for his grandfather. Our people have been on this land for generations. And now I'm leaving them, and all their memories, behind." She opened a trunk that Ben and Sara had just wrestled up from the basement.

"See these blankets? Even these blankets have memories."

"Auntie, they're just old blankets. How can they have memories?"

"Look at them. A good blanket was like gold for trading. These blankets were some of the best." Ben and Sara looked at the worn blankets. It was a little hard to believe. "Aboriginal peoples trapped fur, and they traded the pelts for things they didn't have. The Hudson's Bay Company shipped in blankets to trade for fur."

Now Ben and Sara were sure their aunt was telling them stories. "Auntie, the Bay is just a department store!"

"Oh, maybe it's just a department store now, but once it was 'The Company of Adventurers of England trading into Hudson's Bay.' Men fought and killed each other for the beaver pelts that could buy these blankets." She looked at Ben and Sara and laughed. "I can see that you don't believe me. It is hard to believe, isn't it?"

Ben and Sara looked at the blankets again. Sara thought, "She's either teasing us, or it's true. I'd like to find out." She

As you read, think about

- why the fur trade began
- where the fur trade took place
- who worked for the French fur trade
- who worked for the Hudson's Bay Company

looked at Ben. She could tell he was thinking the same thing. But where would they start?

In this chapter, you will go back a few hundred years, back to the beginning of the fur trade and Samuel de Champlain's first voyage to the New World. You will learn more about the fur trade, who was involved, and how the trade developed. You will look at the beginnings of the Hudson's Bay Company and at how Canada grew because of the fur trade.

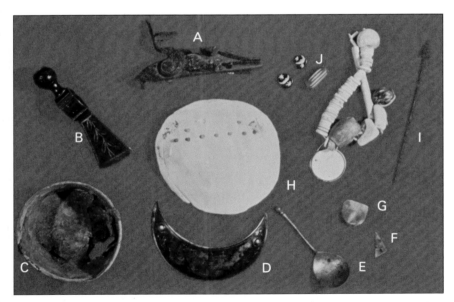

Figure 7.2 Historic trade goods from the early days of the fur trade: A) a French flintlock device for a musket; B) a pipe in the shape of a ceremonial brass axe; C) a brass kettle; D) an English silver gorget; E) a French brass spoon; F) a spear point made from a fragment of a brass kettle; G) a French gun flint; H) a conch-shell and glass-bead pendant; I) an iron spearhead; J) European trade beads from the French period, as well as native stone and shell beads.

The Fashion that Fuelled the Fur Trade

From about 1550 onward, the beaver felt hat was what gentlemen (and ladies) wore to keep themselves dry in the rainy weather of London, Paris, and other fashionable European cities. The beaver hat was so popular that beavers had been hunted, almost to extinction, in Europe and Russia. So far there had been no suitable replacement that worked as well and looked as good.

Right around the time that the beaver shortage might have become a real fashion crisis, European explorers and seafarers started looking for a Northwest Passage to Asia. As you know, they did not find a passage for many years, but they did find lots of beavers. Beavers were very plentiful in North America. Aboriginal peoples used their pelts for blankets and clothing. When the Aboriginal peoples found out that the Europeans were willing to trade items they wanted for beaver pelts, they were pleased to oblige.

To King Louis XIII of France, beaver fur was not gold, but it was the next best thing. He thought that fur would provide France with a source of wealth. That wealth would allow him to expand his colonies, find the Northwest Passage, and become one of the most powerful kings in Europe.

As you read in chapter 4, the early colonies at Port Royal and Quebec were established mainly as fur-trade posts. At first, the economy of New France was entirely dependent on the fur trade. Furs were sent to France. In return, France sent colonists and the supplies and tools that

The beaver hat

The beaver hat was not actually made of fur. It was made of felt. Felt was made by shearing the beaver's short hairs that grew close to the skin. The little hairs were barbed on the end, like a burr, or Velcro. This made beaver especially good for felt that was warm and held its shape in the rain. Because hatters wanted only the short underhairs of a beaver skin, they actually liked getting older, used pelts that already had the longer guard hairs worn off. They liked winter beavers and beavers that came from the north the best, because they had the thickest fur.

"CONTINENTAL" COCKED HAT. (1776)

"NAVY" COCKED HAT. (1800)

ARMY. (1837)

CLERICAL. (Eighteenth Century)

(THE WELLINGTON.) (1812)

CIVIL.

(THE PARIS BEAU.) (1815)

(THE D'ORSAY.) (1820)

(THE REGENT.) (1825)

MODIFICATIONS OF THE BEAVER HAT.

Figure 7.3 A nice beaver hat was expensive. Some hats were even passed on from father to son in wills. This illustration shows eight different styles.

they needed to survive. By the time King Louis XIV took power, the colonies had grown. The colonists who lived there began to support themselves through agriculture and other trades. Yet, the fur trade continued to be an important part of the economy of the mother country.

England also wanted to profit from the fur trade. However, as you saw in chapter 6, the English were not interested in settling British people in these northern lands. They were more concerned with building a good business. Both countries knew they needed strong alliances with the Aboriginal trappers to succeed. This was especially important, because France and England had been enemies for many centuries. The rivalry would continue in the North American fur trade.

There's a good reason for the saying "mad as a hatter." People who made beaver felt hats used a mixture that contained mercury. The fumes caused brain damage that made them slur their words, twitch, and walk with a lurch.

Figure 7.5 Mad Hatter, from *Alice in Wonderland*

Figure 7.4 This fur-trading scene appeared on a map of Canada from 1777.

Rivers and Lakes

One reason the fur trade developed as it did was because of Canada's rivers and lakes. Look at the map on this page. The St. Lawrence River was the main river of the early French settlements of Quebec, Montreal, and Trois-Rivières. If you look farther west, you will see the St. Lawrence River flows from lakes known as the Great Lakes.

From their Aboriginal allies, the French traders heard about lands farther west. They were told that if they travelled inland, they would find more beavers and more riches to send home. They might even find the Northwest Passage.

The simplest way to reach these western lands was by canoe. There were many different types and sizes of canoes, and many different methods of making them. Every Aboriginal group had some sort of canoe. In the far north, frames made out of driftwood were covered in animal skins.

Figure 7.7 This illustration shows what Europeans thought about hunting beavers in Canada in the late 18th century. They believed beavers lived in multi-level dwellings. Hunters could kill the animals easily using either a bow and arrow or a gun.

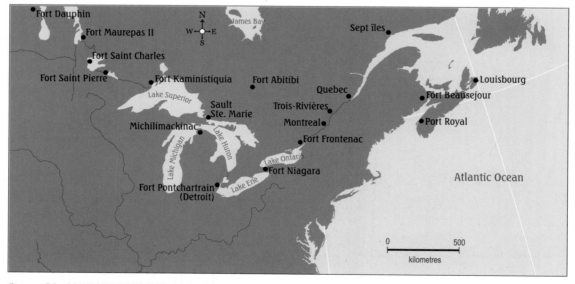

Figure 7.6 EARLY FRENCH FUR-TRADE POSTS

In forested areas, birchbark was used. A small birchbark canoe was light enough to carry from place to place, yet it could hold 100 beaver pelts. If the canoe was damaged, the materials needed to fix it were all around.

As you think about how the fur trade developed in New France, imagine the countryside as it was over 400 years ago. There were no roads, only pathways, and **portages**, that led from one waterway to another. Until you got to the prairies, you were surrounded by rolling (and sometimes very rugged) hills and a lot of trees. The rivers and lakes provided the easiest, quickest mode of travel. They were the highways of the time. Even in winter, it was easier to walk along a frozen river pulling a sled than it was to trudge through the deep snow in the woods.

The land and rivers also supplied the fur traders with the things they needed to live. Their Aboriginal guides taught the Europeans how to hunt and fish for food to supplement the dried corn and salt pork that they brought with them. They taught them which berries could nourish them when food was scarce. They supplied them with pemmican, made from bison or other game, and wild rice that grew in the waterways they travelled. Their Aboriginal partners showed them how to make medicines from the plants in the forests. In winter, fur traders wore warm clothing and moccasins made of animal skins.

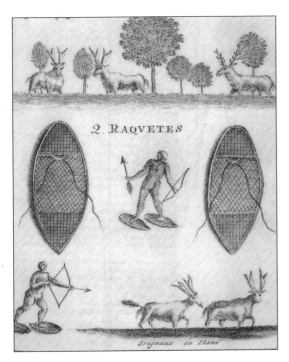

Figure 7.8 This drawing, by Louis Lahontan, a French soldier and adventurer, is from his memoirs, published in 1703. It shows snowshoes and bows and arrows, useful equipment that French fur traders adapted from the Aboriginal peoples and that allowed them to survive on the land.

Figure 7.9 Fur traders relied on canoes to travel lakes and rivers.

The French Fur Trade

Early partnerships and conflicts

The early French traders knew nothing about trapping animals. They did not know much about the land, where to find the animals, or how to survive in the northern wilderness. They needed to rely on people who were experienced in hunting, trapping, and living in the cold climate of North America. They formed a partnership with the Wendat people and their allies, the Algonquin and Montagnais. These Aboriginal allies could bring the French furs of the highest quality from their traditional hunting grounds.

In 1609, Samuel de Champlain and his men fought with their allies against the Iroquois. The Iroquois, who had never seen or heard guns before, were quickly defeated by the small force of Wendat and French, who were armed with guns known as **arquebuses**. This was the beginning of

Figure 7.10 Champlain fires his arquebus. This is the only picture of Champlain that survives from his lifetime.

The Iroquois Confederacy, 1500 or earlier

The Iroquois were one of the most disciplined and organized groups in North America. Well before the Europeans came, a great prophet named Dekanahwideh brought together five warring nations, the Mohawk, Seneca, Cayuga, Onondaga, and Oneida to arrange a peace treaty. They created the **Great Law of Peace**. Each clan had an equal vote, and they had to completely agree on all their decisions. The **Iroquois Confederacy** became the most powerful Aboriginal alliance in North America.

a conflict between the French and Iroquois that would last more than 90 years.

By 1640, however, the Wendat had been weakened by smallpox that they had caught from the Europeans. The Iroquois, now armed with guns from the British and Dutch, took control over former Wendat territory and began to cut off the French fur trade routes. Many Wendat were killed. Others were taken prisoner or forced from their homes. Within 10 years, the Wendat were almost wiped out.

The Great Peace of Montreal, 1701

By the 18th century, the French, their allies the Wendat and Algonquins, and the Iroquois Confederacy wanted peace. Both the fur trade and farms of New France were being affected by constant attacks; and the Aboriginal peoples were being weakened by disease, hunger, and constant war. All knew that to survive they would have to reach an agreement. In the summer of 1701, Louis-Hector de Callière, the governor of New France, invited 1200 representatives from 40 Aboriginal nations to find a way to end the decades of wars. On August 4, after days of talks, a treaty was signed. The Iroquois gained fur trapping and trading grounds, and the French were able to grow their crops without worry. The Iroquois also promised to remain neutral in any battles between the French and the English.

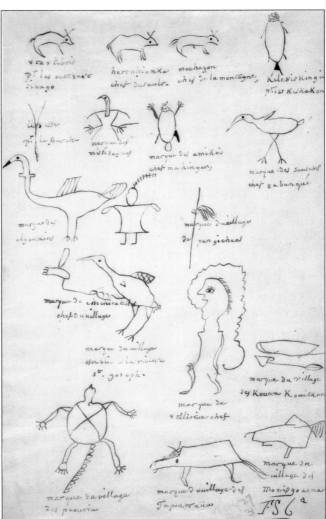

Figure 7.12 Each of the 40 chiefs who took part in the Great Peace treaty signed the document by drawing a picture of the totemic animal of his clan. Many kinds of birds and animals were drawn.

Figure 7.11 Leaders from 40 First Nations met to negotiate peace in 1701. They came from as far as James Bay to the north, the Great Lakes to the West, New York to the south, and the Maritimes to the east.

Roles of the French Fur Trade

Aboriginal trappers

In the winter, Aboriginal trappers trapped animals and prepared furs. In the spring, as soon as the rivers were free of ice, they transported the furs to trading posts on the St. Lawrence River, where they traded for items from Europe. Merchants supplied things such as metal tools, knives, guns, and kettles, in return for the trappers' furs.

Aboriginal guides

European explorers and traders relied on Aboriginal guides, whose ancestors had been travelling the waterways for centuries, to lead them to new fur-trading grounds. The guides, both men and women, also acted as translators and mediators. They supplied explorers with important information about new territories and the people who lived there.

Coureurs de bois

Some French settlers soon realized they could make money by trading for furs themselves, instead of waiting for the Wendat to bring furs to them. They became coureurs de bois, independent fur traders. Coureurs de bois travelled west and north into the interior of the country, trading directly with Aboriginal trappers. The government of the colony wanted sole control over the trade and its profits, however. They viewed the coureurs de bois as outlaws. Still, just about every family had at least one "runner of the woods," who made a much greater profit trading furs than he would have made farming the land as a habitant.

Étienne Brûlé

Étienne Brûlé was the first coureur de bois and is probably the most well known to historians. In 1610, Champlain arranged for Brûlé, a young man of about 18, to live with a Wendat tribe. From them, he learned to speak their language, and he adopted their customs. After several years, Brûlé was brought back to Quebec City. There, he worked as a scout for the fur traders and as an interpreter between the Wendat and the French. Brûlé also explored territory west and south of Quebec City. Champlain regarded him as a son.

In 1624, a Récollet brother named Gabriel Sagard convinced Champlain that Brûlé was working for both France and France's enemies. Champlain and Brûlé had a quarrel, and Brûlé left the colony and returned to live with the Wendat.

The Iroquois twice captured Brûlé. He may have escaped torture the first time, in 1615, because he promised to promote an Iroquois alliance with the French. He was again taken by the Iroquois in 1629, after he had helped the English capture both Quebec and Champlain. Brûlé escaped, and he returned to his Wendat village. When he told the Wendat about his capture, they accused him of trading with the Iroquois. They considered him a traitor and, in 1633, they tortured Brûlé to death.

Figure 7.13 Étienne Brûlé

Figure 7.14 Trappers, guides, traders, merchants, and women were all important to the success of the fur trade.

Voyageurs

Around 1680, the government of New France, in an effort to stop the independent trade of the coureurs de bois, began granting licences to traders. These traders became known as "voyageurs."

Merchants

The merchants of New France were in charge of purchasing pelts from the fur trappers and supplying the trappers with items for trade. The merchants were mainly interested in beaver pelts, but they bought just about any kind of pelt, including wolf, ermine, and fox. Merchants then sent the furs back to Europe in return for money. They could charge a high price for the pelts, which were in great demand from Europeans who used them to make hats or trim fancy clothes.

Dogs

Before they had horses, many Aboriginal peoples used dogs to help them on their journeys. Dogs were excellent companions for trappers and fur traders: they could warn of enemies or wild animals, they could carry furs and supplies on travois or sleds, they helped hunt, and if food got scarce they could be eaten.

The role of women in the fur trade

Aboriginal women were important partners in the fur trade. Women prepared the furs for trade, made food such as ground corn, and sewed clothing and moccasins. Women chopped firewood and tended fires. They also made items that were crucial to the survival of the fur traders, such as snowshoes and fish nets. Most important, they acted as mediators and translators between Europeans and Aboriginal peoples.

Women also prepared pemmican, a mixture of dried meat that was pounded and then mixed with berries and fat. Pemmican was portable, extremely high in calories, and full of protein. Because of the vitamin C in the berries, it warded off scurvy. Pemmican never spoiled. It was the fuel that kept the voyageurs going.

Radisson and Groseilliers

The coureurs de bois Pierre Esprit-Radisson and Médard Chouart Des Groseilliers probably changed the fur trade more than anyone else. They came up with the idea to ship fur to Europe via Hudson Bay. They first went to the French, who were not interested in their plan. Then they went to New England, but they could not get anyone there to back them. So Radisson and Groseilliers travelled to England to see if anyone there would be interested. Although Radisson and Groseilliers were French, they were the ones who opened up the fur trade to the English.

A conversation with Pierre Esprit-Radisson (1640–1710)

Imagine you had a chance to meet Pierre Radisson. This is what he might tell you about himself.

I came to New France with my half-sister when I was just a young boy. I'm not even sure how old I was because birth dates weren't that important back then.

Those were the days of the Iroquois raids. During one of these raids, my sister's husband was killed. In another raid, I was taken captive by the Iroquois. I was lucky. I was young and strong, and an Iroquois family wanted to adopt me.

I learned the language, and enjoyed the Iroquois way of life. It was from them I learned about the forests and rivers of New France. Still, I wanted my freedom, and so I escaped. I was quickly recaptured and then punished. I won't even tell you about that. I'd rather forget.

They would have killed me, but my Iroquois family intervened. I didn't stay long, though. I soon escaped again and returned to Europe.

How drab and dreary it was after my life of adventure in the woods! I had to return to New France.

When I returned in 1654, a short-term peace alliance with the Iroquois gave us just enough time to find out that there were a great many furs available in the northwest. If we wanted to go where the real money was, we needed to find a way. My brother-in-law Groseilliers figured that between the two of us, we'd be able to get our hands on those beaver pelts and the riches that would come with them.

Figure 7.15

A conversation with Médard Chouart Des Groseilliers (1618–1696)

Imagine you had a chance to meet Médard Des Groseilliers. This is what he might tell you about himself.

The English liked to call us Mr. Gooseberries and Mr. Radishes. Yes, it's true, my name does mean gooseberries. But that's nothing to be ashamed of. My family owns land in France, and that's pretty important back there. Owning land, even just a gooseberry patch, means you are a person of wealth. I wanted more adventure out of life than gooseberries, though, and so I went in search of fur.

In 1659, Pierre and I set out with a small group to find the Aboriginal peoples who had plenty of fur, but we didn't dare face the Iroquois to bring it to us. We spent a cold winter around Lake Superior. We went hungry a lot, but the following summer, we returned in triumph! We had so many furs, we needed the trappers to help us bring the furs back with us. Then that governor made me so angry. He said we were illegal coureurs de bois, with no official **sanction** from the government. He confiscated all our fur, made us pay a fine, and threw me in jail. I resolved that one day, I would get my revenge.

Figure 7.16

Figure 7.17 Radisson and Groseilliers meet King Charles II of England in 1670.

The English Fur Trade: "The Company of Adventurers"

Although the French were not interested in Radisson and Groseilliers' plan, Prince Rupert, a cousin of King Charles II of England, was. The prince was also a **privateer** and an inventor. When Prince Rupert met Radisson and Groseilliers, he was eager to back the adventurers and make some money. In 1665, the prince convinced some powerful and influential people to fund an expedition by Radisson and Groseilliers to Hudson Bay.

Figure 7.18 Prince Rupert

It took three years to prepare for the journey. On June 3, 1668, two ships set out from England, with Radisson in one and Groseilliers in the other. Radisson's ship was damaged in a storm, and he had to return to England. Groseilliers' ship, the *Nonsuch*, was able to make the journey in 118 days. The crew spent the winter on the Rupert River, and when spring arrived, approximately 300 Cree traders came to the ship with beaver pelts.

The *Nonsuch* was ready to sail back to Europe in June, but Groseilliers had to wait until August for the ice to leave Hudson Bay. When he returned to England in October, the beaver pelts sold well. The trip did not make much money, but the partners still felt the idea had promise. On May 2, 1670, "the Governor and Company of Adventurers of England trading into Hudson's Bay,"

Figure 7.19 Replica of the *Nonsuch*

as Prince Rupert and his partners were known, were given a royal **charter** by King Charles. The charter granted the company a **monopoly**, or exclusive right, to trade in the lands drained by the waters that flowed into Hudson Bay. Although no one realized it at the time, this land covered close to 7 million square kilometres, or almost 40 percent of present-day Canada. The company would come to be known as the Hudson's Bay Company.

Prince Rupert became the first governor of the Hudson's Bay Company, and all the land draining into Hudson Bay was named Rupert's Land in his honour.

There is a good reason the beaver is on one side of the Canadian nickel. The beaver is a reminder of Canada's early economic history, when the currency of the day was the beaver pelt. The chart (below), found in early documents relating to the Hudson's Bay Company, outlines how many beaver pelts were needed to trade for certain items in 1670.

The STANDARD how the Company's Goods must be barter'd in the *Southern* Part of the *Bay*.

Guns.	One with the other 10 good Skins; that is, Winter Beaver; 12 Skins for the biggest sort, 10 for the mean, and 8 for the smallest.
Powder.	A Beaver for half a Pound.
Shot.	A Beaver for four Pounds.
Hatchets.	A Beaver for a great and little Hatchet.
Knives.	A Beaver for 6 great Knives, or 8 Jack Knives.
Beads.	A Beaver for half a Pound of Beads.
Lac'd Coats.	Six Beavers for one good Lac'd [laced] Coat.
Plain Coats.	Five Beaver Skins for one Red Plain Coat.
Tobacco.	A Beaver for one Pound.
Kettles.	A Beaver for one Pound of Kettle.
Looking-Glasses and Combs.	Two Skins.

Funny money

Another method of paying for goods was by wampum beads, which the Algonquins made of quahog clamshells. Purple wampum beads were more valuable than white wampum, but war and rivalry between tribes often interrupted the flow of wampum. Later, glass beads from France replaced wampum as popular currency. In 1670, people began to use coins from Europe, but wampum was still preferred by many Aboriginal peoples. The supply of coins was also somewhat unreliable — ships were sometimes late, or sank with their cargo on board. This left the government of New France with a problem: how to pay their soldiers' wages? Intendant de Meulles came up with a good idea that lasted until the British took over New France. He collected all the playing cards he could find and assigned amounts to each of them. When real money arrived from France, the colonists could redeem their playing cards.

Figure 7.20 Wampum beads

Figure 7.21 Playing card money, front and back

Life at a Hudson's Bay Company Trading Post

The Hudson's Bay Company set up a different way of trading. Instead of building colonies and travelling inland to get fur, the company built their posts on the shores of Hudson Bay, and convinced Aboriginal trappers to bring their furs to the posts. Within 30 years of its founding, the Hudson's Bay Company had built posts at the mouths of many rivers flowing into Hudson Bay. York Factory, built in 1684 and located between the mouths of the Hayes and Nelson rivers, became the company's main post.

The Hudson's Bay Company was owned by **shareholders** who lived in Britain. The office in Britain was run by a company governor and committee. The governor of Rupert's Land represented the company in North America. **Factors** were responsible for the day-to-day dealings at the fur-trade posts (known as factories) and for the clerks and traders who lived there.

Many of the company men came from the Orkney Islands off the northern coast of Scotland. They were strong, hardy, and good boatmen. They soon settled into a daily routine of chores, gathering wood, and hunting food to add to supplies

Figure 7.22 This drawing by the explorer Samuel Hearne is of York Factory.

that came once a year from England. They constructed the posts' buildings. They traded with Aboriginal trappers who travelled to the forts twice a year. They came in spring with their pelts, and in the fall to get provisions for the coming trapping season.

Daily life was dangerous

The northern lands harboured several dangers. Rapids, wild animals, and cold weather or sudden snowstorms in winter took the lives of many adventurers. Others got lost in the woods and never found their way home. Hunger and illness were also ever-present.

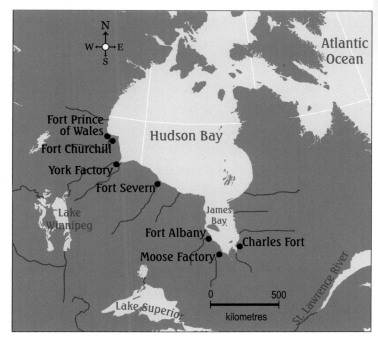

Figure 7.23 EARLY HUDSON'S BAY COMPANY POSTS

> The mosquitoes continue at their post from dawn to 8 or 9 o'clock in the morning. The black flies succeed, and remain in the field until sunset; the mosquitoes then mount guard until nightfall and are finally succeeded by gnats, who continue their incessant attacks until dawn....I was incessantly tormented by venomous flies.
>
> —*John McLean, employee of the Hudson's Bay Company*

In addition to these difficulties, warfare and rivalry between the French and the English took the lives of many people. Early Hudson's Bay Company employees faced constant threats by the French who wanted to take over their forts.

A letter to Governor John Nixon from the company directors in London shows how dangerous life was. Nixon was told that if he should die, Mr. Walter Farr was to replace him as governor. If Mr. Farr should die, then Mr. Bridger was to take his place. The directors also give instructions for replacing the ship's captain if he should die.

Daily life was uncomfortable

Imagine a bed filled with leaves, straw, or, if you were really lucky, feathers. Imagine your hair freezing to the pillow, and imagine having to break the ice in the wash basin to wash your face. Imagine swarms of biting insects and no repellent. You have had a small glimpse of life at a northern fur-trade post.

> Thanks to the Lord I have escaped, Sir, the most dreadful country in the world. I do not think that they will catch me there again.
>
> —*M de Bacqueville de la Potherie, 18th-century historian*

Adventurers, Traders, and Explorers

While the Hudson's Bay Company conducted its trade on the Hudson Bay, it did send out explorers to make new trade alliances with Aboriginal trappers. The company also hoped to find precious metals. The French had their own adventurers who wanted to expand the trade.

Henry Kelsey (1667–1724)

One of the Hudson's Bay Company men who ventured out was Henry Kelsey. He was born in England and began to work for the Hudson's Bay Company when he was around 17 years old. He was the first European explorer to reach the Canadian prairies. He was the first to see bison and the bison hunt, as well as grizzly bears. He liked to write poems, and this is how he described the prairies, the bison, and the grizzly bear in a journal entry of 1690.

The one is a black, a Buffalo great
Another is an outgrown Bear, which is
*   good meat*
His skin to get I have used all ways I can
He is man's food and he makes food
*   for man…*
This plain affords nothing but Beast
*   and grass*
And over it in three days time we past.

Thanadelthur

Thanadelthur, a Dene woman, escaped her Cree captors in 1714 and sought refuge at York Factory. For Chief Factor James Knight, she provided important information about the rich furs and precious metals in the lands beyond the post. She became an important mediator and translator, establishing peace between the Cree and the Dene and creating important trade alliances for the Hudson's Bay Company.

Figure 7.24

Figure 7.25

> She was one of a very high Spirit and of the firmest Resolution that ever I see .. and of great Courage...the most Melancholy [is it] by the Loss of her.
>
> —*James Knight, after Thanadelthur's death in 1717*

Anthony Henday

Anthony Henday (worked 1750–1762; birth and death unknown) left York Factory in June 1754. He paddled up the Hayes River, and walked to present-day Red Deer, Alberta. Check the distance on a map!

He met the Peigan people from the Alberta plains and hunted bison with them. However, he could not persuade them to travel to Hudson Bay with furs. They were happy trading with French traders. Besides, their chief told him, "we do not paddle, we ride." The Peigan used horses as their main method of transportation. Henday travelled back to York Factory, where he was laughed at for telling stories about the people who rode horses. The people at the fur-trade post used dogs as beasts of burden, and the description of horses was hard to believe. Henday also brought back valuable information about the French and their fur-trade alliances along the Saskatchewan River.

Figure 7.26

Figure 7.27 **TRAVEL ROUTES OF HENDAY AND KELSEY**

Both Henday and Kelsey have hydro-electric dams named after them, located near Gillam, Manitoba.

DID YOU KNOW?

Competition

Recollections of Pierre de La Vérendrye (1689–1745)

Imagine what the fur trader, explorer, soldier, and farmer from Trois-Rivières might tell you if you could talk to him today.

I was more interested in finding the Northwest Passage than I was in working in the fur trade. However, I knew that the merchants of Montreal wouldn't pay me to look for the Western Sea. They were paying me to build forts on the trapping grounds of our Aboriginal partners. In that way, the Montreal merchants hoped they could regain some of the fur trade they had lost to the Hudson's Bay Company. What trader would want to paddle all the way to Hudson Bay when he could go to a trading post only a day or two away?

Figure 7.28 Pierre de La Vérendrye (standing)

We set out from Montreal in June of 1731. A few days into our journey, we met some Cree and Assiniboine who were travelling to Hudson Bay. We persuaded them to trade with us, and we got many fine furs. It was like that all the way to Rainy Lake. We reached Rainy River in the fall and built Fort Saint-Pierre. The next spring, we travelled to Lake of the Woods, where we built Fort Saint-Charles.

Of course, we faced many challenges over the next several years. The most difficult one was getting enough money to pay for our expeditions. Another problem was finding enough men who were willing to work hard for months at a time. More than once, some of my men abandoned me.

Despite these setbacks, within 12 years, by 1743, my men and I had built eight trading posts. These posts extended from Rainy Lake to Lake Winnipeg. The Montreal merchants benefited greatly from the strategic locations of the forts. Just as the merchants had hoped,

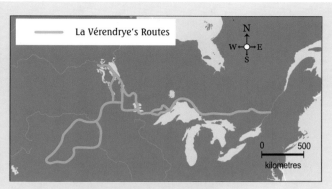

Figure 7.29 LA VÉRENDRYE'S JOURNEYS

La Vérendrye's Routes

many traders brought their pelts to our posts instead of to the English posts on Hudson Bay.

While I didn't find the Western Sea and the route to the East, I strengthened French-Aboriginal friendships. I used all of my skills as a **diplomat** to encourage partnerships with the Cree, Assiniboine, and Mandan. These partnerships cost me a lot. In 1736, one of my sons and several good friends were killed by the Sioux on an island in Lake of the Woods. The Sioux were paying me back, because I had sided with the Cree and Assiniboine against them a couple of years earlier.

Some have said that I didn't have the curiosity or the qualifications to be an explorer. Perhaps I should have spent more time exploring and less time running the forts. I would have realized that the route west was by way of the Saskatchewan River and not the Missouri River. Whatever some people think, I know I played an important role to expand into prime fur-trapping territory.

Pierre Le Moyne d'Iberville

Not everyone thought Pierre Le Moyne d'Iberville was a pirate, but many English settlers did. Born in New France, he attacked English settlements and ships from Hudson Bay to the Caribbean, and he destroyed English fishing villages in Newfoundland. In 1697, d'Iberville turned his attention to the Hudson's Bay Company post York Factory. Aboard the *Pelican*, he battled three British ships and managed to sink one, chase off another, and force the third to surrender. Although the *Pelican* sank, the French were able to capture the fort. They kept York Factory until 1713, when Britain would once again control all the land surrounding Hudson Bay.

Figure 7.30 *The Sinking of the* Pelican

Conclusion

In this chapter, you learned how the fur trade developed. You also read about how the fur trade played such an important role in the growth of Canada. You learned that the Hudson's Bay Company needed to become more aggressive and expand into new areas if it wanted to compete with the Montreal merchants.

In chapter 8, join Ben on his canoe trip. You will learn how the rivalry between the French merchants and the Hudson's Bay Company resulted in the European expansion into the great Northwest.

8

Into the Great Northwest

Ben's arms had never felt so sore. After paddling a canoe for two days, he had had enough.

"How much farther?" he asked. "Just another hour or so, and we'll make camp for the night," the guide replied.

When Ben and his dad signed up for the canoe trip, it had sounded like fun. They would spend five days in the woods with nothing to do but paddle and look for wildlife. So far, they had seen several bald eagles, a couple of turtles, too many deer to count, one bear, one moose, and a bunch of beaver lodges and dams. (Ben was kind of mad at the beavers. Their dams had forced a few unplanned portages.) They had caught some Northern pike that they had cooked over the fire within an hour of pulling them out of the water. Ben had never enjoyed eating fish so much.

Figure 8.1 Ben's canoe trip

The adventure had been a lot of fun, but his muscles were starting to ache. Ben wondered how he'd get through three more days of paddles and portages.

Today, most of us canoe or camp just because we like it. Being in the wilderness is a wonderful way to spend a weekend, and after it is over, we go back to our comfortable homes. During the early days of the fur trade, however, canoeing and camping were not weekend pastimes; they were transportation and lodging. Traders travelled to pick up the furs that provided their livelihood. Handling a canoe was as crucial for the earliest inhabitants of North America as driving a car is for us today.

The voyageurs were a lot tougher than Ben. They had to be able to paddle 16 to 18 hours each day, or for as long as it was light outside. They slept under their canoes in bad weather, and they did without tents. They used wool blankets or tanned hides or furs to keep themselves warm. They did not have waterproof clothing, or protein bars, trail mix, or granola. They ate pemmican or corn mush along the way. If they were lucky, they would catch fish or shoot a bird or an animal to add variety to their meals. They did not have any bug spray or sunscreen.

Although their canoes were light enough to carry, they were still much heavier and more likely to break than modern canoes. The people in the fur trade were some of the best travellers Canada has ever seen. In this chapter, you will read more about the fur trade. You will also be introduced to the only rival and competitor that ever really threatened the strength of the Hudson's Bay Company: the North West Company.

As you read, think about

- **how European fur traders and Aboriginal guides and trappers influenced each other**
- **how the two fur-trade companies were different**
- **how competition between the two fur-trade companies expanded exploration**
- **what new places and settlements arose from the fur trade**

The Beginning of the North West Company

When the Seven Years' War ended in 1763, the French fur trade was over. The French lost their power, and they had to abandon the land they had once claimed. The British took over their territory. The Hudson's Bay Company was now without a rival in the entire northern part of British North America. However, the French settlers and their descendants had not left the country, and many were still able paddlers and traders.

When Scottish merchants began immigrating to Montreal in the middle of the 18th century, they wanted to profit from the fur trade as well. They saw great opportunity. They began outfitting French-

Canadian voyageurs and sending them into new fur-trading territories. For years, the Hudson's Bay Company had camped by the shores of Hudson Bay, and the Aboriginal trappers came to them. The Montreal merchants sent people to the heart of the fur lands and saved the trappers a trip to Hudson Bay. By the late 1760s, the Hudson's Bay Company's monopoly was weakening, as the Montreal merchants pushed farther and farther into the Northwest.

However, the Montreal merchants had a few challenges of their own as they looked to establish themselves in the fur trade.

- They had far greater distances to travel, because they could not use Hudson Bay as a means to ship furs to Europe.

- They had a lot less money than the Hudson's Bay Company.

- Fierce competition among themselves kept them from being strong enough to take on the Hudson's Bay Company.

In 1776, some of the merchants joined together as partners. In 1779, they officially became the North West Company. For 40 years, they

Figure 8.2 *Shooting the Rapids*, by Frances Anne Hopkins (1838-1919). Hopkins was the wife of a Hudson's Bay Company man. During her 10 years in Canada, she went with her husband on at least three expeditions and saw firsthand the life of the fur trader.

challenged the Hudson's Bay Company. During these years, the Hudson's Bay Company seemed to follow the Nor'westers, as the traders of the Montreal company were called. After the North West Company built a fort, the Hudson's Bay Company would build one close by. The rivalry became fierce. The North West Company had the upper hand in every area except one. They did not control Hudson Bay. Without access to the bay, the Nor'westers could not ship their furs to Europe through it. They had to travel the much longer distance to Montreal and ship their furs from there to Europe.

Figure 8.3 North West Company coat of arms

A day in the life of a Nor'Wester

From early summer to freeze-up in the fall, North West Company voyageurs moved furs and trade goods over thousands of kilometres of waterways. Each day before sunrise, they loaded their canoes and set off.

Every hour or so, for a few minutes, the men stopped to smoke a pipe. A distance could be measured by the number of pipe breaks. For example, the time it took to travel the length of a 24-kilometre lake might be measured as three pipes, representing about three hours of travel. When conditions were good, the voyageurs paddled up to 130 kilometres in a day.

After about three or four hours of paddling, the voyageurs stopped for breakfast, which was often leftovers from the previous night's dinner. The voyageurs also carried rawhide *parflêches* filled with pemmican. The voyageurs snacked on pemmican throughout the day.

Whenever the voyageurs had to make a portage, they carried their loads across a stretch of land, then returned to carry the canoes. Sometimes, they had to run the rapids. With the roar of the rapids filling the air, they emptied their loads from the canoes. One or two paddlers rode the lightened canoe through the rushing water, while the others carried the supplies along the riverbank.

After a full day of paddling, between 8 p.m. and 10 p.m., the voyageurs stopped for the night. They cooked their evening meal, perhaps of cornmeal or dried peas, and fish or meat that they traded for or caught along the way. Sometimes they made rubaboo*, a soup of pemmican, flour, and water. They also repaired any damage to their canoes and equipment. After eating by the fire, and sharing stories and songs, the voyageurs took shelter under their overturned canoes, covered themselves with blankets or fur robes, and went to sleep.

* Rubaboo is a word that comes from the sound pemmican soup makes when it is cooking. The Cree people call it *alupapo*.

Figure 8.4 *Voyageurs at Dawn.* In 1871, Frances Anne Hopkins made this painting of voyageurs at the start of their day.

People of the North West Company

The early partners of the North West Company were ambitious men, mostly Scottish immigrants. They did not necessarily like or even trust one another. However, they recognized that by working together, they could become rich. Most of the directors in the North West Company were men who had been west and traded furs. They knew how to handle a canoe and carry their own load.

Figure 8.5 Simon McTavish

They included men like Simon McTavish. He was born into a poor family close to Loch Ness, Scotland, and came to New York in 1764 at the age of 13. He began to work in the fur trade, and by 1776, he was an established and wealthy businessman in Montreal. He paid for the education of his nephew William McGillivray, who was also from a poor family in Scotland and would later head the company.

Figure 8.6 William McGillivray

Benjamin Frobisher was born in England and was the first governor of the North West Company. He died just as the North West Company was gaining strength and making money. James McGill was born in Scotland. He left money in his will to start McGill University in Montreal.

Other North West Company men took a special interest in exploring and mapping new territories. Some of them are discussed below.

Peter Pond (1740–1807)

Peter Pond was an American who began his fur-trading career around Detroit. He got to know some of the Montreal merchants. He explored west of the Great Lakes, mapping the area around Lake Athabasca. He led the way for Alexander Mackenzie, who would continue Pond's explorations. Pond was a good explorer and a hard worker. He had a bad temper, however, and he was suspected in the murder of two men. Because of this, people did not want to work with him. He eventually sold his share in the North West Company to William McGillivray and returned home to Connecticut.

Alexander Mackenzie (1764–1820)

Alexander Mackenzie was born in Scotland and became a very important explorer for the North West Company. He founded Fort Chipewyan, the oldest European settlement in Alberta, in 1788. The following year, he travelled to the Arctic on a river that he called the Disappointment, because it led to the Arctic and not to the Pacific as he had hoped. The Disappointment River was later named the Mackenzie River. Mackenzie's great achievement was to cross North America by land in 1793, arriving near Bella Coola, British Columbia. At the end of the

Figure 8.7 Alexander Mackenzie

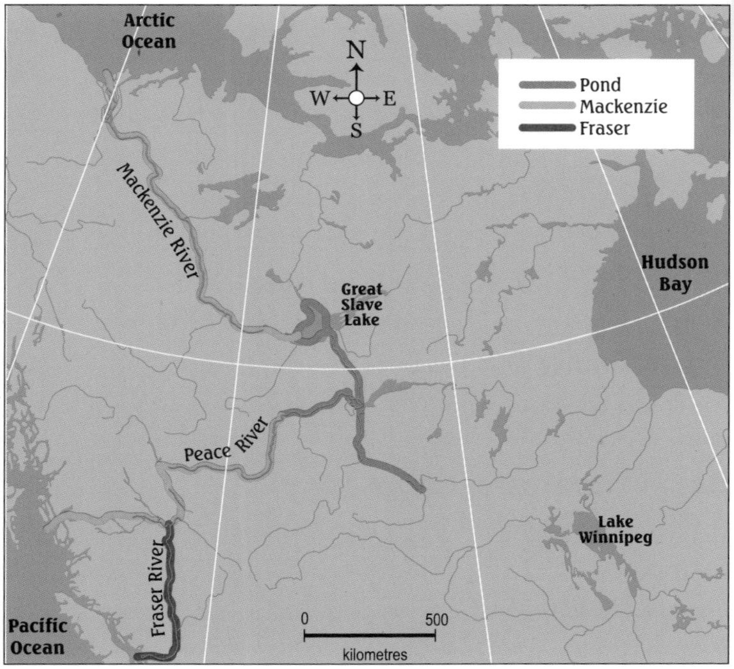

Figure 8.9 THE EXPLORATIONS OF POND, MACKENZIE, AND FRASER

trip, he took some grease and red paint and wrote on a rock, "Alexander Mackenzie, from Canada, by land, the twenty-second of July, one thousand seven hundred and ninety-three."

He had a disagreement with some of the leaders of the North West Company, which led him to found the XY Company. The two companies merged within a few years.

Simon Fraser (1776–1862)

Figure 8.8 Simon Fraser

Simon Fraser was born in Vermont. His family came to Canada after the American Revolution (see p. 164), because they were loyal to Britain. He joined the North West Company when he was 16 years old. He made several

> Here I must again acknowledge my great disappointment in not seeing the main ocean–having gone so near it as to be almost within view. Besides we wished very much to settle the situation by an observation for the longitude. The latitude is 49° nearly; while that of the entrance of the Columbia is 46° 20' [...] This River, therefore, is not the Columbia–if I had been convinced of this truth where I left my canoes, I would certainly have returned from thence.
>
> —Simon Fraser

expeditions between 1805 and 1808, trying to get to the West Coast. As with many explorers, he relied greatly on his Aboriginal guides. They knew the land and negotiated with other peoples along the way, so that Fraser and his party could pass in peace. He considered his trip a failure because he never saw the Pacific Ocean.

Fraser planned to travel down the Columbia River, but he ended up on another river (later called the Fraser). It was full of whitewater rapids, which made it very hard to navigate. When Fraser finally reached the mouth of the river, Vancouver Island blocked him from seeing the open ocean. The Cowichan people who lived there were unwelcoming and chased the expedition back up the river.

David Thompson (1770–1857)

David Thompson joined the Hudson's Bay Company in 1784 at the age of 14. Thompson learned mathematics, surveying, and astronomy with the company, but he soon left. He felt the Hudson's Bay Company would not allow him to do the work he wanted as a surveyor. The North West Company was willing to give him more freedom. In May 1797, in the middle of the night, he crept away from the Hudson's Bay Company post where he was

Figure 8.10
David Thompson
and Charlotte Small

stationed. He travelled 130 kilometres to the nearest North West Company post on the Reindeer River.

Thompson mapped much of the northwest of the continent, nearly 4 million square kilometres worth! He married Charlotte Small, a daughter of a European fur trader and his Cree wife, in 1799. Charlotte travelled with David most of the time. They had 13 children over the course of their 58 years of marriage. Thompson was forced to live with a daughter when he got old, as he had no money. He died in February 1857. Charlotte died three months later. For many years after his death, Thompson was forgotten. In 1914, his journals and maps were discovered and published. He has been called "the greatest land geographer who ever lived."

No living person possesses a tithe of his information respecting the Hudson's Bay countries, which from 1793 to 1820 he was constantly traversing…he had a very powerful mind, and a singular faculty of picture-making. He can create a wilderness and people it with [vivid images], or climb the Rocky Mountains with you in a snow-storm, so clearly and palpably, that you only have to shut your eyes and you hear the crack of the rifle, or feel the snow-flakes melt on your cheeks as he talks.

—*John Bigsby, an English geologist talking about Thompson, whom he once met*

Fort William

Fort William was built on the shores of Lake Superior, by the Kaministiquia River. Named after William McGillivray, it was the company's central shipping post. Canoe brigades met there in August, at the North West Company's annual rendezvous (meeting). Sometimes, close to 1000 people would be in attendance. After the meeting, some people returned to Montreal with furs to ship to Europe. Others, the men of the north, travelled into trapping grounds to spend the winter. Fort William is now in Thunder Bay, where you can visit a reconstruction of the original fort.

Figure 8.11 Fort William

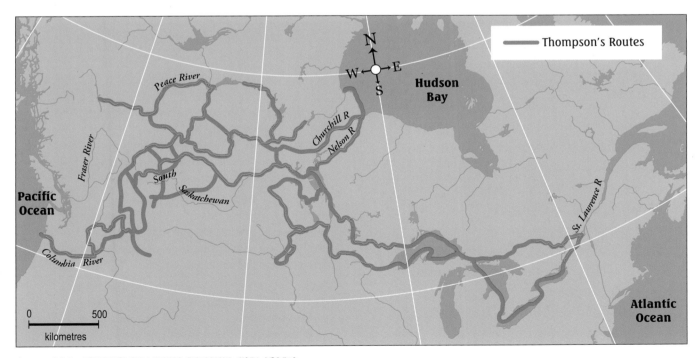

Figure 8.12 THE EXPLORATIONS OF DAVID THOMPSON

People of the Hudson's Bay Company

With the North West Company taking away some of its trade, the Hudson's Bay Company knew it would have to be more forceful. The company sent out men to develop trade with hunters and trappers inland. Below are some of the people who were involved in exploration.

Samuel Hearne (1745–1792)

Samuel Hearne was born in London, England. His first two attempts to reach the Coppermine River failed. The first time, he was deserted by his guides. On his second try, his quadrant, which he needed to navigate, broke. On his third try, in 1771, he succeeded. His success was largely because of the skill of his guide Matonabbee and the Dene women on the expedition who looked after food, clothing, and shelter.

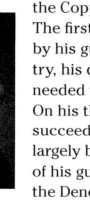

Figure 8.13
Samuel Hearne

Hearne was the first European to travel to the Arctic Ocean, but he did not find the precious metals he wanted.

Hearne was a faithful Hudson's Bay Company man his entire life. He founded the company's first inland post, Cumberland House, in present-day Saskatchewan. He was a very curious man and documented in his journals all that he saw: people, plants, animals, and landscape. He kept many different wild animals as pets, even beavers. When the weather became cold, he was "obliged to take them into [his] house and keep [them] in the sitting room." It is said that when women and children entered the sitting room at Fort Prince of Wales, where Hearne was stationed for several years, the beavers sat up and crawled into their laps.

Matonabbee (1737–1782)

Matonabbee was raised at the Hudson's Bay Company post in Churchill, Manitoba, after his father died. The son of Dene parents, he spoke English, Dene, and Cree, and was a skilled negotiator and guide. Matonabbee offered to guide Samuel Hearne on his third attempt to reach the

Figure 8.14
Matonabbee

The mystery of Sir John Franklin

In Baffin's Bay where the whale-fish blow
The fate of Franklin no man can know
The fate of Franklin no tongue can tell
Lord Franklin with his seamen does dwell.

—*from the ballad "Lord Franklin,"* traditional

In 1845, the explorer Sir John Franklin and his crew of 134 men set out in two ships, the *Erebus* and *Terror*, to find the Northwest Passage. They had packed supplies for three years, yet no one returned alive. The mystery of the expedition's disappearance captured the imagination of the public in both Europe and North America.

In 1859, the bodies of many of the crew, frozen on King William's Island, were discovered. Also found were two letters saying Franklin and others had died on ship from starvation and scurvy. The ships have never been found.

Historians are still trying to figure out what happened. Some think that everyone was poisoned with lead from the tins that food was stored in. Others think that the men were not prepared for the harsh northern climate. The search for answers about how they died continues to this day.

Figure 8.15 John Rae

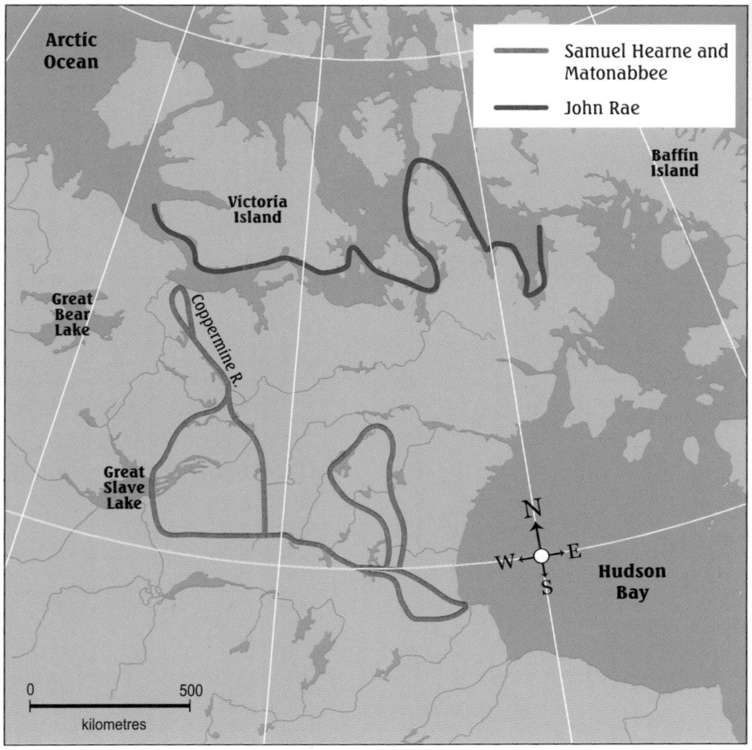

Figure 8.16 THE EXPLORATIONS OF HEARNE, MATONABBEE, AND RAE

Coppermine River, convinced his previous guides had lacked the necessary knowledge and skills for successful expeditions. On the next try, Hearne, guided by Matonabbee, finally reached the Coppermine. Matonabbee also brought his wives along to ensure the success of the journey.

Hearne greatly admired his guide, whom he called "the most sociable, kind, and sensible Indian I had ever met."

Dr. John Rae (1813–1893)

Dr. John Rae was born in Orkney and joined the Hudson's Bay Company in 1833. He loved the outdoors, and as the doctor at Moose Factory, he became attracted to "the wild sort of life to be found in the Hudson's Bay Company service." Rae learned all that he could from the Cree people about how to survive in a cold climate. He learned how to hunt and store food, and he became very skilled at snowshoeing. Later, Rae and his Inuit guides made four expeditions to the Arctic, mapping much of the coast. Rae travelled mainly on foot – between 1846 and 1854, he walked more than 16 000 kilometres! Rae also found out from some Inuit people about the death of Sir John Franklin and his expedition, which had disappeared while searching for the Northwest Passage in 1845. Rae's great admiration for Canada's Aboriginal peoples made him a controversial figure in his day, as they were often dismissed as inferior to Europeans. However, because he learned their ways, he became a pioneer of Arctic exploration.

Differences between the companies

	NORTH WEST COMPANY (NWC)	HUDSON'S BAY COMPANY (HBC)
Governors	Mostly inhabitants of Canada, Scottish businessmen who were living in Montreal. They often participated in exploration or trading in the wilderness.	British gentlemen who almost never came to Canada. They governed through "factors" in their North American posts.
Employees	French-Canadian voyageurs.	Mainly men from the Orkney Islands, off the coast of Scotland.
Attitudes about women	Marriage to Aboriginal women was encouraged.	Officially, marriage to Aboriginal women was not allowed but it did occur. White women were not allowed at HBC posts until early 19th century.
Buildings/Forts/Factories	Inland along important waterways. 342 posts scattered throughout the west.	By the bay, until they had to move inland. 242 posts usually following NWC posts.
Attitudes toward trappers	We'll go to you and collect your furs in your territory.	You come to us, and we'll buy your furs.
Exploration	Far reaching.	Only when necessary.
Vessels	Canoes.	York boats and canoes.
Turnover time (the time it took to get furs from trapping grounds to Europe)	24 months or more.	About 14 months.
Distances	Two to four times that of HBC.	More manageable because they controlled Hudson Bay.
Payment to employees	Commission. The more you work, the more furs, the more money.	Salary. You will always make the same amount of money.
Food	Easier to get in the more southern areas. Less problems with supply — lots of bison along the plains.	Sometimes known as the "hungry belly company," there was not enough 'portable' food around the bay. People more often struggled with scurvy and hunger in the north.
Land holdings	Rivers and waterways in "southern" Canada.	Land drained by rivers and waterways running into Hudson Bay.
Trade goods	Used alcohol in trading; other trade goods were sometimes of poorer quality.	Reluctantly used alcohol in trading, to keep up with the Nor'westers. Other trade goods were often better quality than NWC.

Figure 8.17 Voyageur of North West Company with canoe. The canot de maitre was a large birchbark canoe up to 12 metres long and paddled by 8 to 12 voyageurs. Smaller canoes held 4 to 6 men.

Song of the voyageur

Voyageurs sang as they paddled. It helped them keep in rhythm, but it also must have helped pass the long 16 to 18 hour days. The following is a traditional voyageur song:

Mon Canot

Assis sur mon canot d'écorce
Assis â la fraiche du temps;
Oui, je brave tous les rapides,
Je ne crains pas les bouillons blancs!

Je prend mon canot, je le lance
A travers des repid's, des bouillons blancs,
Et là, à grands sauts, il avance.
Je ne crains mêm' pas l'océan.

Un laboureur aim' sa charrue,
Un chasseur, son fusil et son chien,
Un musicien aim' sa musique
Moi, mon canot, c'est tout mon bien.

My Canoe

Seated in my bark canoe,
Seated in the coolness of the day;
Yes, I brave all the rapids,
I do not fear the white foam!

I take my canoe and launch it
Across the rapids, the white foam
And then by great leaps it advances
I am not even afraid of the ocean.

A farmer loves his plough,
A hunter his dog and gun,
A musician loves his music,
As for me, my canoe is everything.

Figure 8.18 Hudson's Bay Company trader and York boat. Based on the Orkney fishing boat, the York boat was used mainly on lakes and major rivers. Sometimes it could be fitted with a sail. It could not be carried on portages, but was rolled over logs. It had a crew of 6 to 8 men.

The Fur Trade in British Columbia

As competition grew, people began looking farther and farther north and west for fur. Many countries became interested in the west coast of North America. Spain had explored and traded there. Russia had explored south from the coast of Alaska. Britain was sending people as well.

James Cook (1728–1779)

Captain James Cook was born in England. As a member of the Royal Navy, he had fought during the siege of Quebec in 1759. He later became known as an excellent sea captain and cartographer. In 1778, he sailed up the west coast of North America from California to Alaska, mapping and charting the whole way. He made a stop at Nootka Sound where he traded for sea-otter skins with the Aboriginal peoples there. Despite the presence of the Aboriginal peoples, Cook claimed the area for Britain. He also explored and mapped huge areas in the Pacific Ocean, from the Easter Islands to Australia to the Sandwich Islands (Hawaii). He was able to sail for long distances and his crew did not suffer from scurvy, because he

Figure 8.19 James Cook

Figure 8.20 This picture of the Nootka was done by the artist on board Cook's expedition. Most expeditions included an artist who recorded the people and places visited.

required his men to eat sauerkraut and citrus fruits. He led the way for George Vancouver to further explore the coast in 1791.

George Vancouver (1757–1798)

George Vancouver was only 15 when he sailed along the west coast of North America with Captain James Cook. Years later, he continued Cook's work, mapping and charting the West Coast in 1793. This was the same year that Alexander Mackenzie completed his overland route. If Mackenzie had been a month earlier or Vancouver a month later, they might have bumped into each other on a beach!

Figure 8.21 George Vancouver

The sea otter

Sea otters have the thickest fur of any animal in the animal kingdom. They were prized for their pelts, which were worth 10 times the price of a beaver pelt. As soon as sea otters were discovered by European traders along the West Coast, they were hunted to extinction. Sea otters can be found along the coast once again, but they are the descendants of Alaskan sea otters that were imported in the late 1960s to early 1970s. Otters have sensitive front paws, love shellfish of all kinds, and need to eat 30 percent of their body weight every day in order to be able to regulate their temperature in the cool ocean waters.

Figure 8.22 Sea otter

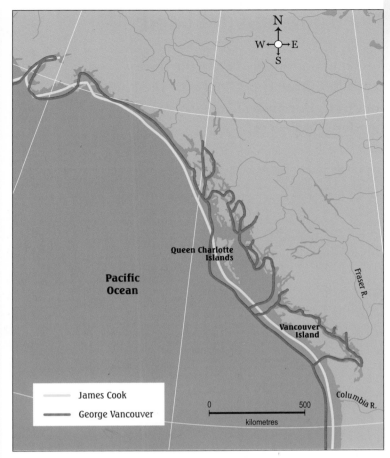

Figure 8.23 WEST COAST EXPLORATIONS OF COOK AND VANCOUVER

Disputes

The **czar** of Russia had granted fur-trading rights in 1799 to the Russian-America Company. The company established fur-trading posts throughout present-day Alaska. When the Hudson's Bay Company wanted to build a post there, they were warned off by the Russians.

The companies came to an agreement. They could both use the land, but the Hudson's Bay Company had to pay rent and supply the Russians with fresh produce. However, the two companies were soon in court to determine who controlled the land north of Vancouver Island. Eventually they

Teen traders

David Thompson was 14, George Vancouver was 15, Simon Fraser was 16, and Henry Kelsey was 17 when they began their working lives. In those days, teenagers were considered adults, and were given many adult responsibilities. How different are things today?

reached another agreement, although there continued to be some problems. American settlers from Oregon were moving into the Hudson's Bay Company territory and did not recognize the company's claim that it was the legitimate government of its territory.

Fur Trade and the Land

Seven main regions of the fur trade stretched from the Atlantic to the Pacific, and from the Arctic Circle to the American border. They were:

BRITISH COLUMBIA. The fur trade in British Columbia centred around the sea otter. The North West Company traded out of Fort Astoria. The main post of the Hudson's Bay Company was Fort Vancouver. From here, smaller posts were administered. Both Fort Astoria and Fort Vancouver were on the Columbia River, in Oregon country, an area shared by Britain and the United States. In 1849, the Hudson's Bay Company moved its Pacific operations from Fort Vancouver to Fort Victoria.

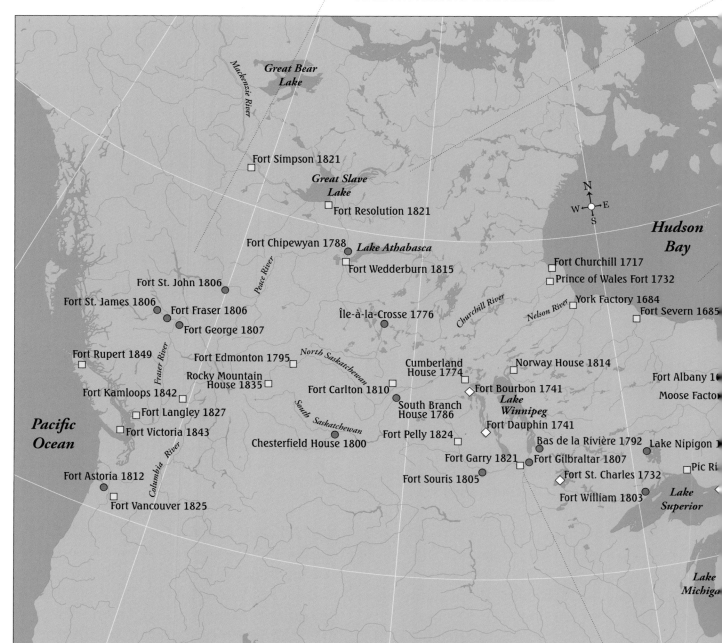

Figure 8.24 **MAIN FUR TRADE POSTS.** The date after the fort's name indicates the year the fort was built.

THE ATHABASCA REGION. The region around Lake Athabasca and north along the Mackenzie River was a rich fur-trading area. Because of the cold climate, the furs were thick and of top quality. For the North West Company, it was a very long trip back to the headquarters in Montreal, but the quality of the furs made the trip worthwhile. Later, when the Hudson's Bay Company established posts in the region, traders could transport their furs to Europe through Hudson Bay.

THE BOTTOM OF THE BAY and HUDSON BAY. The Bottom of the Bay, now called James Bay, was home to some of the earliest Hudson's Bay Company trading posts, such as Moose Factory and Fort Albany. Other posts, such as York Factory, Fort Prince of Wales, and Fort Churchill, were built farther west, out of the reach of the French. The Hudson's Bay Company's first inland post, Cumberland House, was built in 1774.

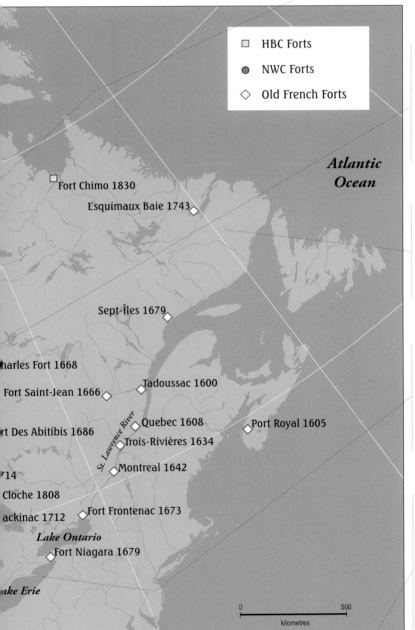

Legend:
- □ HBC Forts
- ● NWC Forts
- ◇ Old French Forts

Atlantic Ocean

□ Fort Chimo 1830

Esquimaux Baie 1743 ◇

Sept-Îles 1679 ◇

harles Fort 1668

Fort Saint-Jean 1666 ◇

rt Des Abitibis 1686

Tadoussac 1600 ◇

St. Lawrence River

◇ Quebec 1608

◇ Port Royal 1605

Trois-Rivières 1634 ◇

'14

◇ Montreal 1642

Cloche 1808

ackinac 1712   ◇ Fort Frontenac 1673

Lake Ontario

◇ Fort Niagara 1679

ake Erie

0 — 500
kilometres

THE KING'S POSTS. West of Labrador and north of the St. Lawrence River was a vast area that extended to the watershed of Hudson Bay. Under the French, this region was known as the King's Domain (Domaine du Roi). The king of France granted fur-trading rights to private companies, who built trading posts known as the King's Posts. In 1842, the posts were taken over by the Hudson's Bay Company.

LABRADOR. The Hudson's Bay Company began trading in Labrador in the 1830s, when Inuit and Montagnais trappers brought furs to more than 20 posts established by the company. The best furs came from Esquimaux Baie. The "EB" mark on a fur was a sign of very high quality at the fur auctions of London.

THE GREAT LAKES and THE PAYS D'EN HAUT. Around 1640, many First Nations people, escaping from the Iroquois, moved west of Lake Michigan between the Ohio River and the Great Lakes, and as far southwest as Louisiana. The French soon followed, establishing such posts as Fort Frontenac and Fort Michilimackinac. Trappers, traders, and their families settled along rivers that ran into the lakes.

THE FORKS of the Red and Assiniboine rivers. The place where the Assiniboine River flows into the Red River was a key location, because all of the east-west canoe routes passed through it. It was also the northernmost point where the bison came, making it an important food depot for the fur-trade brigades. The bison-rich land around The Forks became home to the Métis. In 1821, when the North West Company and Hudson's Bay Company merged as one company, many fur traders retired to Red River, the settlement at The Forks.

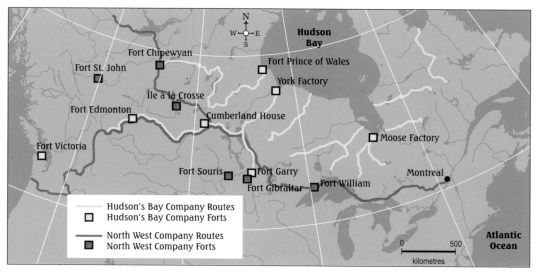

Figure 8.25 FUR TRADE ROUTES. The North West Company and Hudson's Bay Company used different routes to explore their fur-trade territories. Between them, they covered the breadth of the country. Many of their posts became permanent settlements that still exist today.

Place names

Among the great legacies of the First Peoples and of the fur trade are Canadian place names. Below are just a few examples of each.

ABORIGINAL PLACE NAMES

- Winnipeg: Cree for "muddy water"
- The Pas: Cree for "narrow between high banks"
- Manitoba: Cree for "the strait of the spirit of Manitobau" or Assiniboine for "Lake of the Prairie"
- Ottawa: Algonquin for "to trade"
- Wawa: Ojibwe for "wild geese"
- Lake Ontario: Iroquoian for "beautiful lake"
- Saskatoon: Cree for "early berries"
- Saskatchewan: Cree for "swift-moving river"
- Nunavut: Inuktitut for "our land"
- Iqaluit: Inuktitut for "place of fish"
- Tuktoyaktuk: Inuktitut for "reindeer that looks like caribou"

Early names are often changed. In 1975, Quebec decided to replace the Inuit names for northern lakes with names of early French settlers and explorers. In response, the Inuit suggested that some other places might be renamed in Inuktitut. Montreal, for example, could be called Sanikuvik, which means "large garbage dump." In some provinces, an Aboriginal name has replaced the European name. Ottawa was called Bytown until 1855. In 1987, Frobisher Bay officially became Iqaluit. Years earlier, Port Brabant in the western Arctic became Tuktoyaktuk.

FUR-TRADE PLACE NAMES

- Fraser River, British Columbia: named after Simon Fraser
- Portage la Prairie, Manitoba: marks the location where fur traders had to make a portage on their way from the Assiniboine River to Lake Manitoba
- Edmonton, Alberta: named after Fort Edmonton
- Dauphin, Manitoba: named after Fort Dauphin
- Prince Rupert, British Columbia: named after Prince Rupert

The fur trade is also responsible for the more than 660 Canadian places that have *moose* in their names. Some examples are Moose Jaw (Saskatchewan) and Moose Factory and Moosenee (both in Ontario). *Beaver* is also in hundreds of place names, including Beaverton (Ontario) and Beaverlodge (Alberta).

French fur traders were responsible for western place names using *butte* ("small hill" in French) and *coulee* (from couler, "to flow" in French). A small town in Manitoba is called Plum Coulee.

Fur-trade names are also used for streets, buildings, and other institutions. For example, one of the main streets in Gillam, Manitoba, is named after the great guide Matonabbee. McGill University, in Montreal, is named for James McGill, one of the founders of the North West Company. La Verendrye School in Winnipeg is named for the explorer Pierre de La Vérendrye.

Canada was just one of several names proposed for the land north of the United States at Confederation in 1867. Perhaps the most unusual suggestion was *Efisga*. It stands for a combination of the first letters of the countries of origin of most people living in British North America: **E**ngland, **F**rance, **I**reland, **S**cotland, **G**ermany, and **A**boriginal lands.

Figure 8.26 This painting, *At the Portage* (1882), shows Hudson's Bay Company employees preparing to carry their loads using tumplines.

Portaging

Voyageurs paddled up to 130 kilometres a day. That distance did not include portages. The portage was the most difficult and energy-draining part of the trip. A voyageur was responsible for six pieces of the load, plus his personal gear. Each piece weighed about 40 kilograms, and personal belongings weighed about 18 kilograms.

Voyagers did not strap their loads onto their backs. They used tumplines. A tumpline is a strap or sling that wraps around the bottom of a pack at one end and the forehead at the other end. Using a tumpline, a voyageur could carry two pieces, and sometimes more, at a time.

A voyageur was able to carry an 80-kilogram load about 0.8 kilometres. If a portage was longer than that, he set his load down and returned for the next load. A voyageur might walk five kilometres a day (half of it carrying at least 80 kilograms) in addition to paddling over 100 kilometres.

Hudson? Hudson's?

European explorers liked to name places after themselves. Often, they named a place possessively, as if it belonged to them – Hudson's Bay, not Hudson Bay, for example. Around 100 years ago, Canadian mapmakers decided it was not right to name places like that, and they changed "Hudson's" Bay to "Hudson" Bay. The Governor and Company of Adventurers of England Trading into Hudson's Bay did not change their name, however.

Effects of the Fur Trade

For the nation of Canada

The fur trade, in many ways, allowed Canada to exist as it does today. Without the far-ranging explorations of the Hudson's Bay Company and North West Company, American colonizers would have moved into the western regions of Canada. Almost all our early maps were drawn because of the fur trade. Fur-trade employees explored the Arctic. Three early trading posts, Fort Garry (Winnipeg), Fort Edmonton, and Fort Victoria became capitals of their provinces. The Hudson's Bay Company sold its territory in the west to the newly created country of Canada in 1870, which allowed Canada to stretch from "sea to sea."

For the Aboriginal peoples

The fur trade and European contact brought about huge changes to the Aboriginal way of life. Some of them are discussed below.

Figure 8.27 Encampment at Red River, 1868

Weapons and tools. The Aboriginal peoples quickly gave up their use of stone arrowheads and axe heads. Metal ones were much sharper and could be purchased ready-made. Guns were a new weapon they could use for hunting, although bows and arrows were still used much of the time.

Alcohol. Aboriginal peoples had never had alcohol before the fur trade. When it was first introduced, priests spoke out against it. At times, people tried to control the use of liquor as a trade item. Even so, liquor became an important trade item of the fur trade. Traders took advantage of many Aboriginal peoples by getting them drunk before trading so they could get cheaper furs. In some places, alcohol was the only item offered for trade.

Settlements. Many Aboriginal groups moved from season to season to places where food was available. They followed animal migrations. Those who farmed, moved their village every 30 to 40 years when the land became less fertile. As more and more Europeans moved into North America and claimed land, Aboriginal peoples' settlement patterns and traditional routes were disrupted.

Disease. Aboriginal peoples had no immunity to many of the diseases the Europeans brought with them. Diseases such as smallpox and measles wiped out entire villages and groups of people. Aboriginal peoples died in such large numbers that they could not resist European settlement.

For the beaver

Aboriginal peoples had many stories and legends about the beaver. Among the Anishinabe, the beaver played a part in the creation of the world. To the Algonquin, the beaver's tail made the sound of thunder. The beaver was valued and respected among First Peoples.

Figure 8.28 This picture of beavers, by the artist J.J. Audubon, was drawn from nature in 1844. By that time, beavers were no longer endangered.

Aboriginal peoples hunted the beaver for its meat and its pelts. The Europeans were far more interested in beaver pelts than meat. The demand for beaver fur was high in Europe, and traders sold as many beaver pelts as they could to the hat makers there. Aboriginal peoples came to depend on the different trade goods they could get for the pelts. For years, men fought each other for control of the beaver trade.

The year 1823 was a bad year for beaver. That was when a trapper named Sewell Newhouse invented the easy-to-use steel trap. With this new invention, a man or woman could catch up to 150 beavers a day, just walking the trap line. Newhouse's trap almost caused the beaver to become extinct. By 1840, however, beaver-felt hats were no longer popular, as silk hats became more fashionable. With less demand for beaver fur, the number of beavers slowly increased.

For a new nation

A whole new group of people arose out of this time in history. The Métis were the result of the intermarriage of European immigrants and the Aboriginal inhabitants of North America. The combination of these two backgrounds created a new culture and way of life.

Conclusion

In this chapter, you learned a lot about the fur trade. You found out how European fur traders and Aboriginal guides and trappers influenced each other. You learned the importance of Aboriginal women to the trade. You learned about the differences between the North West Company and the Hudson's Bay Company and about some people who worked for them.

In chapter 9, join Sara and Ben as they learn about a new people – the Métis.

9

A New Nation: The Métis

Sara and Ben were visiting Le Festival du Voyageur, a winter carnival that celebrates the life of the people who lived at the Red River settlement during the days of the fur trade. Many of the people who lived at the settlement were Métis, children of European men and Aboriginal women. The Métis made their living off the fur trade. They trapped and traded fur, and supplied items needed for the fur trade, like pemmican.

Sara ducked into a little cabin. Inside, a small fire was burning. The temperature in the cabin was warmer than it was outside, but just barely.

A park interpreter, dressed in a blue coat wrapped with a multi-coloured Métis sash, stood by the door. He was talking about the life of the Métis – as if he were one of them. Sara asked him why such a small fire was burning on such a cold day.

"This is how we built fires," the interpreter answered. "We didn't want to waste wood by making the fire larger than it needed to be. Most of the trees close to the fort had been chopped down to build homes and make fires. Every winter, we had to travel upstream, cut wood, pile it on the frozen river, and wait for the ice to melt to transport the wood back to the fort. If we didn't cut enough wood one winter, we would surely pay for it the next!"

Sara shivered and held her hands closer to the fire. It had been a lot of work back then just to cook and stay warm.

Still, Sara noticed, the Métis seemed to have found time for making things beautiful. Their clothing was colourful and combined European fabrics such as wool with

Figure 9.1 A Métis family on the prairie

traditional Aboriginal beading. Even the sash combined the Aboriginal craft of finger weaving with the European textile, wool.

As Sara and Ben wandered around the festival grounds, they learned the Métis also had time for fun. The music at the festival celebrated some of the traditional instruments of the Métis and the voyageurs such as fiddles and spoons and wooden boxes used as drums. The maple-syrup taffy, made by pouring boiled syrup into the snow and rolling it onto a stick, was as delicious as any candy Sara and Ben had ever tasted.

The Métis, they learned, was a unique culture, forged from the fur trade.

Figure 9.2 *A Man and His Wife Returning with a Load of Partridge,* a painting by W. Richards

Origins of the Métis

When the Europeans first came to North America, almost all the newcomers were single and male. Most women they met were Cree, Ojibwa, or Saulteaux. Many of these European men married Aboriginal women. The men were young and lonely. The Aboriginal women they met could perform many useful tasks to make the Europeans' lives more comfortable. Marriage was also a way to build alliances with Aboriginal groups.

These people did not marry according to European customs. Few priests and ministers who performed marriages lived in North America. Instead, the couple married *à la façon du pays* – according to the "custom of the country." The marriages were called "country marriages," and wives became known as "country wives."

The "country born" referred to children born to Aboriginal mothers and English-speaking fathers, often traders with the Hudson's Bay Company. The term *Métis* referred to people descended from Aboriginal mothers and French-speaking fathers, often traders of the North West Company and their Aboriginal wives. Today, Métis refers to anyone of European and North American Aboriginal descent.

Many European men spoke fondly of their country wives, and they often had large families. However, some men left their country wives behind when they returned to Europe. Some husbands supported the wives and children they left behind, while

As you read, think about

- **how the Métis people came to be**
- **where and how the Métis lived**
- **what threatened the Métis way of life**
- **what the Métis wanted**

others did not. Some took their children to Europe to be educated.

Many men, however, decided to stay in North America with their families after their working contracts were over. Journal writer and fur trader Daniel Harmon wrote this about his country wife: "Our connection has been cemented by work and faith. We have wept together over the death of our children, and we have children still living who are dear to us both. How could I spend my days in the civilized world and leave my beloved children in the wilderness? And how could I tear them from a mother's love and leave her to mourn over their absence?"

Most country wives helped their husbands adapt to a new way of life. Their hunting skills, their ability to sew moccasins and make snowshoes, and their understanding of Aboriginal customs aided their husbands' careers. These women played an important role in the growth of the fur trade. Until recently, however, their stories were rarely mentioned in history textbooks.

Later, men brought women from Europe with them to their postings. Very few European women thrived in the way that country wives did, however.

The home guard

Just outside the walls of the forts on the Prairies were villages of Cree people. These Cree became known as the "home guard." They hunted, trapped, and fished to supply food to the post, and they helped with other work.

Traditional Life

The Métis way of life combined both Aboriginal and European cultures. From the First Peoples, they took the skills necessary to live in the wilderness, prepare traditional medicines, and pass on oral traditions. From the Europeans, they took many tools and adapted them to the North American way of life. From both cultures, they inherited a love for storytelling, music, and dance. They spoke the languages of their fathers and of their mothers, and they learned the spiritual systems of both parents.

The semi-annual bison hunt was very important to the Métis. The bison hunt began as a means for Aboriginal peoples to obtain animal hides for clothing and shelter, bones for making tools, and meat to survive through the long, cold winters. By the early

Figure 9.3 Almost all parts of the bison were used by the Métis. Bison hides were used to make warm winter coats, like the one at right.

1800s, the Métis needed the bison hunt to make pemmican that they traded to the North West Company in return for goods essential to their survival.

The bison hunt

The Métis hunted bison very differently from their Aboriginal ancestors, who herded them over cliffs or corralled them into ravines. The Métis hunted herds of bison from the backs of galloping horses. At first, they used bows and arrows. Later, with the arrival of firearms, they used rifles.

The bison hunt was always an important event. By the middle of the 19th century, however, it had become a huge event in which hundreds, and, sometimes, thousands of people gathered. In 1840, for example, the hunt at Red River was attended by 620 men, 650 women, and 360 children. With them they brought 586 oxen, 655 cart horses, and 403 horses suitable for running the bison. According to the census of that year, fully a third of those living in the settlement attended the hunt. Spring hunts lasted for up to three months. In the fall, smaller hunts were held. The meat from these hunts – 500 000 kilograms or more – was dried for pemmican, and the skins were made into clothing.

To keep order during these large gatherings, the Métis made a series of laws that governed the hunt. A president was elected, and captains and policemen selected by the president ensured that the rules of the hunt were followed.

Figure 9.4 Each day after the hunt, bison meat was dried on wooden racks.

Rules of the Hunt

1. No buffalo to be run on the Sabbath-Day.

2. No party to fork off, lag behind, or go before, without permission.

3. No person or party to run buffalo before the general order.

4. Every captain with his men, in turn, to patrol the camp, and keep guard.

5. For the first trespass against these laws, the offender to have his saddle and bridle cut up.

6. For the second offence, the coat to be taken off the offender's back, and be cut up.

7. For the third offence, the offender to be flogged.

8. Any person **convicted** of theft, even to the value of a sinew, to be brought to the middle of the camp, and the crier to call out his or her name three times, adding the word "Thief," at each time.

Paul Kane (1810–1871), a painter and traveller, described the bison hunt in his journal, which was later published (see box at right).

We all walked our horses towards the herd. By the time we had gone about 200 yards [183 metres], the herd perceived us, and started off in the opposite direction at the top of their speed. We put our horses to full gallop, and in 20 minutes were in their midst.

The scene now became one of intense excitement; the huge bulls thundering over the plain in headlong confusion, while the fearless hunters rode recklessly in their midst, keeping up an incessant fire at but a few yards' distance from their victims. Upon the fall of each buffalo, the successful hunter merely threw some article of his apparel – often carried by him solely for that purpose – to denote his own prey, and then rushed on to another. *

The chase continued over an area of five or six square miles [13 to 16 square kilometres], where might be seen the dead and dying buffaloes, to the number of 500. In the meantime, my horse, which had started at a good run, was suddenly confronted by a large bull. He was taken by surprise and

Figure 9.5 When Paul Kane was on the Plains, he took part in a bison hunt. This painting by Kane captures some of the activity during the hunt.

sprung to one side, getting his foot into a badger hold. I was thrown over his head with such violence that I was completely stunned, but soon recovered my recollection. Some of the men caught my horse and I was speedily remounted, and soon saw reason to congratulate myself on my good fortune, for I found a man who had been thrown in a similar way, lying a short distance from me quite senseless, in which state he was carried back to the camp.

I again joined in the pursuit; and coming up with a large bull, had the satisfaction of bringing him down at the first fire. Excited by my success, I threw down my cap and galloping on, soon put a bullet through another enormous animal. He did not fall, but stopped and faced me, pawing the earth, bellowing and glaring savagely at me. The blood was streaming from his mouth, and I thought he would soon drop. I could not resist the desire of making a sketch. I dismounted and had just commenced when he made a dash at me. I had hardly time to spring on my horse and get away from him, leaving my gun and everything else behind.

When he came up to where I had been standing, he turned over the articles I had dropped, pawing fiercely as he tossed them about, and then retreated towards the herd. I recovered my gun and soon planted another shot in him; and this time he remained on his legs long enough for me to make a sketch. This done I returned with it to the camp, carrying the tongues of the animals I had killed, according to the custom, as trophies of my success as a hunter.

*Early travellers misidentified bison as buffalo. This misidentification continues today.

Figure 9.6 Paul Kane

Wandering artist

Paul Kane (1810–1871) was born in Ireland and came to Canada as a child. He learned to draw and paint as a child in Toronto, Ontario. As a young man, he set out on a two-and-a-half year adventure west, to the Great Lakes, Prairies, and West Coast, taking with him his notebooks, pencils, and paints. His pictures of early Aboriginal life and plant life showed North America before it became changed by European contact. His illustrated book of his travels, *Wanderings of an Artist Among the Indians of North America*, was a bestseller. Kane can be compared to a modern-day photojournalist. In the days before photography, Kane's paintings and writings were important documents of North American life.

Food

Pemmican. As you have read, pemmican was the staple food of the fur traders and voyageurs. Sir John Franklin (see p. 128) described pemmican in the following way: "A very little of this rich, solid food satisfies one's appetite. It is eaten, not because it tastes good, for it does not, but to live. It is almost like eating tallow candles. One must have a sharp appetite to eat it the way it is usually prepared."

Pemmican was made by cutting bison meat (or meat from deer, moose, or other large animal) into long thin strips and letting the strips dry in the sun. In later years, the meat was dried over a small fire burning under the rack of meat. When the meat was dry, it was pounded into a granular powder and put into hide bags. Hot bison fat was poured into the powder and mixed well. The bags were then sewn shut and pressed into flat bundles and left to cool. If wild berries were available, they were added to the mixture to give it flavour.

Bannock. Like pemmican, bannock, a type of bread, was a staple of fur traders and voyageurs. Bannock was easy to transport, easy to prepare, and could last a long time without spoiling. Traditionally, bannock was cooked several ways. In one method, the dough was buried in hot sand close to the fire. When the dough was cooked, the sand was brushed off, and the bannock was eaten. Another method was to form the dough onto a stick and hold it over a fire. Settlers introduced baking powder and cooked the dough in cast iron pans. Bannock could then be cooked on a stove, and the baking powder made it fluffier.

Figure 9.7 A scene of Métis life

Clothing

Métis clothing combined both Aboriginal and European heritage. Women wore European-style dresses, and moccasins decorated with floral beadwork unique to the Métis. Men wore a coat with a hood, and pants with an opening at the hip. Their clothes were often made of wool, with flannel or bright cotton shirts. They wore leggings decorated with beadwork on their shins, moccasins, and a sash.

Traditionally, the sash was tied at the waist to hold a coat closed. Its fringed ends and the threads in the fringe could be used as an emergency sewing kit. The sash itself had many other uses; for example, as a support to the back for lifting, as a tourniquet for injuries, as a wrap for a broken bone, as a washcloth or towel, as a marker left on a killed bison to identify the shooter, or as a rope to tie up a canoe.

Red River cart

The two-wheeled Red River cart, invented by the Métis, was used for transporting goods on land. The two wheels were up to two metres in diameter each. These large wheels enabled the cart to roll over bumps without tipping and to go through mud without getting stuck. The wheels could be removed and strapped to the bottom of the cart so that it could float across a river. The cart was light, sturdy, and easy to make and repair. The carts were extremely noisy because the wheel axles could not be greased. Trails were usually very dusty. Grease on the axles would become coated with sand, causing the wheels to stick. Some people said that every cart had its own special squeal. The carts were especially helpful for hauling meat after bison hunts – a horse or ox could pull the cart and a 450-kilogram load. The Hudson's Bay Company used Red River carts as well, for travelling to St. Paul, Minnesota, and to Fort Edmonton.

Michif

Many Métis children grew up speaking two languages – French and Cree. In time, these languages evolved into a completely new language called "Michif." Michif is a blend of French nouns, Cree verbs, and some vocabulary from languages such as Saulteaux and Dene. Today, Michif is an endangered language, spoken by less than a thousand people. Some Michif words are *lī blôwån* (blueberries), *nimâmâ* (mother), and *moshkwa* (bear).

The term *Michif* may also refer to the Métis people.

Arrival of the Selkirk Settlers

Since the late 1700s, Lord Selkirk had been looking for a place where poor, homeless families from Ireland and Scotland could resettle. He decided the Red River area in Rupert's Land looked like a good place to start an agricultural settlement. To fulfill his dream, Lord Selkirk became a shareholder in the Hudson's Bay Company. He convinced the company to grant him approximately 300 000 square kilometres of land in Rupert's Land (see map, p. 151). In return, Selkirk promised he would create a settlement and supply employees of the Hudson's Bay Company with servants from Scotland and Ireland.

The North West Company traders and the Métis were not happy when they learned about Selkirk's plans for a colony at Red River.

Figure 9.8 Thomas Douglas, the Fifth Earl of Selkirk (1771–1820) was born in Scotland, and became earl after the death of his father in 1799. As a young man, Lord Selkirk had been shocked to see the farmers of the Scottish Highlands uprooted from their homes. He became a fervent supporter of emigration, and thought that the Highlanders would adapt well to the rigours of North America. He started a colony in Prince Edward Island in 1803, and by 1811, his plans for an agricultural settlement at Red River were well under way. Selkirk did not foresee the hardships that his settlers would face, nor the anger of the Métis at Red River. Before he died, he spoke sadly of the settlement as a place "where we had the prospect of doing so much good."

Many Métis families were already living on land he claimed for the settlement. As well, the settlement was to run alongside the North West Company's most profitable trade route. Settlement would ruin the fur trade by cutting Métis off from their fur-trading grounds farther west. Another great worry was that settlement land included territory traditionally used in the bison hunts. The Nor'Westers and Métis tried their best to make Lord Selkirk reconsider. They argued that the Red River area was too isolated. They tried to convince him that travelling there from the east was too difficult. They also argued that produce would go bad on long trips east, south, and west.

Lord Selkirk refused to listen to them. In 1812, the first settlers arrived from Scotland. Under the leadership of Governor Miles Macdonell, they set up camp close to the junction of the Red and Assiniboine rivers (present-day downtown Winnipeg). There, they prepared for another group of settlers – 120 men with women and children – who arrived with sheep, seeds for planting, and not much else.

The colony was doomed from the start. The long trek made it impossible for the settlers to bring farm tools. Most did not even have a plough. They could plant only small gardens. They had to hunt and fish for most of their food. During the winter, the settlers struggled to get enough food, and they were forced to eat their sheep. The Nor'Westers and the Métis, who resented the arrival of these settlers, did nothing to help them. The Saulteaux who lived nearby, however, helped them enough to keep them from starving to death.

Figure 9.9 The Selkirk settlers began to arrive at the Red River settlement.

The Pemmican Wars

Miles Macdonell, the governor, wondered why his settlers were going hungry, when so much bison meat was available as pemmican. When he found out that the Métis were sending almost all of the pemmican to far-ranging posts of the North West Company, he issued the Pemmican Proclamation. This stated that no food could be exported from the colony. The Métis were very upset, because they depended on making and selling pemmican to the fur traders to earn a living.

Macdonell also demanded that all North West Company employees in Rupert's Land leave their forts within six months. The Nor'Westers were angry. They decided to do all they could to end Selkirk's colony:

- They persuaded many of Selkirk's colonists to leave for **Upper Canada** by offering them free land and free transportation.

- They got the Métis to harass the settlers.

- They arrested Miles Macdonell for "Illegal Pemmican Seizure" and sent him back to Montreal for a trial, leaving the colony without a leader.

Newcomers

Jean Luc peeked out from behind the bushes. He saw a boy, about his age, and a younger girl. Their hair was red, and he imagined the sun would soon redden their thin faces, as well.

His own dark skin was used to the sun, and his hair was black. He was sturdy and well fed on his mother's garden and the meat from the bison his father hunted each year. He reached in his pocket and nibbled at the pemmican he almost always carried. Some days, he wandered far from his home while he played, and he didn't always want to return home for lunch.

As he ate, he saw the boy and girl eyeing his food. He could tell they wanted to try some, but were afraid to approach.

"Voulez-vous manger mon pemmican?" he asked. They didn't respond. He realized they couldn't understand him. He held out his pemmican and offered it to them, showing them that they could take it. He knew that there was more food for him at home, and these children looked hungry.

He decided that they must be with the people Lord Selkirk was bringing to the settlement. His father was against the new settlement. He was worried that the bison hunt would be ruined. His father sounded angry when he talked about the settlers, and Jean Luc had wished that they would leave.

But these strangers seemed nice, and it was hard for Jean Luc to imagine that they would cause problems. They said "thank you"

Figure 9.10

many times over, and Jean Luc knew that it meant *merci*. Soon they traded words while gesturing. They started laughing at each other's pronunciations.

"Sky."

"Ciel."

"Grass."

"Herbe."

"Feet."

"Pieds."

It was time to go. Jean Luc knew that his older brother would come looking for him any minute now, and he wanted to keep this meeting a secret. He wanted his new friends to understand that he needed to leave, and he hoped that they could play together again.

"A demain."

"Tomorrow."

Figure 9.11 Robert Semple (1777–1816) was born in Boston, Massachusetts, to Loyalist parents. Semple moved to England with his family during the American Revolution. He became a merchant and travelled throughout Europe, Africa, South America, and the Middle East. Semple wrote several books about his travels, and he even had a novel published. In 1815, he was appointed governor of the Hudson's Bay Company territories by Lord Selkirk.

The calm before the storm

By 1815, only 13 families remained in the Red River settlement, and they took refuge on the shores of Lake Winnipeg. Meanwhile, some Métis destroyed farms, trampled the fields, and burned buildings.

That fall, to create peace in the area, the Hudson's Bay Company and the Métis signed a treaty. According to the terms of the treaty, it sounded like the Hudson's Bay Company would never again try to establish a settlement at Red River. However, it was not long before Robert Semple, the new governor, arrived in Red River with another group of settlers.

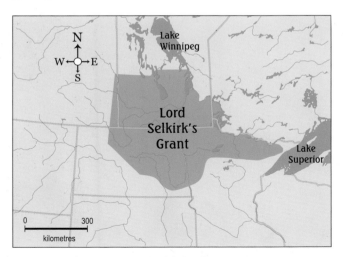

Figure 9.12 LORD SELKIRK'S LAND. Present-day boundaries show the extent of land granted by the Hudson's Bay Company to Lord Selkirk, land that had traditionally been used by Métis.

Treaty between the Hudson's Bay Company and Métis, 1815

1. All Settlers to retire immediately from this river, and no appearance of a colony to remain.

2. Peace and amity to subsist between all parties, traders, Indians, and freemen, in future, throughout these two rivers, and on no account any person to be molested in his lawful pursuits.

3. The honourable Hudson's Bay Company will, as customary enter this river, if they think proper, from three to four of their former trading boats, and from four to five men per boat as usual.

4. Whatever former disturbance had taken place between both parties, that is to say, the honourable Hudson's Bay Company and the *Métis* of the Indian Territory, to be totally forgotten and not to be recalled by either party.

5. Every person retiring peaceable from this river immediately shall not be molested in their passage out.

6. No person passing the summer for the Hudson's Bay Company, shall remain in the buildings of the Company but shall retire to some other spot, where they will establish for the purpose of trade.

Signed

Cuthbert Grant, Bostonais Pangman, Wm. Shaw, Bonhomme Montour, The Four Chiefs of the *Métis*, James Sutherland, James White

Red River Indian Territory, Forks, Red River, 25 June, 1815.

The Rise of the Métis

Tensions were growing between the Hudson's Bay Company and the North West Company. The Hudson's Bay Company was still interested in settling the land around the Red and Assiniboine rivers. The North West Company wanted to keep the land for fur trading and hunting. In the spring of 1816, the Hudson's Bay Company captured Fort Gibraltar, the stronghold of the North West Company. The North West Company answered back by capturing Brandon House. Some of the North West Company men then marched to Fort Douglas.

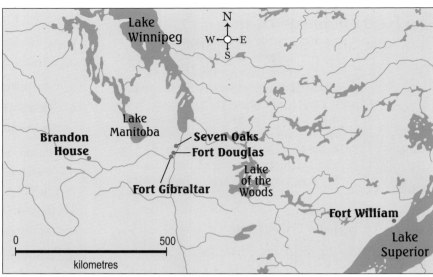

Figure 9.14 SITES OF CONFLICT BETWEEN NWC AND HBC

Figure 9.13 At the Battle of Seven Oaks, Métis supporters of the North West Company fought with the settlers of Red River.

The Battle of Seven Oaks

Governor Robert Semple had ignored warnings about the Métis' concerns. As the Métis approached the fort on June 19, 1816, he went out to talk with them. They met at Seven Oaks, which the Métis called the "Frog Plain" because so many frogs lived there. After a brief conversation, fighting broke out between Semple and his group of

settlers and the Métis, led by Cuthbert Grant. The Métis were the better **marksmen**.

Figure 9.15 The Métis created their own flag in 1815, just before the Battle of Seven Oaks. The infinity symbol represents the joining together of Aboriginal and European cultures into a single people.

They were used to shooting bison while riding horses. They were also more experienced fighters. When the fighting ended, 21 settlers, including Semple, were dead. One Métis had been killed.

The leaders of the Métis were sent to Upper Canada to stand trial for Seven Oaks, but no one was ever convicted. For the next five years, the North West Company and the Hudson's Bay Company engaged in many fights as each struggled for control of the territory. A Royal Proclamation called it "open warfare in the Indian Territories." It was a time of "anything goes." Young beavers were trapped, liquor was used in ever-increasing quantities, and employees and supporters of both companies fought and killed each other, and captured forts.

Bard of the Métis

Pierre Falcon, a Métis poet, composed a song about the battle at Seven Oaks. Here are the first two verses, in French, as he wrote it, and an English translation.

**Voulez-vous écouter chanter
Une chanson de vérité?
Le dix-neuf de juin, la band' des Bois-Brûlés
Sont arrivés comm' des braves guerriers.**

**En arrivant à la Grenouillère
Nous avons fait trois prisonniers;
Trois prisonniers des Arkanys
Qui sont ici pour piller not' pays.**

**Would you like to hear me sing
Of a true and recent thing?
It was June nineteen, the band of Bois-Brûlés
Arrived that day.**

**Oh the brave warriors they!
We took three foreigners prisoners when
We came to the place called Frog, Frog Plain.
They were men who'd come from Orkney
Who'd come, you see,
To rob our country.**

Figure 9.16 Pierre Falcon

The Enemies Unite

By 1820, profits were at an all-time low for both the Hudson's Bay Company and the North West Company. The companies were stuggling because of their constant fighting and the drop in demand for furs. Something had to be done.

In 1821, representatives of the two companies met at Fort William to discuss the terms of a **merger**. On March 26, they agreed to join together as one company. The Hudson's Bay Company had more money to see them through years of losses, and so the new company kept the name Hudson's Bay Company. It was now the largest trading company in the world. Many people were not happy with the merger, however.

- The new company had no competition. Across the northern part of North America, the Hudson's Bay Company was the only company that bought pelts, and the only company that sold supplies. This meant it could pay less for fur and charge more for supplies.

- There were a lot of extra forts and traders. Forts needed to be closed and employees laid off.

Figure 9.17 Cuthbert Grant's father worked for the North West Company. His mother was Métis. When Cuthbert Grant (1793–1854) was only six, his father died. William McGillivray, the head of the North West Company, became his legal guardian and sent Cuthbert to Scotland for school. Cuthbert later rose through the ranks at the North West Company. In 1814, he was appointed the "Captain General" of the Métis at the Red River settlement. Sadly, his body lies buried under a Manitoba highway near the town that originally bore his name.

Scottish-born George Simpson was appointed governor of Rupert's Land and given the responsibility of making the Hudson's Bay Company profitable again. He crisscrossed the country, visiting every post and closing down the ones that were less efficient. He fired over half the work force, and he replaced canoes with York boats and even steamships wherever he could.

Because of George Simpson's cost cutting, many people who once worked for the Hudson's Bay Company and North West Company returned to Europe. Most of those who stayed were married to country wives and had families. At the time, the Red River settlement was a perfect place for them to raise their families. There was little of the racism they would experience farther east.

Now that the fighting between the North West Company and the Hudson's Bay Company had ended, the people of the Red River settlement enjoyed a time of relative peace. There were some conflicts over the bison hunt between the Métis and the

Figure 9.18 George Simpson was governor of the Hudson's Bay Company from the time of its merger in 1821 until 1856. He expanded the company and made it more profitable than ever. Knighted in 1841, he was often called "the Little Emperor."

Dakota, but most of the time, people were able to get along.

In 1828, the Hudson's Bay Company appointed Cuthbert Grant as Warden of the Plains. With this title, Grant was recognized as leader of the French-speaking Métis. Eleven years later, he was appointed to the Council of Assiniboia, which governed the Red River settlement.

Grant's Old Mill, located by Sturgeon Creek in Winnipeg, was built in 1829 by Cuthbert Grant. It was the first time anyone had used hydro power in Manitoba. Grant Avenue in Winnipeg, and Grantown (now the town of St. Francois Xavier) were also named for Cuthbert Grant.

DID YOU KNOW?

Figure 9.19 *View of the two Company Forts on the level prairie at Pembina on the Red River*, by Peter Rindisbacher, shows the HBC's Fort Daer (left) and NWC's Fort Pembina (right). Fort Daer was originally established by Miles Macdonell and Red River colonists in 1812. Following the merger of the two companies in 1821, it was torn down, and its lumber was floated down the Red River to Fort Douglas.

The Colony Grows

In the 1820s, the settlers at Red River faced many challenges – failed crops, grasshopper infestations, and, in 1826, the worst flooding on record. Despite these problems, the colony continued to grow. People farmed and hunted, and built churches, hospitals, and schools.

The Hudson's Bay Company was both the biggest employer in the area and the government. Not all of the people living in Rupert's Land approved. To the Métis, the Hudson's Bay Company had too much power. The Métis were used to making decisions based on the consent of all, not the orders of one person. They were upset that they were not well represented in the colony's government.

The Hudson's Bay Company also wanted to keep its monopoly on the fur trade. By the 1840s, however, many Métis were trading with others.

Figure 9.20 Red River settlement c. 1820s. At left is St. Boniface Cathedral. At right is the Grey Nuns' Convent, which still stands. The oldest building in the city of Winnipeg, the convent is now home to the St. Boniface Museum.

Guillaume Sayer

In 1848, the Hudson's Bay Company had a chance to test if its monopoly was legal. That year, Guillaume Sayer, a Métis from the Red River settlement, was arrested for illegal trading. He had been trading directly with a merchant from North Dakota rather than with the Hudson's Bay Company. Sayer believed he should be able to trade with whomever he chose. The Métis and independent traders supported him.

During the trial, Sayer admitted he was trading. However, he said that the furs he was trading had been a "present exchange," which was an Aboriginal tradition. He was found guilty, but the court did not punish him. This decision was important. It meant that the trading monopoly of the Hudson's Bay Company could no longer be enforced.

Figure 9.21

Conclusion

The Métis engaged in many struggles. For example, with the increasing number of European immigrants moving into the Red River area, the Métis were sometimes discriminated against. Their struggles would continue later in the century as they tried to hold onto their territory and traditions.

Today, Manitoba has a large Métis population. Métis people also live across Canada, and throughout North America. The Métis continue their fight to have their traditional lands recognized through land claims.

In part 4, you will learn more about the settlement of English-speaking Canada. In chapter 10, join Sara and Ben as they learn about the British Empire Loyalists.

PART 4

From British Colony to Confederation

1783
The Revolutionary
War in the U.S. ends.
Approximately
45 000 Loyalists migrate
to British North America.

1791
The Constitutional
Act divides Quebec
into Upper and
Lower Canada.

1814
On December 24,
the Treaty of Ghent
ends the War of 1812.

1834
Slavery is
abolished in
Britain and its
colonies.

1839
The Durham Report
recommends
Responsible
Government and
a united province of
Canada.

10. A Question of Loyalties **11. A Colony's Growing Pains** **12. Rebellion and Reform**

1784
New Brunswick
and Cape Breton
break off from Nova Scotia
to become separate
provinces. The
Six Nations Reserve is
formed in Ontario.

1812
Sir Isaac Brock
is killed in the Battle
of Queenston
Heights.

1832
Construction on
the Rideau
Canal is completed.

1837
Rebellions
break out in
both Upper and
Lower Canada.

1841
The Act of Union
joins Upper
and Lower Canada
into the united
Province of Canada.

1848
Responsible
Government is
granted to Nova Scotia
and soon
follows in Canada.

1864
Conferences are
held in Charlottetown
and Quebec to
discuss Confederation
of the British colonies
in North America.

13. From Colony to Country

1845
Blight destroys
the potato crop
in Ireland, causing
widespread famine.
Thousands of victims
emigrate to
North America.

1857
Queen Victoria
chooses Ottawa
as the capital
of Canada.

1867
The British
North America Act is
passed, which unites
New Brunswick, Nova
Scotia, Quebec, and
Ontario into the Dominion
of Canada.

10

A Question of Loyalties

Ben and Sara were ready for a long car trip: they had their snacks, their games, their books, and a pillow each. They were excited to be going somewhere they'd never been before. Within an hour of starting the trip, however, they wondered why they were stopping.

"Customs," their dad said. "We're at the border."

Have you ever taken a trip to Niagara Falls? The Niagara River is shared by the United States of America and Canada. The river serves as a border between the two nations. In other places, like Manitoba, the border is often just a stopping point in the prairies. Windsor, Ontario, and Detroit, Michigan, also share a river, but Brown Road is home to both a Canadian and Americans because it swerves back and forth along the border between New Brunswick and Maine.

Figure 10.1 Loyalist refugees escape to Canada.

Figure 10.2 This painting of Niagara Falls was done in 1797. The border between Canada and the United States was first decided in 1783, after the American War of Independence. Some people who left their homes in the United States settled near Horseshoe Falls, on the Canadian side of Niagara Falls.

Have you ever thought about why borders exist? How did it happen? When Britain won the Seven Years' War and swept French power out of North America, why did the colonies divide and two countries, instead of one, emerge?

If you continue along the border, you will find that almost all of Canada's most populated areas are within just a few hours drive of the American-Canadian border.

Today, crossing the border may take time, as border guards check people coming and going. During the late 1700s, however, crossing the border was often a matter of life and death. In 1775, the Thirteen Colonies decided they wanted to form their own country. They started a war against Britain,

As you read, think about

- why some people in the Thirteen Colonies wanted to remain British
- what hardships they suffered by being loyal to Britain
- what changes their arrival caused in the British colonies of North America
- how the Loyalist migration affected the French and Aboriginal peoples

the Revolutionary War, also known as the War of Independence. People who remained loyal to Britain were forced to flee to the colonies that wanted to stay under British control.

Unrest in the Colonies

Why did people want to revolt?

The Thirteen Colonies did not suddenly declare their independence from Great Britain in 1776. Several events during the 1760s and 1770s led up to this point. Some people in the colonies wanted to **revolt** against the government of Great Britain and form their own government. They called themselves "Patriots." The British called them "rebels."

There were many reasons people wanted to revolt against British rule, but the two main ones were:

1. People in the Thirteen Colonies were tired of paying British taxes, when they did not have a voice in the British government. After the Seven Years' War, Britain had a huge debt to pay. To make some money, the British government introduced the Stamp Act and the Tea Tax. Many people in the colonies did not want to pay for the war. They wanted to collect their own taxes and keep money in the colonies. They said that there should be "no taxation without representation."

2. The Quebec Act of 1774 gave the Ohio River Valley, just west of the Thirteen Colonies, to the province of Quebec. The people of the Thirteen Colonies wanted to expand and farm in that area.

Boston Tea Party

American colonists were angry, because Britain was charging lots of taxes to import tea. When colonists started smuggling their own tea into the colonies, Britain made its tea cheaper. The smugglers and their supporters got so angry that they stormed the decks of the British ships carrying tea and threw it all overboard into Boston Harbour. This incident became known as the Boston Tea Party.

Figure 10.3

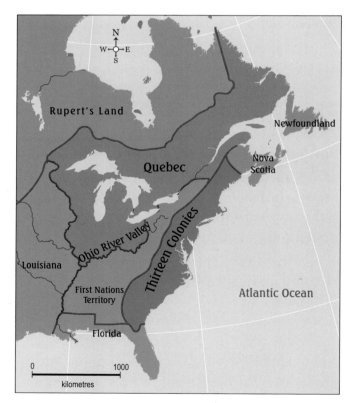

Figure 10.4 THE 13 COLONIES AND OHIO RIVER VALLEY AFTER THE QUEBEC ACT, 1774

Why did some people remain loyal?

Some colonists had been in North America for generations. Others were recent immigrants. Many felt that living under British rule had helped them. These people called themselves "Loyalists." The rebels called them "Tories." This was meant as an insult, because people who were unable to change or try something new were called Tories. People wanted to remain loyal to Britain for five main reasons, discussed below.

Figure 10.5 The Society of Friends, or Quakers, did not support the American cause. Like the Mennonites, they refused to fight in any war. They did not consider themselves Loyalists to the British Crown, but knew they could practise their religion freely under British rule.

1. They had been loyal to Britain and the monarchy their entire lives. They trusted Great Britain.

2. They distrusted the new American ideas. They were concerned about being independent, about being without a **monarch**, and about the kind of democracy the rebels wanted. Some Loyalists were afraid that democracy and elected governments would give too much power to "the mob" (people who were not educated or considered important).

3. They felt that it was the best way to preserve their freedom. They could always petition the monarch and ask for help if they felt they were being treated unfairly. They believed the British monarch would defend their interests. They did not trust American democracy. For instance, although the American Declaration of Independence stated that all men were equal, American male slaves were not regarded as free men by the state.

4. Aboriginal peoples knew that the Thirteen Colonies wanted to take over their lands. They believed the British monarch would defend their interests and allow them to keep their traditional lands.

5. The Loyalists believed that there was more tolerance for people of other religions and belief systems under British rule. Many colonists had come to North America seeking freedom from persecution. They knew that this freedom would continue under British rule, but were not sure what would happen if the **revolution** was successful.

The Revolutionary War

The invasion of Quebec

In 1775, the rebels were ready to make bold steps to separate from Great Britain. They declared war against Britain, and invited the people of Quebec to join their side. Most people in Quebec did not want another war. They had just finished rebuilding after the Seven Years' War. To them, this revolution seemed to be a quarrel between the British Crown and the people of the Thirteen Colonies.

The people in French Canada did not join the rebels. They did not join the British, either. When Governor Guy Carleton called for recruits for the defence of Quebec, only about 600 men showed up. This hurt Carleton's feelings, because he felt he had always been fair to the people of Quebec. Why were they not willing to help?

Late in 1775, General George Washington, commander of the rebels, sent two attack forces to the province of Quebec. Victory there would give the Americans control of a major shipping route – the St. Lawrence River. One force captured Montreal. The other force tried to overtake Quebec on December 31, 1775, during a snowstorm. Travelling through the confusing streets, the Americans got lost and were fired on by the British. The attack on Quebec failed, and the British drove the Americans away.

Loss

For the American colonists who remained loyal to the British, the war years were terrible. The rebels considered them traitors, and fought against them. The rebels **banished** the Loyalists from their homes and took their property and land, sometimes farms they had tended for generations. The British, grateful for the support of the Loyalists, promised them land in Canada if they helped Britain in its fight against the rebels. Many Loyalists became soldiers in the British army.

Figure 10.6 The American general George Washington believed that the French in Canada would join them in their revolution against Britain.

Although the British won Quebec, they could not stop the rebels from taking over the Thirteen Colonies. In 1776, the rebels created the United States of America. When fighting ended in 1783, the Americans had won their independence from Britain. The Loyalists lost all hope of ever returning to their homes, and became refugees to Canada.

Tarred and feathered

During the Revolutionary War, many Loyalists were tarred and feathered. This was one way that Patriots could publicly punish and humiliate Loyalists. Hot tar was poured on the body, and feathers were shaken out to stick to the tar. The tar was hot enough to blister the skin, and the feathers were simply a way to further bother the victim. Removing the tar and feathers was very difficult. People would have to bathe in turpentine or some other solvent to get the tar off their tender skin.

Figure 10.7 Tarring and feathering

Taking Flight

Mama told me to run to Uncle Jeb's and tell him that tonight would be the night. We had to leave the 13 colonies quickly. The American rebels were getting bolder all the time, and everyone in the county knew that Papa had gone to fight for the king of England.

Papa thought we would be safe, because he said his own neighbours would never hurt a woman and her children. He had been wrong. In the next county, a woman had been thrown out of her home and her farmhouse burned when her husband went to fight for the British.

When I got there and told Uncle Jeb we were ready to go, Aunt Laura exploded.

"Why are you putting yourself into such danger?" She grabbed Uncle Jeb's arm. "If the rebels discover what you're doing tonight, you'll be in danger of being tarred and feathered, or worse."

It hurt me to know that she was angry. I had been named for her, and I had always gone to her house to play. Mostly, though, I was afraid that Uncle Jeb would change his mind.

Uncle Jeb spoke up. "I ask you, Laura, how can I let my sister cross that river alone with two children in the dead of night? I may not agree with her politics, but we're still family. Do you forget that her husband helped me buy this farm? And that she cared for our children when you were sick?"

Uncle Jeb would not back down. He grabbed his coat and his gun, saddled up his horse, and slung me up behind him. I used to love riding behind Uncle Jeb, but not today. Today, I was afraid.

I was afraid of how far we would have to travel to find safety. I was afraid Papa would get killed in the war. I was afraid that I wouldn't be able to go to school once we got to Nova Scotia. I was afraid of crossing the river at night. I was afraid for Josiah. I was 11 years old, but he was only 7. How would he manage the trip?

Uncle Jeb galloped for home where Mama was preparing for our journey. I thought of how the distance between our houses had always been such a pleasant walk. But now I was going away, and I wondered if I would ever see Aunt Laura again. Would my last memory of her always be of an angry woman who didn't want her husband to help us?

I didn't understand why the grownups couldn't get along, and I didn't understand why we were no longer welcome in our own town.

I just hoped that Papa would be able to find us, wherever we were going.

Figure 10.8

Who Were the United Empire Loyalists?

The United Empire Loyalists were a diverse group. They came from all walks of life. They were farmers, businessmen, soldiers, and slaves. Some were educated, and others were not. They came from different ethnic backgrounds, including Swiss, Dutch, German, Aboriginal, British, and African-American.

American-born colonists. Many of the American-born colonists were farmers from the northern states of New York and Pennsylvania. Although some of them were wealthy landowners, others were poor. They felt that Britain offered them a better way of life than a revolutionary government would.

Figure 10.9 *Coming of the Loyalists, 1783,* by Henry Sandham. This painting was completed in 1925. It shows the Loyalists arriving in Nova Scotia in very fine clothes and footwear. Do you think this picture is accurate?

Immigrants. Some Loyalists were recent immigrants from Britain. They had come to North America after the Seven Years' War ended in 1763. They did not like the American ideals of democracy. They believed the monarchy was the best way to preserve their rights. Many of them came from Scotland.

Other Europeans. Groups that had come to North America to escape religious persecution also stayed loyal. Mennonites and Amish people who had come from Germany did not believe in war. They were known as **pacifists**. They were thankful to Britain for providing them with a place to practice their religion without persecution, and they were not sure how they would fare apart from the monarchy. Also living in North America was a small number of Jewish people from Portugal. They were afraid that they might be persecuted in a country without a monarchy or British justice system.

African-Americans.

Some African-Americans were slaves belonging to Loyalist families from the south. These families settled in Quebec and Nova Scotia, where slavery was legal. Others were known as **free Blacks.** They became Loyalists because they were promised freedom and land in Nova Scotia if they joined the British. Approximately 3000 Black Loyalists came to Nova Scotia. However, life in Nova Scotia was not as good as they had hoped, and many of them faced discrimination and hatred. When a colony for freed slaves was established in Sierra Leone, Africa, approximately half of the Black Loyalists moved there, hoping for a better way of life.

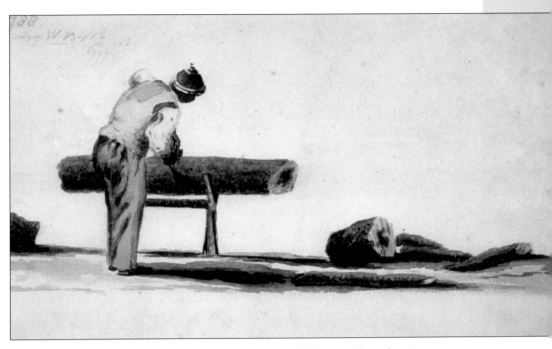

Figure 10.10 This watercolour, *A black woodcutter at Shelburne, Nova Scotia,* was painted by William Booth in 1788. It may be the oldest portrayal of an African-American Loyalist in Nova Scotia. Many descendants of these Loyalists still live in the province today.

Aboriginal peoples.

Many Aboriginal peoples sided with the British. They feared the American thirst for their traditional lands and thought that the British were more likely to preserve their rights to those lands. Approximately 2000 of them followed Thayendanegea (Joseph Brant) to British North America after the Revolutionary War.

Women. The American Revolution was especially difficult for many women who remained loyal to Britain. They were left alone and without protection as their husbands went to fight. Many set out alone with their children to find safety in British North America during and after the war.

United Empire Loyalists

Lord Dorchester, governor of Quebec, decided that the Loyalists who had sacrificed so much to support Britain should receive special recognition. In 1793, he decreed that the Loyalists could use the initials U.E. beside their names, showing their support for "Unity of Empire." These refugees from the Revolutionary War became known as United Empire Loyalists, and their present-day descendants can still use the initials beside their names.

Figure 10.11 The inscription under this picture says: "Encampment of the Loyalists at Johnston, a New Settlement, on the Banks of the River St. Laurence [*sic*] in Canada, taken June 6 1784." The settlement of Johnston became the city of Cornwall, Ontario. What would these settlers have to do next to build a town?

Loyalists' Stories

William Schurman

William Schurman's family had been in North America since the 1650s, when the Dutch and French Huguenots (Protestants) came to escape persecution in Europe. Schurman was born in 1743 in New York. He was a prosperous farmer and merchant when the Revolutionary War broke out.

Schurman tried to remain neutral throughout the revolution. By 1782, however, he knew that the rebels would win, and he would have to leave his home. He was luckier than many Loyalists who fled the United States with nothing. He was able to sell his farm to his brothers-in-law, who wanted the land to remain in the family.

He left with his wife, five children, and two family slaves. They eventually found land in Bedeque, Prince Edward Island. William cleared land, built a gristmill, and opened a store. He sold everything from clay pipes to moccasins, and guns to sugar. He mapped out the first road that led from Bedeque to Charlottetown. He began to build ships. When he died in 1819, he owned 3000 hectares of land, two sawmills, a store, a gristmill, a forge, his farm, and a shipping and lumbering business.

Boston King

Boston King was born in 1760 near Charleston, South Carolina. He was the son of slaves, though as a driver, his father had more responsibilities and privileges than some. Boston King learned to be a carpenter.

During the Revolutionary War, a horse that Boston King had in his care was stolen by another apprentice. Boston knew that he would be blamed, then beaten or even killed. He decided to flee to the English who were fighting in Charleston. Although he was sad about leaving the only way of life he had ever known and his friends and family, he found that he loved freedom.

The British encouraged slaves like Boston King to leave their plantations. Every slave who deserted left the Americans with fewer workers, and the British desperately needed tradespeople to help them. The British promised to protect the former slaves and not send them back to their masters if they supported Britain.

As promised, the Black Loyalists who came to Nova Scotia and the surrounding areas were granted land. It was usually such poor land, however, that they had trouble growing crops. Many former slaves, including Boston and his family, struggled to survive, especially during a famine in 1789.

When Britain offered to move the Black Loyalists to Sierra Leone in Africa in 1792, Boston and his wife decided to move there. More than 1100 Black Loyalists left Nova Scotia for Sierra Leone.

Koñwatsiãtsiaiéñni (Molly Brant) and Thayendanegea (Joseph Brant)

Molly Brant, a Mohawk woman, was born in 1736, probably in what is now Ohio, an area controlled by the Six Nations at the time. She was married to Sir William Johnson, and they had eight children. After her husband died in 1774, Molly lived in New York and ran a store.

When war broke out, Molly declared loyalty to Britain. She helped Loyalists who were on the run. She also passed on information to the British about rebel battle plans. She encouraged Iroquois warriors to fight for the king. If the British won the war, she believed, the Aboriginal peoples would get their land back and be able to live the life they, not someone else, chose.

After the war, the members of the Iroquois Nations realized how much land

Figure 10.12 Thayendanegea (Joseph Brant)

and power they would lose. Molly, along with her brother Joseph Brant, continued to speak on their behalf. The Brants were granted land by the Canadian government, and Molly settled in Cataraqui, which is now Kingston, Ontario. Molly died in 1796. She was remembered and honoured by all who knew her for her passionate loyalty to her people and to Britain.

Joseph Brant, Molly's younger brother, was born in 1742. He fought with the British during the Revolutionary War. He also acted as a negotiator among many different First Nations. Concerned that his people would lose their independence, he travelled to Britain several times to discuss his concerns with King George III. The king assured him that his peoples' traditional lands would remain under their control and that they would be **sovereign** within the British colony.

Because of his military service, he received a pension and a land grant in Burlington, Ontario. Brantford, Ontario, is named after him.

Sarah Sherwood

The women who remained loyal to Britain are sometimes called the "invisible loyalists." They had very little political power and were often treated badly by neighbours when their husbands or sons went to fight for the British. Sarah was born in Connecticut in 1754. After she was born, her family moved to Vermont, which was a frontier area at the time. There, she met and married her husband in 1774.

In 1776, Sarah's home was broken into by rebels. Her husband had to flee, and she was forced to move several times. After months of trying to stay close to her home, she made her way to Fort St. Jean in Canada. She was eight months pregnant and accompanied by her slave and her two young children. Shortly after arriving in Fort St. Jean in December 1777, she gave birth to her third child.

Figure 10.13 This portrait of Loyalist Willet Carpenter was painted in 1820. Mr. Carpenter fled from New York to Queens County, New Brunswick, in 1777. In a letter dated April 6, 1786, in the British Public Record Office, Carpenter asks the British government to pay him for his land in New York, which he lost after supporting the British.

Figure 10.14 This tintype (photo printed on metal) of Nancy and George Miller was taken at the time of their marriage, around 1860. Nancy Loyst and George Miller were the children or grandchildren of German Loyalists. The name Miller was originally Mueller. Like many early Loyalists, the Mueller family intermarried and adopted British names and ways.

Until the end of the war she lived at the fort, caring for her family and other refugees.

After the war ended and her husband rejoined the family, they faced a final deadly enemy: smallpox. They were all able to fight off the disease. They later struggled during The Hungry Years. The drought that affected Boston King in Nova Scotia in 1789 also caused shortages along the St. Lawrence River where the Sherwoods lived.

By 1791, the Sherwood family was doing well on their farm in Augusta, Upper Canada. Sarah Sherwood outlived her husband and retired to Montreal where she died in 1818.

The End of War

The Treaty of Paris, 1783

With the end of the Revolutionary War came the need for another treaty. Britain had to concede defeat and acknowledge that the Thirteen Colonies were now free states. The treaty established borders between the two countries, and worked out details like fishing rights and the release of prisoners. Aboriginal peoples and Aboriginal lands were not mentioned in the treaty, and this worried their leaders like Molly and Joseph Brant. The king of Britain had promised them their lands if they fought for him, and now they sought it.

The Gun Shot Treaty, 1792

The Gun Shot Treaty survived in oral history for many years before papers were discovered confirming its existence. This treaty was signed between representatives of the British king and the Aboriginal peoples who lived close to and around the Bay of Quinte, on the north shore of Lake Ontario. The treaty promised that as long as the "sun shone in the sky" the Aboriginal peoples would be able to fish on all the waterways, and hunt on land adjacent to lakes, rivers, and streams equal to the distance that a gunshot could be heard. In return, the Aboriginal peoples promised to "surrender" or "share" the land that had traditionally been theirs.

Figure 10.15 This house was built in 1787 by Loyalist David Nairn, who was a barrel maker, or cooper. It is now home to the Shelburne County Museum in Nova Scotia.

Six Nations Reserve

Following the Revolutionary War, Britain was forced to give up land it controlled west of the Mississippi River, land they had promised to the Mohawk people for supporting them in the war. Thayendanegea (Joseph Brant) insisted that the British fulfill their promise. In 1774, the Mohawk were granted 385 000 hectares of land on either side of the Grand River north of Lake Erie, where close to 2000 Mohawk Loyalists settled. However, the land they received was far less than what Brant had originally agreed to. The Six Nations Reserve is still there today.

Where the Loyalists Settled

The Loyalists had a great impact on the history of Canada. After the Revolutionary War, approximately 45 000 settled throughout North America in the areas that remained loyal to Britain. (Others went to Britain or British colonies in the Caribbean.) In 1784, the population of Canada and Nova Scotia was approximately 125 000. The challenges of managing the huge population increase that came with the influx of Loyalists caused the British government to divide up the area that was known as Nova Scotia into three separate colonies: Cape Breton, (present-day) Nova Scotia, and New Brunswick. Quebec was divided into Upper Canada and **Lower Canada**, with the Loyalists going mainly up the St. Lawrence to the land north of Lake Ontario and the other Great Lakes.

Cape Breton Island. Approximately 1000 Loyalists settled on Cape Breton Island, which forced Britain to establish a government there in 1784. It operated as a separate colony until 1820, when it reunited with Nova Scotia.

Island of St. John (renamed Prince Edward Island in 1798). Approximately 500 Loyalists made their way to Prince Edward Island, but because

Figure 10.16 This shipbuilding crew takes a break at the R.W. Freeman shipyard at Jordan River, Nova Scotia, in 1880. The second from right in the front row is master shipwright James Cox, great grandson of Loyalist James Cox who settled in Shelburne around 1790. Many Loyalists who settled in Nova Scotia made their living in the shipyards, as well as in the lumber or fishing businesses, as do many of their descendants today.

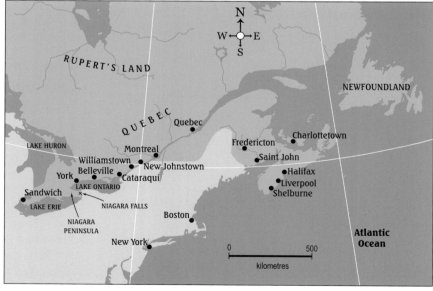

Figure 10.17 LOYALIST SETTLEMENTS. Approximately 45 000 Loyalists settled in the places shown on this map. How would the arrival of so many new people affect the future of British North America?

of the way the government mismanaged their land grants, many of them left.

Nova Scotia. Many Loyalists from New York arrived in Nova Scotia and received land grants, including Black Loyalists like Boston King. Shelburne was a major Loyalist community of more than 10 000 people that sprang up in the year 1783. The Loyalists there were mainly farmers, however, and the poor soil and isolation of Shelburne made it difficult to make a living. Many of them gave up and moved elsewhere, and after 10 years only about 300 remained. Those who did stay got involved in shipbuilding, fishing, or the lumber trade.

New Brunswick. Approximately 20 000 Loyalists were granted land in New Brunswick, and, in 1784, the British government appointed Loyalists to govern the province.

Quebec. The colony of Quebec saw an influx of approximately 10 000 Loyalists. For the first time the English-speaking, farming population outnumbered the French-speaking population. The Loyalists had strong ideas about government, and they were unfamiliar with French language and French laws.

The French were also nervous about losing their voice and their power to the new immigrants. With the Loyalists living primarily in two places, west of Montreal in Cataraqui (Kingston) and in the Niagara Peninsula, the British government divided the colony of Quebec into two separate provinces. In 1791, Upper Canada was formed for the Loyalists, and Lower Canada remained French.

Conclusion

The coming of the Loyalists changed British North America forever. The many English-speaking immigrants had backgrounds different from the French of Canada. The Loyalists had suffered hardships that those already in the colonies had never known. They had different ideas about government, favouring the British system over the French. Now the British North American colonies had large numbers of English-speaking people, as well as French and Aboriginal peoples. It also included people from other backgrounds, such as German, Swiss, and African-American. Mainly, the map of North America had changed in ways that no one could have foreseen, with the United States of America to the south, and the new provinces of Upper Canada and Lower Canada carved out of Quebec.

After the Revolutionary War, the Constitutional Act of 1791 established the new boundaries for each of the colonies. It replaced the French seigneurial system with a new land ownership system, and it gave some, but not much, power to elected councils. It had been designed to help the French and the English get along. With the separation of Upper and Lower Canada, the French Catholics were able to maintain their way of life, and the English Protestants were exempt from living under French-style laws.

In the next chapter, join Ben and Sara as they discover how loyalties to Britain were tested when its North American colonies were threatened.

A Colony's Growing Pains

Queenston Heights is a great place to have a picnic, hike on a trail, visit the Laura Secord homestead, or climb the Brock Tower. There are trees and gardens, and a butterfly conservatory is nearby. It's hard to imagine that this area saw some of the bloodiest battles on Canadian soil, but that's what Ben and Sara discovered on their trip to Niagara Falls.

The history of Canada is everywhere – they just had to look around.

Just west of the falls is Lundy's Lane, which leads down to the Niagara River. Two hundred years ago, Lundy's Lane was just a farm. The Lundy family provided British soldiers with tea and snacks while they fought the Battle of Lundy's Lane.

Ben and Sara, along with their parents, had fun riding the *Maid of the Mist* and exploring the tunnels behind the falls. They then decided to do some investigating beyond the noise of the waterfall. While they were looking for a place to picnic, they discovered the Brock Monument.

Figure 11.1 Soldiers and their allies at the Battle of Queenston Heights

Figure 11.2 Queenston Heights rises above the Niagara River approximately 100 metres. This was the site of a famous battle in the War of 1812, where Sir Isaac Brock died while defending Upper Canada from American soldiers. In the picture (above), you can see the original monument built to honour General Brock. It was bombed in 1840. Figure 11.3 A replacement (right) was completed in 1856.

They decided to climb the steps, and while they climbed, they counted.

"Two hundred thirty-five! At least coming down will be easier than going up!" The view from the top of the tower was amazing. They could see the river snaking through forests that probably looked quite a bit like they did in 1812.

The spiral staircase was so narrow, they both got dizzy, and they were glad that few people chose to climb the stairs. There was barely enough room to squeeze by another person. They noticed that the walls were damp, and ladybugs liked to rest on the walls. There were hundreds of them. Once they had climbed back down, they realized that the monument was where Sir Isaac Brock, commander of the British army and hero of the War of 1812, was buried. His remains lie in the base of the tower, along with those of his trusty second-in-command, John Macdonell.

The monument was first built in 1824 as a memorial to Brock, who died in the Battle of Queenston Heights, but it was bombed in 1840. The tower that Ben and Sarah climbed was built in 1854. It stands as a reminder of a time when there were people willing to risk their lives to protect their land even before Canada was a country.

As you read, think about

- why British North America and the U.S. fought the War of 1812
- what the effects of the war were on the people of British North America
- who came to British North America after the war, and why they came

Figure. 11.4 *Attack of Fort Oswego, on Lake Ontario, North America.* On May 6, 1814, the British attacked the U.S. *Fort Oswego* to cut off supplies to American troops and to secure more territory on the Great Lakes. The lakes were an important transportation route, and the land surrounding them was of great value to the British, First Nations, and Americans.

Causes of the War of 1812

On June 18, 1812, James Madison, president of the United States, signed the Proclamation of War against Great Britain. The United States planned to attack the closest British colonies, Upper and Lower Canada, just to the north.

President Madison had not really thought things through, however. The American army was not well equipped or well trained. The British army, though small, was well organized and prepared. As well, Britain's Aboriginal allies were valuable to their war effort. They were disciplined and fierce fighters, and the Americans were almost paralyzed with fear when facing them in battle. The Americans would have a much more difficult time during the War of 1812 than they had thought.

There were three major issues that caused the War of 1812 and led President Madison to declare war.

1. **Trade.** Britain and France were at war. The United States wanted to remain neutral and trade with both sides, but Britain was stopping other countries from trading with France.

2. **The Sea.** Britain had a very large and powerful navy. Britain also bullied the Americans at sea. British ships would regularly stop American ships to look for and remove British citizens who might be sailing on them. The Americans felt that this was unfair harassment.

3. **The Great Lakes Region.** The United States wanted to control land around the Great Lakes. Although the territory south of the Great Lakes had been transferred to the United States after the Revolutionary War, the British still occupied many of the forts in the region.

The Americans had fought for this land, because their farmers wanted to move into it. The War Hawks, a group of American politicians, convinced President Madison to declare war against Britain so they could have complete control over the Ohio River Valley.

The Aboriginal peoples fought back. The land was theirs for hunting and fishing, and they did not want farms and settlements interfering with their way of life. The British sided with the Aboriginal peoples and even supplied them with guns and weapons. The British relied on the Aboriginal peoples to guard against the Americans. The Canadian fur traders also supported this idea. They wanted to protect their livelihood, and the American push to settle and farm would harm their trade.

Tecumseh

"Live your life so that the fear of death can never enter your heart. When you arise in the morning, give thanks for the morning light. Give thanks for your life and your strength. Give thanks for your food and for the joy of living. And if perchance you see no reason for giving thanks, rest assured the fault is in yourself." — Tecumseh

Tecumseh, chief of the Shawnee people, with his brother Tenskwatawa, led a movement to build a **confederacy** of First Nations, from the Great Lakes to Mexico. He believed this was the only way to prevent the United States from taking over Aboriginal lands. He travelled to many different First Nations, and persuaded them not to give in to the United States. Tecumseh commanded an impressive army of Aboriginal soldiers, and became a trusted friend of Sir Isaac Brock, the British commander.

Tecumseh died in battle in October 1813, a year after his great friend died in the Battle of Queenston Heights.

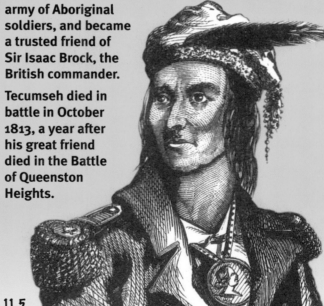

Figure 11.5

Events of the War of 1812

Upper Canada

Most fighting in the War of 1812 took place in Upper Canada. The American Brigadier General William Hull invaded Upper Canada on July 12, 1812, at Detroit. He had far more soldiers and weapons than the British. Tecumseh and British Major General Isaac Brock knew they would need their forces to appear more powerful than they actually were, so Brock sent Tecumseh a fake letter and made sure it was captured by the Americans. The letter said that British needed "only" 5000 Aboriginal warriors to capture Detroit.

In reality, there were only about 600 warriors available to fight. To make it seem like there were more, Tecumseh marched the same group through a clearing in the woods several times.

Hull was sick, and so were many of his troops. He was also terrified of the Aboriginal warriors. Before Brock and Tecumseh could attack, Hull surrendered at Detroit on August 16, 1812.

This easy victory strengthened Upper Canada's morale. Many settlers and Aboriginal peoples were encouraged and decided to support the British after the capture of Detroit. The Americans realized that taking the land would not be "a simple matter of marching," as former President Thomas Jefferson had predicted.

Sir Isaac Brock's horse was named Alfred.

DID YOU KNOW?

Figure 11.6 Isaac Brock was a distinguished soldier in the British Army when he was posted to British North America in 1802. There, he trained the militia and commanded the British regular army. When war broke out in the United States in 1812, Brock became partners with the Shawnee chief, Tecumseh. Together, they claimed many victories for the British. Brock was knighted following his victory at Detroit.

Battle of Queenston Heights, October 13, 1812

Sir Isaac Brock heard that a large American force was marching on Queenston, and so he moved a force of 1000 men to meet them there.

The Americans captured the hill known as Queenston Heights, and killed both Brock and his second-in-command, John Macdonell. The Americans took the British cannons and turned them on the British troops.

Their success did not last long, though. John Norton, a Mohawk chief, climbed through the woods with a small group of Aboriginal fighters and attacked the Americans from the rear. The Americans retreated, and the British won the battle. The Americans did not attempt to invade Upper Canada again that year, but they would try later.

The Battle of Queenston Heights was a crucial victory for the British in the Niagara region, even though Sir Isaac Brock died before the battle was over. Although the

Figure 11.7 Sir Isaac Brock's jacket, recovered from the battlefield, shows the hole made from the bullet that killed him.

Figure 11.8 On October 13, 1812, the Americans, led by General Stephen Van Rensselaer, attacked British forces and Canadian militia at Queenston Heights, on the Canadian side of the Niagara River. Although the British were outnumbered by American soldiers, they won the Battle of Queenston Heights. However, the British lost their great general Sir Isaac Brock, who was killed in the battle.

British numbered 1300 soldiers to the Americans' 6000, only 14 British soldiers died, compared with 100 Americans.

Results of the war

Two more important battles were fought in Lower Canada in 1813: the battles at Chateauguay and Crysler's Farm. The war continued into 1814, with battles at Chippewa, Lundy's Lane, and elsewhere. Yet neither side could

Figure 11.9 John Norton was born in Scotland, the son of a Scottish woman and a Cherokee father who had been adopted into a Mohawk tribe. He was well educated and worked as a schoolteacher and a missionary, as well as an advocate for Aboriginal rights. In addition to Queenston Heights, he led a fighting force at the battle of Lundy's Lane in late July 1814 and at the unsuccessful British assault on Fort Erie in mid August.

win. On December 24, 1814, American and British delegates signed the Treaty of Ghent in Belgium. Although Britain promised to stop blockading the Americans, the borders were left exactly as they had been at the start of the war. The War of 1812 was sometimes called "the war that no one won."

Figure 11.10 KEY BATTLES OF THE WAR OF 1812

Effects on British North America

The War of 1812 had important effects on the British North American colonies.

Identity. It confirmed that British North America would stay separate from the United States of America. The war showed that the people of British North America were still loyal to Britain, and that they were on their way to forming their own identity. There was a new Canadian pride and nationalism. Pierre Berton, a famous Canadian writer, said that without the War of 1812 and the invasions that occurred, the colonies would have been quietly swallowed up by their American neighbours as more and more Americans moved into British North America. The War of 1812 made them aware that they wanted to be different. The war also made it clear that there must be a border between the two countries.

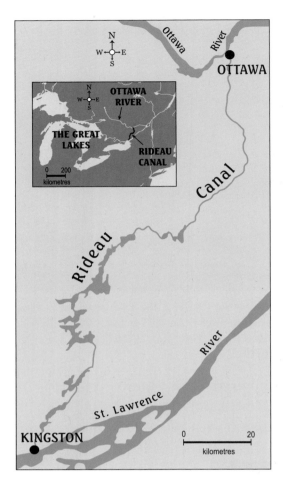

Figure 11.12 **RIDEAU CANAL**

Unity. The French and English in North America had fought together along with the Aboriginal peoples against a common enemy for the first time. This promoted unity within the colony.

The Rideau Canal. During the War of 1812, the British worried that the Americans would take the St. Lawrence River and cut off the British supply route to Upper Canada. The Americans never did, but this concern led the colonies to build the Rideau Canal, which would provide an alternate route.

Figure 11.11 *Entrance of the Rideau Canal, Bytown (Ottawa), Upper Canada, 1839.* The Rideau Canal was built between 1826 and 1832. It provided a secure route for supplies between Montreal and the Great Lakes in case the United States attacked Upper Canada. The waterway still runs between Ottawa and Kingston. It is the oldest continuously operated canal in North America.

Figure 11.13 This picture shows American forces attacking British and Aboriginal forces at the Battle of Moraviantown (also known as the Battle of the Thames), on October 5, 1813. The Americans won the battle, which took place near present-day Chatham, Ontario. It gave them control of Aboriginal lands to the northwest. The Aboriginal peoples also lost their great leader, Tecumseh, who was killed in the battle.

Losses for Aboriginal peoples

Aboriginal peoples lost much in the aftermath of the War of 1812.

The Americans resumed their westward expansion into Aboriginal territory in the Ohio River Valley Region, and pushed the First Nations farther west and north.

The confederacy of First Nations that Tecumseh had built collapsed, and with it went the movement toward a larger union of Aboriginal nations. The Aboriginal peoples lost their power and could no longer defend their lands. The French, the British, and the Americans no longer needed them as allies. Nor did they need them for the fur trade, as warriors, or as guides to living in North America. The First Nations people were increasingly losing their influence and status.

Peaceful solutions

One good outcome of the War of 1812 is that it ended war as a means to settle differences between Britain and the United States. Although some smaller raids and arguments occurred, after the War of 1812, the two countries negotiated and discussed their differences and came to peaceful solutions. For instance, the Convention of 1818 was an orderly meeting that established a border from the Great Lakes to the Rocky Mountains at the 49th parallel.

Immigration

Europeans had been coming to North America to settle since the beginning of the 1600s. Many of them had chosen to settle farther south in the Thirteen Colonies, but some had settled in the part of British North America that would become Canada. Because completely accurate records are hard to find from these early days of colonization, the chart below will give you some approximate numbers.

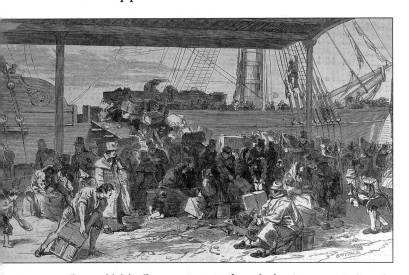

Figure 11.14 These emigrants from Ireland prepare to board a ship for a new life in North America. Between 1825 and 1850, more than 800 000 Irish people immigrated to British North America. Many others went to the United States, Australia, and New Zealand.

By the end of the War of 1812, immigration was starting to increase in British North America and around the world. People came in greater numbers, because it was a time of peace. The Atlantic would be free of warships until the American Civil War in the 1860s. Travel was still dangerous, and the conditions on board ships could be terrible, but at least people did not have to worry about being attacked by enemy ships.

Many immigrants came to British North America from Great Britain in what came to be called the "Great Migration." Others came in smaller numbers from the United States and China. People left their homelands for four main reasons, discussed below.

1. Food shortages

Europe had experienced food shortages for centuries, and many people there could not escape hunger. Now they could move somewhere more promising. Many places, such as Australia, South Africa, Russia, as well as North America, offered free or cheap land to immigrants. Poor people had few opportunities to own land in Europe. Emigration promised a chance to build a better life, where Europeans could own their own farms and provide for their families.

Immigrants, 1665–1814

YEAR	NUMBER	FROM	COLONY
1665–1680	20 000	France, mostly	New France
1758	6000	Europe	Nova Scotia
1760s	10 000	13 Colonies	Nova Scotia
1760s	several hundred	13 Colonies	Quebec
1770s	several hundred	Scotland	Nova Scotia, Island of St. John
1780s	45 000	13 Colonies	Nova Scotia, Quebec
1790–1814	5000	Scotland	British North America (Some went West)

a) Scotland and Ireland. In the mid 1800s, both Scotland and Ireland were affected by the Great Potato Famine. Potatoes were the staple crop for both countries, and peasants relied on them for all their food. An adult male could eat up to seven kilograms of potatoes per day! But in 1845, a mysterious fungus, called **potato blight**, began to destroy potato crops. The tubers rotted in the ground, and they were impossible to eat. Many people starved to death. Others moved away if they could. Sometimes their landlords sent them away, because they did not want to look after them or pay for their care. The ships the emigrants left on became known as "coffin ships," because so many people died coming over to North America.

Once the immigrants arrived at their destination, they continued to suffer. They were weak or infected with disease, and were often not welcomed by the established settlers. In Quebec, each ship stopped at Grosse Isle, which served as a place to **quarantine** the sick. The numbers of sick were so great, and the doctors so overwhelmed, that they often could not tend to a person for several days. It was deathly cold in the winter, and blazing hot in the summer. There was not enough fresh water on the island, and a doctor who had requested funds to care for and feed the people was only given 10 percent of what he needed.

b) China. Food shortages were also a problem in China. Chinese immigrants first came to British Columbia in 1788 when British Captain John Meares brought 120 of them to work in the

Sorrowful song

Following are the first two verses of a song that was written in the early years of the Irish Potato Famine:

**Give me three grains of corn mother, only three grains of corn
It'll keep the little life I have till the coming of the morn
I'm dying of hunger and cold mother, yes dying of hunger and cold
And half the anguish of such a death my lips they never told**

**It grieves my heart like it was mother, it was bad as forceful blood
And all the day and the livelong night I cried for the want of food.
I dream of bread in my sleep mother, the sight it was heaven to me
But I woke with an eager famished thirst but you have no bread for me**

Figure 11.15 This picture shows the launch of *North West America*, the first fur-trade ship ever built on the British Columbia coast. It was built by Chinese workers hired by Captain John Meares in 1788 to collect sea-otter pelts.

fur trade. They built a trading post on Vancouver Island and a ship. Beyond that, no one is sure what happened to them. Some people think that some of them stayed, married Aboriginal women, and worked in the western fur trade.

More Chinese immigrants came in 1858 because of a gold rush in the Fraser River Valley, and later to help build the cross-Canada railroad. They also cleared land and worked in mines. Some Chinese opened stores and restaurants, and soon areas known as "Chinatown" sprang up.

By the late 1800s, mistrust of the Chinese immigrants by the European settlers resulted in a loss of rights for Chinese-Canadians. They could not vote and were often treated unfairly. The government began charging a Head Tax on each Chinese immigrant, so that when people wanted to help their families come to Canada, they had to pay an extra tax that other immigrants did not have to pay.

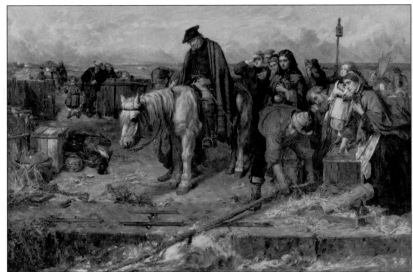

Figure 11.16 *The Last of the Clan*, by Thomas Faed, 1805, shows farmers from the Scottish Highlands forced to leave their homes.

2. Agricultural changes

The traditional farming and landholding systems changed greatly in Great Britain in the 1800s. Most people did not own land, but farmed it for landlords who did. Many generations of families had worked and lived on these plots of land for centuries. When the **tenants** were no longer needed to farm the landlord's property, they were forced to leave.

In Scotland, traditional farming of small plots of land was being replaced with large sheep farms. Landlords began to charge their tenants rent money. In the past, farmers had been able to pay rent on their property with a portion of their crops. Paying cash was impossible for many tenants, and they moved to cities or left Scotland entirely. These expulsions became known as "The Highland Clearances." The Selkirk settlers (whom you read about in chapter 9) were victims of these clearances.

3. Industrial Revolution

The Industrial Revolution began in Europe in the late 1700s when many new inventions, such as the steam engine, were created. Machines took over jobs that men and women had done for many years. These innovations changed the world forever.

For instance, cloth had always been woven by weavers on looms in their homes. The invention of motorized weaving machines meant good quality cloth could be produced in large quantities, and factories began springing up. People who had worked as weavers were no longer needed to make cloth.

As well, less skill was needed to produce items. With the machines doing the work, factory owners could hire women, children, and other people with little or no training.

Figure 11.17 Industrial weaving machine, London, 1835

Since fewer people were needed to make goods, many people found themselves out of a job. They decided to move and try to find work elsewhere. Some people came to North America looking for a livelihood that would provide them with a better way of life.

4. Escaping slavery

Many African-American people came to British North America from the United States to escape slavery. Slavery was made illegal in the British Empire by 1834, so the colonies provided a haven for slaves from the United States.

The Underground Railroad was not really underground, and it was not a railroad either. It was a secret system of routes to British North America and safe places to stay along the way. The routes were kept as secret as possible. That was because American people known as "bounty hunters" were paid to retrieve slaves before they crossed the border. Although exact numbers were never kept, people believe that approximately 20 000 former slaves left the United States and settled mostly in Upper Canada.

Although they escaped bondage, American slaves did not escape hardship. They were not always treated fairly or equally by the white settlers in their new country. Still, they came, and soon the Canadas had their first Black craftsmen, teachers, doctors, and lawyers.

Harriet Tubman

"If you're tired, keep going, if you're hungry, keep going, if you're scared, keep going, if you want to taste freedom, keep going." — Harriet Tubman

Harriet Tubman was born into slavery in 1820. She escaped to British North America in 1849 and settled in St. Catharines, Ontario. From there she became a conductor on the Underground Railroad. She made 11 return trips to the United States, risking her own life as she guided approximately 300 people to freedom. She was called "Moses," and many people thought she was a man, because they could not believe a woman could accomplish what she did. This was probably to her advantage. At one point there was a $40 000 **bounty** on her head, and if the bounty hunters were looking for a man, she was just a little bit safer.

Figure 11.18 Harriet Tubman, far left, with some of the people she helped escape from slavery to a new life in Upper Canada.

Mary Ann Shadd Cary

Mary Ann Shadd Cary was born into a free Black family in Delaware in 1823, and she came to Upper Canada in 1850. She started the first integrated school in the British colony. She became North America's first Black editor when she started

Figure 11.19

the newspaper, the *Provincial Freeman*, which promoted ideals of anti-slavery and self reliance. She returned to the United States and recruited people to the Union Army during the American Civil War (1861–1865). She became the first Black female lawyer in the United States when she graduated from law school in 1870.

Singing toward freedom

Many songs were sung about freedom and travelling on the Underground Railroad. "Follow the Drinking Gourd" was a secret code, telling people to follow the Big Dipper and the North Star, north to the British colony.

When the Sun comes back
And the first quail calls
Follow the Drinking Gourd.
For the old man is a-waiting for to carry
    you to freedom
If you follow the Drinking Gourd.

The riverbank makes a very good road.
The dead trees will show you the way.
Left foot, peg foot, travelling on,
Follow the Drinking Gourd.

The river ends between two hills
Follow the Drinking Gourd.
There's another river on the other side
Follow the Drinking Gourd.

When the great big river meets the little river
Follow the Drinking Gourd.
For the old man is a-waiting for to carry
    you to freedom
If you follow the drinking gourd.

Figure 11.20 Mi'kmaq people (detail of a painting by Mary Chaplin, 1839)

Effects on the First Nations

Throughout the 1800s, many immigrants began to make British North America their home. They came looking for work, cheap land, and to escape persecution, slavery, and hunger. They came looking for new opportunities. While life was often difficult, many of them found a better life. However, for the Aboriginal peoples, opportunities were starting to narrow. They were being pushed to marginal lands to make room for the new settlers.

A letter to Queen Victoria, written by Louis-Benjamin Peminuit Paul in 1841, appears on the next page. It gives an idea of how Aboriginal peoples felt.

To the Queen

Madame: I am Paussamigh Pemmeenauweet... and am called by the White Man Louis-Benjamin Pominout.

I am the Chief of my People the Micmac Tribe of Indians in your Province of Nova Scotia and I was recognized and declared to be the Chief by our good friend Sir John Cope Sherbrooke in the White Man's fashion Twenty Five Years ago; I have yet the Paper which he gave me.

Sorry to hear that the king is dead. I am glad to hear that we have a good Queen whose Father I saw in this country. He loved the Indians.

I cannot cross the great Lake to talk to you, for my Canoe is too small, and I am old and weak. I cannot look upon you, for my eyes cannot see so far. You cannot hear my voice across the Great Waters. I therefore send this Wampum and Paper talk to tell the Queen I am in trouble. My people are in trouble. I have seen upwards of a Thousand Moons.

When I was young I had plenty: now I am old, poor and sickly too. My people are poor. No Hunting Grounds – No Beaver – No Otter – no nothing. Indians poor – poor for ever. No Store – no Chest – no Clothes.

All these Woods were once ours. Our Fathers possessed them all. Now we cannot cut a Tree to warm our Wigwam in Winter unless the White Man pleases.

The Micmacs now receive no presents, but one small Blanket for a whole family. The Governor is a good man but he cannot help us now. We look to you the Queen. The White Wampum tells that we hope in you. Pity your poor Indians in Nova Scotia.

White Man has taken all that was ours. He has plenty of everything here. But we are told that the White Man has sent to you for more. No wonder that I should speak for myself and my people.

The man that takes this over the great Water will tell you what we want to be done for us. Let us not perish. Your Indian Children love you, and will fight for you against all your enemies.

My Head and my Heart shall go to One above for you.

Pausauhmigh Pemmeeauweet, Chief of the Micmac Tribe of Indians in Nova Scotia. [His mark] +

Conclusion

The War of 1812 made most people living in British North America aware that they wanted to be separate from the United States and connected to Britain. However, by the 1820s, the rules for governing the country were flawed. They did not apply to everyone living in British North America at the time, especially the new immigrants.

The main challenge that would next affect the British colonies was the move to **Responsible Government** – a government that fulfilled the wishes of the common people. Although many of the residents of the British colonies wanted to remain loyal to Britain, they also wanted a voice in their own government and through representatives who would act on their behalf.

In the next chapter, join Ben and Sara as they learn about some of the people who forced Britain to change the way they governed their North American colonies.

12

Rebellion and Reform

en, Sara, and their parents drove into Toronto. On their way, Sara noticed an old-style house among the modern buildings. She asked what it was, and her dad said it was William Lyon Mackenzie's old house. It was a museum now. Ben asked who William Lyon Mackenzie was, and Mom said he was a journalist, a former mayor of Toronto, and the leader of the 1837 Rebellion in Upper Canada.

Ben and Sara argued about where Upper Canada was, but neither of them knew what a **rebellion** was. Their parents decided to stop and let the museum staff answer all of their questions. Sometimes parents don't know all of the answers.

Figure 12.1 Rebels marching in Upper Canada

Carol, the woman who worked at the museum, explained that a rebellion happens when people get so angry at their government that they refuse to obey the government's laws. In 1837, the people thought that the government wasn't paying any attention to them. In Upper Canada, people were so angry that they armed themselves with pitchforks, shovels, and hoes, and fought the soldiers that the government sent to make them obey.

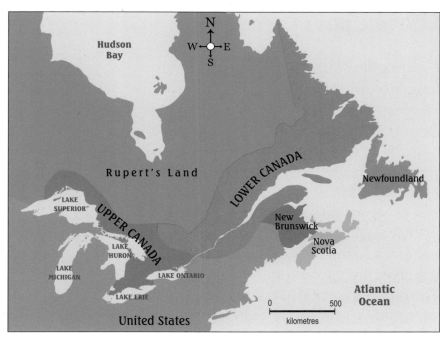

Figure 12.2 UPPER AND LOWER CANADA

Ben and Sara were impressed by this story. They thought rebellions only happened in other countries. Ben wanted to know what had made the people so angry.

Carol took Ben and Sara around the museum, showing them pictures, newspapers, and other artifacts. "Try to imagine what it was like to live in Upper Canada in 1837," she said.

First of all, she told them, Upper Canada was the name given to the southern part of what is now the province of Ontario. It included the settlements along the Great Lakes, from Cornwall to Fort William. Most of the events of the Upper Canada Rebellion took place in the areas bordering lakes Erie and Ontario. About 430 000 people lived in Upper Canada at that time. Some of the people lived in York (Toronto) and some in settlements such as Kingston and London. Most people lived on farms out in the countryside.

These people had come from many countries, hoping to find free land and the freedom to take part in their government. The settlers spoke many different languages at home, but English was the language of business and government. They worked very hard and didn't want to be pushed around. Many had lived in the United States and wanted to have some of the rights that the Americans had fought for. People wanted their government to listen to them and to be responsible to them. *Responsible* is another word for *answerable*, so the people wanted the governor and the councils to do what the people wanted.

As you read, think about

- **what life was like in Upper Canada and Lower Canada in the 1830s**
- **what Responsible Government was, and why people wanted it**
- **what happened as a result of the Rebellions**

Life in Upper Canada

Country life in Upper Canada was tough. People worked hard to make a living. Farmers usually lived on the edge of the forest and had to clear the trees out before they could sow crops. At first their crops were just enough to feed the family. But by the 1830s they were growing wheat and other products that they could sell. At that time there were several poor harvests. Farmers became upset, because the government was not helping them. The farmers found that they could not take over more land to grow more crops, because the land had been given to the Church of England or was held by the Crown.

Just doing the farm work and keeping the family clean, clothed, and fed meant that everyone had to work long hours. Farm children worked just as hard as adults, and were often treated like little adults. If the school was nearby and there were enough people to do the farm work, some children could go to school. They might go for six years and learn reading, writing, arithmetic, and some geography and history. Many children never went to school, because there was no school nearby, or the roads were too poor for travel. Every landowner had to help to keep the roads in good shape. If the church or the Crown owned land opposite the roads, there would be no one there to help maintain the roads.

Children who could not go to school regularly learned only a little reading and writing at home. Some children never learned to read and write at all because their parents could not read or write. School was

DID YOU KNOW?

Next time you bite into a MacIntosh apple, remember that it was developed in Upper Canada by John MacIntosh, an immigrant who found 20 apple trees in the forest while he was clearing land for his farm. He transplanted them, and his son Allan began experimenting so that by 1835, the family had one of the first commercial orchards in Canada.

not required until after Confederation in 1867. Some children had to work to help feed their family, so they could not go to school. The children of the wealthy town families got a better chance at education and were likely to get all of the good jobs in government. Many poorer families thought this was unfair.

Most people went to church services on Sunday. Church played a central role in almost everyone's life. In those days, people had to go to a church to be baptized, married, or buried. There were many different churches in Upper Canada: Methodist, Quaker, Presbyterian, Roman Catholic, Church of England, and others. The Church of England was the only church in Upper Canada that received government money and land.

Figure 12.3 Bishop John Strachan was an Anglican minister and teacher from Kingston, Ontario. A member of the Executive Council, he was leader of the Family Compact in Upper Canada.

Figure 12.4 Farm on Cataraqui Creek, near Kingston, Ontario, c. 1834

People who belonged to other churches thought that was not fair.

Everything in the colony was decided by a group called the "Family Compact" (sometimes called Tories.) This was a small group of wealthy and educated families who belonged to the Church of England, disliked Americans, and liked the British system of government. They did not want to change anything, because they had most of the power in the community.

There was an elected assembly, but a person had to own a lot of property to be a member or to vote for a member, so very few people could take part (see chart, p. 196). Even if the Assembly voted for a law, the governor could disagree with it. He appointed the Executive Council, so its members would always agree with him. When a legislative council was added to the government, the situation was even worse, because the council members were appointed for life by the governor. The governor was always an important man from England, and most governors did not talk to ordinary people very often. People had to pay whatever taxes the government ordered, even if they did not have a say about what the money was used for. Ordinary people wanted to change the government, saying that they deserved to have more rights to decide about things that were important to them. The British government refused. People were getting angrier.

Figure 12.5 Sir Francis Bond Head was governor of Upper Canada from 1836 to 1838. He supported the Family Compact and ignored the General Assembly in Upper Canada.

Talking About Reform

In a time when there was no radio, television, or Internet, how did people get a chance to learn about the world around them and talk about the changes they wanted? Men and women met and talked about local concerns after church, at card parties and dances, and at "bees." When a family needed to build a house or a barn, all of their neighbours would get together at a bee to do the work. The men would build, the children would carry tools and run errands, and the women would feed everyone. Women also got together at quilting bees. Men talked together at the mill while they waited to have their wheat ground into flour or when they went to the sawmill to get lumber. They also talked at the tavern when they met to have a drink.

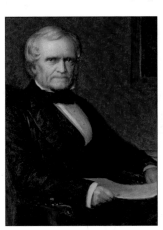

Another way that people heard about the problems was through newspapers such as the *Constitution*.

William Lyon Mackenzie used his newspaper to try to persuade people to bring

Figure 12.6 William Lyon Mackenzie was born in Scotland in 1795. He started his first newspaper, the *Colonial Advocate*, in Toronto, in 1824. After a trip to the United States in 1829, he came to admire the American government, and wanted a more democratic government in Canada. In his newspaper, the *Constitution*, he attacked members of the Family Compact. He became mayor of Toronto in 1834, and, in 1837, led the rebellion in Upper Canada. He fled Canada to the U.S., and returned in 1849. He became a member of the Assembly of Canada from 1851 to 1858. He died in 1861.

Printing a newspaper in the 1800s was hard work! Metal type, representing letters, had to be formed into words, words into paragraphs, paragraphs into columns, then placed on the press to be printed. To put a whole newspaper together took a long time. Newspaper publishers like William Lyon Mackenzie would have done a lot more than set type: they wrote, edited, sold, and delivered their newspapers as well.

Figure 12.7 Printing press from W.L. Mackenzie's time

about Responsible Government. He was so successful, that in 1826, after Mackenzie had moved his family to Toronto, some Family Compact supporters got so tired of his rants about them that they vandalized his office and threw all of the metal type for his printing press into the lake. This made Mackenzie a celebrity, and he ended up winning a seat in the Assembly. He also got a settlement of £625 when he sued, and it helped him pay off his debts. (That would be worth about Cdn $85 000 in 2006.)

Mackenzie was a bit **eccentric**. He wore several coats during the Rebellion, thinking that the extra layers would ward off bullets. He wore a red wig that he took off and threw around when he was making a speech and became agitated. His teacher had noted that, as a child, he liked to read, but he did not like being told what to do.

What people wanted

Different groups of people in Upper Canada had different ideas about change.

Average colonists. These people made up the biggest group. The average colonist at this time was suffering. Crops had failed for a few years in a row, and the economy was not doing well. The colony was also in debt. The leaders had not spent money wisely, and

the way the government was set up cost a lot of money. These people were angry, but most of them did not believe in acting violently to get what they wanted.

Colonists: We are hungry. We came to this country looking for a better life. With the crop failures and struggles that we are facing, and with the Family Compact giving all the best land to themselves and their friends, we wonder if a better life will ever come.

Moderate reformers. People like Robert Baldwin and his father, William, believed

that **reform** could take place reasonably, without violence. Although they agreed with the complaints of radicals like William Lyon Mackenzie, they did not agree with his methods.

Moderates: We believe that we can work within the present system to bring about reform and Responsible Government.

Radical reformers. People like William Lyon Mackenzie and his followers believed that the only way to true freedom was to do away with the British system of government entirely. They favoured any means that

would release them from the British, including allying themselves with the United States. Mackenzie often chose unusual allies. His friend Benjamin Lett blew up the first Brock's Monument because he hoped that the United States would be blamed. Then

Britain and the United States would declare war on each other. If this happened, there was a chance that Canada would be invaded by the Americans and be freed from British rule.

Radicals: We want to be heard, and we want to be heard now. Throw off the tyranny of the British! Where's our shovels? We need weapons so that we can do battle!

Family Compact. Members of the Family Compact often belonged to the Executive and Legislative Councils, or were powerful and influential businessmen. Almost all were related to one another (which is why reformer Mackenzie called them "Family

Compact"). They lived in the Toronto area, and many had fought in the War of 1812. They believed that British ways were superior to all others and that they knew what was best for their colony and its inhabitants.

Family Compact members: A strong central government under the authority of a governor is best for the colony. We are loyal to the Crown, and Britain will always be there to help us. Sure we allocate finances in ways that will improve our own land and business interests, but if we succeed, the colony will succeed, and that will be good for everyone.

Events of the Rebellion

William Lyon Mackenzie was a better writer than a soldier. In his newspaper, he had argued that it was time to change the way the colony was governed. He did not think it was fair that Upper Canada was run by a few wealthy men who cared only for their own interests. It was time for a rebellion to overthrow the government, and then install a new one that acted in the interests of its citizens.

On December 5, 1837, Mackenzie and about 700 men marched down Yonge Street on their way to Toronto.

The rebels were not well armed. They had mostly farm implements and just a few muskets. They were not well trained, either. They turned and ran when they saw a wagon full of wood coming toward them that they had mistaken for a cannon. Many of them deserted before any battles took place.

Mackenzie, their leader, stopped on the way to Toronto to have a bite to eat and to negotiate a truce with the lieutenant governor. When the lieutenant governor saw how poorly equipped the rebels were, he decided to fight instead of talk.

Two days later, the government's soldiers confronted the rebels at Montgomery's Tavern, where about 500 of them were camped out. A government force of 1500 fired a cannonball into the tavern, and the rebels panicked. The "battle" lasted about 30 minutes. The surviving rebels fled, Mackenzie included.

The troops burned Montgomery's Tavern down. The government offered a reward of $4000 for Mackenzie's capture. He had fled to the United States, however, where he tried to keep the Rebellion going by publishing a newspaper and promising rebels free land if they joined him.

The Rebellion in Upper Canada

	ELECTED ASSEMBLY	EXECUTIVE AND LEGISLATIVE COUNCILS
POPULAR NAME	Reform Party	Family Compact
LEADERS	William Lyon Mackenzie; Robert Baldwin	Governor Sir Francis Bond Head; Family Compact leader John Strachan
SUPPORTERS	Farmers and less-wealthy colonists	Wealthy, landowning "gentlemen" Tories
ACTION AND RESPONSE	500-page report on grievances written by Mackenzie	Type for printing presses thrown into the lake

EATH OF COL. MOODIE.

Figure 12.8 On December 5, 1837, rebels led by William Lyon Mackenzie met at Montgomery's Tavern to march against the government. Colonel Robert Moodie, a British soldier, was on his way to tell the governor about the demonstration, and fired his pistol to clear the way. The rebels shot back and killed Moodie. The incident sparked a rebellion that took place three days later.

After the Upper Canada Rebellion

No one was willing to follow Mackenzie's radical Reformers after the Rebellion. Mackenzie had fled, and two rebels, Peter Matthews and Samuel Lount, were hanged as traitors on April 12, 1838. More moderate Reformers like Robert Baldwin began to lead the Reform Party. Although the Rebellion was over, people still hoped for change, and they wondered what the British government would do.

These were the reasons the Rebellion did not succeed:

- The rebels were poorly armed and poorly trained.

- Many of the ordinary people were angry at the government but not angry enough to fight them.

- Mackenzie fled the country and never had the same influence again.

- Mackenzie and others expected at least some support from the United States and did not get it.

Government in the Canadas, 1791 to 1841

The rules for governing Upper and Lower Canada had been set out by the Constitutional Act of 1791. The governor or lieutenant governor acted on Britain's behalf within Upper and Lower Canada. He represented the power of the monarch within each province. In Upper and Lower Canada, the power to make laws and collect taxes resided with Executive and Legislative Councils. Both Councils worked together, and some people sat on both Councils. The Assembly that was elected by the voters had very little power. Any law that threatened the privileged position of the Executive or Legislative Councils was quickly denied.

The governor (Lower Canada) and lieutenant governor (Upper Canada) represented the monarch and British government. They had the power to make decisions about all the laws in the colonies.

Executive Council members were appointed for as long as the governor decided. They advised the governor about laws that needed to be passed and plans for the colony, such as where to put roads.

The Legislative Council members were responsible for writing laws and presenting them to the governor. They were appointed for life by the governor.

The Assembly, elected by the voters, could suggest laws to the Legislative Council. The Council did not have to follow the Assembly's suggestions, however.

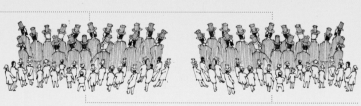

Voters had to be male, own property, and be British subjects 21 years and older. Women, men who did not own property, and Aboriginal peoples were not allowed to vote.

Figure 12.9

Life in Lower Canada

Sara and Ben started to read about the 1837 Rebellion and found that there had been two rebellions. In fact, the Rebellion in Lower Canada had started even earlier than the one in Upper Canada. To find out why people in Lower Canada wanted to rebel, Ben and Sara thought they should find out what life was like there.

Lower Canada was the southern part of the province that we now call Quebec. It included both sides of the St. Lawrence River and part of what is now Labrador. Most of the events of the Rebellion took place along the St. Lawrence, Richelieu, and Ottawa rivers. About 700 000 people lived in Lower Canada at the time. English criminal law and French civil law were used there.

By the 1830s, large groups of both French- and English-speaking people were living in Lower Canada. The French-speaking people included the habitants whose families had lived in the rural areas for a long time, and a large group of professional people such as doctors and lawyers who lived in the cities and towns. The English-speaking groups included the merchants and businessmen who had come to the area after New France became a British colony. There were also United Empire Loyalists and other English-speaking farmers. They had settled on land in the Eastern Townships set aside for English-speaking people.

Country life in Lower Canada was much like life had been in New France. People worked hard and paid their dues to the seigneur. People lived in low, broad houses with whitewashed outside walls and steep, pitched roofs. However, land was becoming scarce as the population grew, and farms were further divided among the sons. As farms got smaller, many children had to move to towns or to the United States for jobs.

Figure 12.10 *Habitants playing at cards*, by Cornelius Krieghoff, 1848

Talking About Reform

People met at church and at social events. Men gathered at the mills, at work in towns, and at taverns. Newspapers were also important ways to get information in towns. Quebec City's *Le Canadien* and Montreal's *La Minerve* spoke out for reform, while English-language papers in the cities spoke for the English business class.

Just as in Upper Canada, in Lower Canada society was becoming divided. During the 1820s and 1830s, there were crop failures, and wheat sold for low prices. Many people almost starved. People needed more land to keep their farms going, and land was not available. Their government did not seem to be able to help them. More and more English-speaking people were coming to Lower Canada, so farmers worried about their future and about losing French language privileges. If more English-speaking people came, many habitants feared that the Roman Catholic religion would also disappear. People were afraid for the future.

What people wanted

Several groups in Lower Canada had different ideas about change.

French-speaking professional people. These people, who lived in towns and cities,

wanted to be leaders of the French-speaking people. They wanted a separate French-Canadian nation that would keep their traditions. They wanted to keep the French language, the Roman Catholic

French professionals: We have our own laws, language, and culture, and we want to make sure they are preserved.

faith, and the agricultural way of life. They did not see why their system of laws should be changed because of these new people. This group was afraid that the British newcomers would change everything, so they formed a political party called the "Parti Canadien."

English-speaking merchants and business people. These people wanted to make Lower Canada more businesslike. They wanted English to be the main language, and they wanted British civil laws for their business contracts. These people wanted

the government to build lots of new harbours and canals. They wanted the roads improved, so that it would be easier for them to do business.

Merchants: British ways are best for business.

French-Canadian habitants. Habitants wanted to preserve their language, religion, and culture. However, whoever they elected into office had no real power to protect their interests. They were concerned that

the British people who ruled the colony wanted them to give up their language and culture.

Habitants: We're not interested in battles or fights, but we want the government to change so that we can have a voice in the running of our own country.

English-speaking farmers. Farmers, such as the Loyalists, were used to having elected assemblies and a bigger say in government. They were unhappy because the French language was being used, and they thought

198   People and Stories of Canada to 1867 • Chapter 12

that English should be the only language. They did not like following French civil law. These people were mainly Protestant, and their church was very important to them. Many of them did not like to see the Roman Catholic Church getting privileges from the government.

Château Clique. This was a small group of wealthy and powerful people. They were of British background or were wealthy French-Canadians who sided with the British. They wanted the British system of government and more English-speaking settlers. They wanted the Roman Catholic

Church to keep its privileges as long as it supported them. They did not want to change the government, because they controlled it.

Château Clique members: We know what's best for the colony and for the habitants. A strong economy will improve their situation. What does it matter if they lose their language?

Elected Assembly. Just as in Upper Canada, there was an elected assembly. A person had to own a lot of property to be a member or to vote, so very few people could participate.

Even if the Assembly voted for a law, the governor could decide not to agree to it.

As in Upper Canada, the governor was an important person from Britain who

Elected Assembly member: I became educated in law so that I could speak on behalf of my people. Of course, I can speak English, but French is the language of my heart. I want to enact laws that will benefit the French habitant and protect our seigneurial system, but the Château Clique stops us every time.

usually only talked to the members of his councils. Ordinary people could grumble, but they had to pay taxes and obey the law. The Assembly asked for changes, but they did not get them. People were getting angry.

As the weakness of the present form of government became more apparent, the movement for reform grew. One of those who

led the reform movement was Louis-Joseph Papineau, leader of the Assembly in Lower Canada and the Parti Canadien. Later on, when these people wanted reform, they called themselves the "Parti Patriote."

Figure 12.11 Louis-Joseph Papineau (1786–1871) was a lawyer and politician. He was a gifted orator, who believed that the French-Canadian culture and language should be maintained. As leader of the Parti Patriote, he influenced those involved in the Rebellions in Lower Canada. Papineau fled to France, and returned to Canada following a government pardon in 1844.

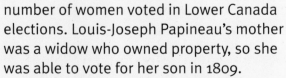

The Constitutional Act of 1791 defined voters as people with property. It did not say that they had to be men. In the 1820s, a number of women voted in Lower Canada elections. Louis-Joseph Papineau's mother was a widow who owned property, so she was able to vote for her son in 1809.

There were many complaints about women being able to vote, and in 1829, the Assembly passed a law saying that women could not vote. Women in this area next voted in 1917.

Events of the Rebellion

Between 1822 and 1836, the Legislative Council rejected 234 bills proposed by Louis-Joseph Papineau and the Assembly. The Assembly tried to block some changes that the councils wanted to make. The government was not working very well.

The habitants' discontent was made worse by years of bad crops, little money, a cholera epidemic, and a slowdown in the timber trade.

Early in November 1837, pro-British members of the Doric Club and the French rebel group Les Fils de la Liberté fought each other in the streets, and a mob surrounded Papineau's house. The British army helped him escape.

An unlikely leader in the Rebellion was Dr. Wolfred Nelson, son of a Loyalist mother and a British father. He and Papineau worked together, but it was Nelson who led the Patriotes in battle against a British force at St. Denis. The Patriotes won the battle, but their success did not last. Two days later, the British army killed 35 rebels. Nelson was arrested shortly afterward, and Papineau escaped to the United States.

In December, a group of Patriotes barricaded themselves in a church, which the British army then attacked and set on fire. They shot 70 Patriotes as they tried to escape. The 118 surviving rebels were rounded up, imprisoned, and sent to trial.

Figure 12.12 *Cholera Plague, Quebec,* by Joseph Légaré, 1832. Cholera was a common disease in North America during the 1800s. It was caused by poor sewage and water that was not clean. Having cholera is like having a bad case of the flu, but it is very dangerous. Some people die within hours of showing symptoms. In Lower Canada, cholera spread in poor neighbourhoods that had no sewage or garbage collection. Thousands died, and many people blamed the British government.

Figure 12.13 *Back View of the Church of St. Eustache and Dispersion of the Insurgents,* by Lord Charles Beauclerk, 1840. The Battle of St. Eustache began with the destruction of the village church and the Patriote fighters who took shelter there. British troops then bombarded the rest of the village, burning 60 homes to the ground, and killing the remaining rebels.

The Rebellion in Lower Canada

	ELECTED ASSEMBLY	EXECUTIVE AND LEGISLATIVE COUNCILS
POPULAR NAME	Parti Patriote	Château Clique
LEADERS	Louis-Joseph Papineau	Governor Sir Archibald Gosford followed by Baron John Colborne
SUPPORTERS	French habitants, as well as Irish farmers and some farming, democracy-minded British	Wealthy, usually British or Scottish businessmen
ACTION AND RESPONSE	92 Resolutions outlining why the government should be controlled by the Assembly	10 Resolutions making the governor's powers even stronger than before
PARA-MILITARY ORGANIZATION	Les Fils de la Liberté was inspired by the American Revolutionary War and began practicing without weapons.	The Doric Club was made up of Anglophone Tories who were later recruited by the governor to fight against the Patriotes with the British army.

After the Lower Canada Rebellion

In all, about 1350 rebels were arrested, and most spent some time in jail. Of the 99 who were sentenced to death, 12 were hanged. The others were banished to Australia and Bermuda or set free. One year later, in 1838, a second uprising was also defeated, and the Rebellion came to an end.

After the Rebellion, more moderate leaders like Louis-Hippolyte LaFontaine led the government and worked together with other moderate leaders.

The Rebellion in Lower Canada did not succeed for several reasons:

- The Patriotes were not very well armed or organized.

- The Patriotes did not agree among themselves. Some thought violence was the only way to get what they wanted, while others believed that violence should not be used.

- Papineau fled the country, leaving the Rebellion with no effective leader.

- The Roman Catholic Church did not support the Rebellion and warned the habitants that anyone who fought in it would be excommunicated, or cast out of the church. That meant that anyone who fought would be barred from the most powerful social institution of the day.

- The Patriotes expected help from the United States but were disappointed because the president did not want another war with Britain.

Change and Responsible Government

The Rebellions were a great nuisance to Britain. A new ruler, Queen Victoria, had just ascended the throne, and Britain wanted to sort things out quickly and start a new era.

In February of 1838, Britain ordered the governor to rule without any elected representatives, giving the people less of a voice than ever. But in May, Lord Durham arrived from Britain. His job was to listen to all those involved, discover the reasons behind the Rebellions, and make a recommendation to Britain about what could be done.

Lord Durham

Lord Durham was an interesting man to send to Canada. In Britain he was called "Radical Jack" and was considered to be a rather unusual person. He was a lord, from the upper class, yet he believed in radical ideas such as:

- the common man should have the vote
- education should be available to everyone
- the middle class was important
- Catholics should have the same rights and privileges as Protestants

He had heard about the Rebellions. When the British government promised him that he could make any changes he wanted, he decided to come to Canada.

He found himself in a very bad situation. Some people had already been executed, and he knew that if he hanged anyone else, the situation would never calm down. He had the top eight ringleaders admit their guilt and sent them to Bermuda. As for those leaders who had escaped to the United States, he warned them that if they dared come back, they would face death. He released the rest.

People in Canada were happy with his actions, but his own party in England was not. He resigned from politics, but still wrote his report when he returned to London. In it, he criticized the members of the Family Compact and Château Clique. He felt they did not keep the best interests of the people in mind.

Figure 12.14 John George Lambton, Lord Durham, was a wealthy British aristocrat. However, he supported many reform ideas that would allow common people to be involved in government and society. When Britain's prime minister promised him full power to make any changes he wanted to in British North America after the Rebellions, he accepted the post of governor of the British North American colonies.

Lord Durham's report, 1839

Lord Durham's solutions for the problems in Upper and Lower Canada still affect us today. Our government is based on some of his recommendations. Three of his main recommendations were:

1. **Unite Upper and Lower Canada into one province.** Lord Durham felt that if the two colonies were combined, the French-Canadian people would have to adopt British ways, which he believed were superior. Lord Durham did not believe

that most of the French habitants were educated enough to govern themselves. By combining the two provinces, he thought that the larger British population could control the smaller French-speaking population.

2. **Separate British affairs from local Canadian affairs.** Lord Durham believed that if the Canadian people ran their own local affairs, they would be satisfied and feel like they had some control over their own lives. Britain would continue to control the colony's **constitution** and its relationships with other countries.

3. **Grant Responsible Government.** Responsible Government meant that the governor had to answer to the voters who elected the Assembly. The governor would need to accept their decisions, even if he disagreed with them. Lord Durham thought that the Executive Council members should be chosen from the party that had the most seats in the Assembly. If the party lost its elected seats, it would lose its Executive Council seats as well. This gave the Assembly more power than ever before and limited the power of the governor and Executive Council. The British government would not allow Responsible Government for some time, but it did come eventually.

Figure 12.15 *The Insurgents at Beauharnois, Lower Canada.* Sarah Jane Ellice was taken prisoner by Patriote forces when they attacked her father-in-law's estate at Beauharnois on November 4, 1838. She and other members of the household were freed November 10. She painted this picture of the rebels while she was imprisoned.

You may have noticed that Durham's report did not mention Aboriginal peoples, their languages, religion, or education. They were not taken into account at this time.

The Act of Union, 1841

The British government thought that uniting the provinces and trying to **assimilate** the French was a good idea. This was attempted through the Act of Union of 1841. Through the Act of Union:

- Upper Canada became known as Canada West and Lower Canada became Canada East.

- The united Province of Canada had a governor general, an appointed executive and legislative council, and an elected assembly. Both regions received 42 representatives in the Assembly, even though the population of Canada East was larger. (In 1840, the population of Canada East was 670 000, and the population of Canada West was 480 000.)

- When the two colonies united, they also shared their finances. Canada East (Lower Canada), which had previously not owed any money, found itself saddled with a large debt that Canada West (Upper Canada) had brought into the union. This did not seem fair to the people of Canada East, either.

The first united Parliament met in Kingston in June 1841, but its members spoke only English. The Act of Union had banned the French language within the government, and restricted it in schools.

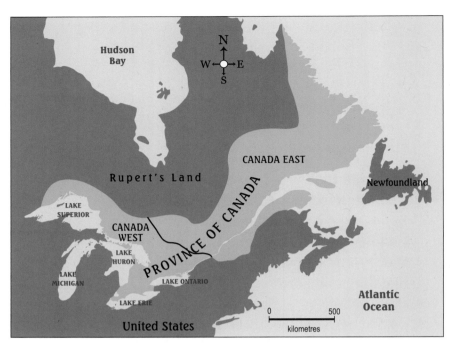

Figure 12.16 **PROVINCE OF CANADA, 1841.** Notice that the Act of Union made one large province, divided into two regions, Canada West (formerly Upper Canada) and Canada East (formerly Lower Canada).

The British thought that with the ban, the French would assimilate more quickly.

The Act of Union stopped short of granting Responsible Government, however. Instead, it just reinstated an elected assembly as it had been before the Rebellions. The leaders in the colony were not sure they wanted to carry out the voters' wishes, and so they decided to continue with the Executive and Legislative Councils holding most of the power of government.

French-British Cooperation

In general, the British of Canada West thought that Lord Durham's report and the British government's reforms were about right. The French of Canada East were not happy, though. They knew the British government was trying to end their language and culture, and they were not going to let it go easily.

There were also some people in English Canada who believed that Responsible Government was necessary. These new Reformers, who wanted change but who were not willing to resort to violence, began to work for Responsible Government. Their main opposition came from British-sent governors, the Family Compact, and the Château Clique.

Figure 12.17 Robert Baldwin (left) was an Anglican and wealthy landowner. He would have been an excellent member of the Family Compact. Instead, he followed in his father's footsteps and led the way for reform. He joined French-Canadian politician Louis LaFontaine (Figure 12.18, right). Together, Baldwin and LaFontaine built bridges of cooperation between the French and the British.

Two Reformers, one French and one British, realized that they would have to work together to bring about change. Louis-Hippolyte LaFontaine was born in 1807 in Lower Canada and educated as a lawyer in Montreal. At first, LaFontaine followed Papineau. In 1837, when Papineau used violence as a way to bring about reform, LaFontaine decided not to become involved in the Rebellions. Instead, he travelled to London, England, to plead his case for reform. Although he was arrested when he got back to Canada in 1838, he was released without being charged. He continued to speak French in the Assembly, even after it was outlawed. He refused to stop, and eventually Britain removed the restriction on French.

In 1848, LaFontaine and Robert Baldwin formed a partnership so that they could push for reform and Responsible Government. The Reformers had won a majority of seats in both Canada East and Canada West in the election that year. Lord Elgin, the new governor general, asked Baldwin and LaFontaine, the Reform leaders, to appoint the Executive Council. In this way, the council would be based on the wishes of the Assembly rather than on the wishes of the governor.

Responsible Government Is Tested

The test for Responsible Government came in 1849. That year, LaFontaine introduced the Rebellion Losses Bill. The bill stated that the rebels should be paid back for the property and goods they had lost during the 1837 Rebellion. Members of the Château Clique and the Family Compact were furious, and they debated against the bill for days. However, because the Reform Party had a majority in the Assembly, the bill passed.

The bill was sent to Lord Elgin, the governor general, who was advised by the Executive Council (remember, it had been appointed by the Assembly) to sign the bill into law. Although Lord Elgin did not agree with the bill, he signed it because it was his duty under Responsible Government.

Figure 12.19 *The Burning of the Parliament Building in Montreal,* by Joseph Légaré. After the Rebellion Losses Bill was passed, an angry mob rioted and burned down the government's home.

Riots broke out, people demonstrated in the streets, and some of the business elite proposed that Canada join the United States. The law held, however, and a year later, when the economy began to improve, people calmed down.

Meanwhile, in the Maritimes, people wondered what all the fuss was about. Nova Scotia and New Brunswick were granted Responsible Government in 1848, Prince Edward Island in 1851, and Newfoundland in 1855. None of these provinces experienced violence on their way to Responsible Government.

> **April 25, 1849**
>
> **Montreal Parliament Buildings ... were set fire to and burnt, by Alfred Perry, leader of the mob, on account of the Governor-General sanctioning the Indemnity Bill[1]. I was in Montreal College, from where we contemplated the conflagration with awe and terror from vague reports we received of outside political troubles.**
>
> — *From the journal of Jean Bruneau, student, Montreal*
>
> [1] Rebellion Losses Bill.

Government in united Canada after Responsible Government

The British government, representing the Queen, chose the governor general for the colony.

The governor appointed the Executive Council to run the country. However, the representatives in council were chosen by the members of the Elected Assembly.

The Assembly was elected by voters to represent their interests and to make laws. Canada West and Canada East each had 42 members in the Assembly. If Assembly members did not approve of the actions of the Executive Council and the governor, they had the power to remove them from office.

Only men of European background who owned a certain amount of property could vote.

Figure 12.20

Figure 12.21 James Bruce Elgin was the governor general of Canada from 1847 to 1854. He believed that granting Responsible Government to Canada (and all British North American colonies) was the best way to solve the problems they were having. Even though he met a lot of opposition, he signed the Rebellion Losses Bill. In 1854, he negotiated the Reciprocity Treaty with the United States, which set fishing rights and some free trade between the United States and Canada. When the treaty was cancelled in 1866, it made British North Americans aware of their need for Confederation.

Conclusion

Achieving Responsible Government had been hard. However, it had strengthened the power of the Assembly. Now, many elected representatives set their sights on something much bigger. Their next goal was to make the colonies stronger in **Confederation**, a union of all the British colonies in North America. This was also not an easy task, and it was one on which many representatives would stake their political lives.

In the next chapter, join Ben and Sara as they learn what life was like in British North America in the 1860s, and how Canada became a country.

13

From Colony to Country

"The Prince of Wales is coming to visit!"

For children living in 1860, this news was very exciting. In a time where there were no rock stars or movie idols, there were few greater celebrities than a prince. He was only 18. Although his reputation as a fashion trendsetter hadn't begun, it was still a thrill to see him.

Canadian officials had invited his mother, Queen Victoria, to come and celebrate the opening of the first-ever bridge that spanned the St. Lawrence River. She declined, but thought it would be a good idea to send young Albert Edward, the Prince of Wales. The visit would give him a chance to

exercise his royal duties. On August 25, he would officially open the Victoria Bridge, and, on September 1, he would lay the cornerstone of Canada's new Parliament Buildings in Ottawa.

Imagine what "Bertie" (as Prince Albert was known) would have experienced when he came to Canada. He would have crossed on a ship that had steam power as well as sail. Wooden-hulled ships were becoming obsolete, replaced by those with iron hulls. The Grand Banks were still full of fish, and his first scent of North America would have been the fish warehouses that lined the shores of St. John's, Newfoundland. He arrived there on July 23, and toured the Maritime provinces before travelling to Canada.

The prince met a young Mohawk leader on his visit to Canada. Oronhyatekha had been chosen by his elders to make a short speech welcoming the prince. Prince Albert was impressed and invited

Figure 13.1 *Landing of the Prince of Wales under the Triumphal Arch Erected by the Harbour Masters, at the Bonsecours Wharf, Montreal, 1860*

Figure 13.2 Oronhyatekha was a Mohawk born in Brantford, educated at Oxford, and married to the great-granddaughter of Joseph Brant. He was the first Aboriginal person in North America to receive a medical degree at the University of Toronto.

Oronhyatekha to study at Oxford, one of England's most prestigious universities.

However, the royal visit came at a time when Aboriginal rights were at risk. In 1857, An Act to Encourage the Gradual Civilization of Indian Tribes in Canada and to Amend Laws Respecting Indians was passed. The act was based on the way people thought at the time. The government of the Province of Canada believed that everyone would benefit by adopting European values and lifestyles. The act encouraged Aboriginal peoples to give up their special rights and assimilate with the rest of society.

The Prince of Wales visited Niagara Falls, and for the first time, the falls were lit up at night, an event that has since become a tradition. He watched Charles Blondin walk over the Niagara River on a tightrope.

Prince Albert travelled some of the time by railroad. In 1860, over 3200 kilometres of track had been laid in the British North American colonies. The prince's visit reflected the pride and hope people felt about their homeland.

Figure 13.3 On June 13, 1859, French acrobat Charles Blondin became the first person to cross Niagara Falls on a tightrope, 335 metres long and 49 metres above the water. He would recreate his feat for the visit of the Prince of Wales in 1860.

DID YOU KNOW?

People from British North America began waving the maple leaf during the prince's visit. Soon the maple leaf became a favourite symbol of Canada. It adorned the dishes the prince used, and many people wore maple leaf pins along his parade route. The prince planted a maple tree for the Toronto Horticultural Society. By the time Alexander Muir wrote *The Maple Leaf Forever* in 1867, the maple leaf was firmly **entrenched** as a symbol of Canada.

As you read, think about

- **why people wanted to join together as a country**
- **why some people objected to Confederation**
- **what roles different people played in bringing about Confederation**
- **how Confederation came about**

The Roots of Confederation

By the time of Prince Albert's visit, the Rebellions were over, and the reforms in government had been made. However, for a number of reasons, the British colonies of North America began to think that they should unite in a **confederation**.

Events and changing attitudes in the 1860s moved the idea from talk to action. Six of them were:

1. **Britain's growing disinterest.** Britain was losing interest in its colonies like Canada. Colonies cost money to govern and defend. The British began reducing the size of their army and navy in British North America, and they cut as many expenses as possible. They wanted their colonies to be more self-sufficient.

2. **New visions of the nation.** Canada West wanted to take over Rupert's Land from the Hudson's Bay Company and open up that territory for agriculture. Canada East was more interested in preserving their way of life and their French-Canadian traditions. Becoming two separate provinces again meant they could pursue their own visions.

3. **The railroad.** The railroad could move people and goods long distances faster than ever before. Track was laid throughout the Canadas, and could be linked to the Maritimes. None of the colonies could afford the railroad individually. If they joined together, the cost could be shared among them. A connected railroad would help the economy grow through trade.

Figure 13.5 This locomotive, built by the Grand Trunk Railway in 1858, showed the growing importance of the railway to trade and the economy.

4. **Trade agreements.** The British colonies needed to find new trade partners. The Reciprocity Treaty was a trade agreement between British North America and the United States, which had been in effect for about 10 years. It had been a good source of income for the British colonies, but now it had ended. As well, Britain had begun buying its wheat, fish, and timber from other sources, so if it wanted its colonies to continue to grow, they had

Figure 13.4 *Manitobah settler's house,* 1862. In 1857, the government of the province of Canada sent an expedition to explore the route to Red River (Manitoba) and study the potential for farming in the region.

Figure 13.6 *Fenians at Battle of Ridgeway.* On June 2, 1866, the Fenians, who opposed British rule in Ireland, attacked British troops near Fort Erie, Canada West. This painting shows the British and Canadian forces in red. In fact, they were dressed in green, and the Fenians fought from behind a fence. The Fenians were victorious, but soon British forces ran them back to the U.S.A.

to find new trading partners and new trade agreements. The colonies thought they could trade with each other.

5. **Border problems with the U.S.A. (1).** When the American Civil War broke out, Britain remained neutral. Some Americans, however, started talking about replacing the southern states, which had withdrawn from the United States, with northern British territory. Even after the war, people in British North America knew that many Americans were interested in **Manifest Destiny**, the idea that all of North America should belong to the United States. The Americans had already

gained Texas and Louisiana, and started moving into Red River territory. People of British North America were worried that the Americans wanted the whole continent.

6. **Border problems with the U.S.A. (2).** The Fenians were Irish Americans who believed that Ireland should be a separate country from Great Britain. They were bitter about British rule, so began to lead raids across the border into the British colonies as a way to attack Britain. These raids frightened the people in border towns. They knew that they needed help to beat the Fenians.

The Great Coalition

By 1860, Britain had seven colonies in North America: Newfoundland, Prince Edward Island, New Brunswick, Nova Scotia, Canada (divided into Canada East and Canada West), British Columbia, and Vancouver Island. Separating the colonies was the huge expanse of Rupert's Land and the North-Western Territory, land the Hudson's Bay Company governed and claimed to own.

Each colony faced its own problems. No one, it seemed, was able to bring about unity. The governments in Canada East and Canada West had been at a standstill for years. Conservative parties dominated in the East; parties that supported reform dominated in the West. With an equal number of seats on each side, neither side was able to gain power and get anything done. They could not even agree on where to put the new nation's capital. Queen Victoria compromised and chose Ottawa.

In 1864, George Brown of Canada West had waited long enough for Confederation. He recognized that unless he worked with his political rivals, the Confederation of British North American colonies would never happen. In a jaw-dropping move, he stood up in the Legislature and announced that all the political parties must quit their squabbles, and join together to bring about a union of the colonies. He proposed a Great Coalition of all the different political parties in the province of Canada. He convinced the members of his party, the Clear Grits, to join with the Liberal-Conservatives of Canada West and the Bleus of Canada East to support his plan for federalism. John A. Macdonald, leader of the Liberal-Conservatives, and George-Étienne Cartier, leader of the Bleus, agreed to his plan. In the next few pages, you will learn about some of the main politicians who came together to create the country of Canada. They are known as the "Fathers of Confederation."

The Fathers of Confederation

John A. Macdonald
Leader of the Liberal-Conservative Party from Canada West/Ontario

Figure 13.7

John A. Macdonald was born in Scotland in 1815, and settled in Kingston with his family when he was five years old. His father was a dreamer and a drinker. The family often had money problems, and his father always came up with a new scheme to get out of debt. It rarely worked. Macdonald was unable to get the money to go to university, but he studied with a lawyer. Because of his skill and ambition, he was managing two law offices by the time he was 19.

He was elected to government as a Liberal-Conservative in 1854 (it would later become the Conservative Party). Although his law practice was profitable and would have made him a lot of money, Macdonald liked politics. He was a great storyteller, quick witted, and full of jokes. He also liked a good party and was known for his tendency to drink too much. He became Canada's first prime minister after Confederation, and believed that Canada should extend west as far as the Pacific Ocean. He stayed in politics until his death in 1891.

George Brown

Leader of the Clear Grit Party from Canada West/Ontario

Figure 13.8

Some people say that it was George Brown's wife who made the difference. Before he married, he was seen as a firebrand, an angry man who would never back down or compromise. Two years after his marriage, he brought about the Great Coalition. George Brown was born in Scotland, immigrated to the United States, and then came to Canada because he found

Toronto the most exciting city he had visited in all his travels. He joined the Clear Grit Party (which later became the Liberal Party) and began publishing the *Globe*, which would later become the *Globe and Mail* newspaper.

DID YOU KNOW?

Hugh John Macdonald, Sir John A.'s son, moved to Winnipeg in 1882. He set up a law practice. In 1899, Hugh John became premier of Manitoba. The Dalnavert Museum in Winnipeg was once Hugh John's home, and shows what life was like for the Macdonald family at the beginning of the 20th century.

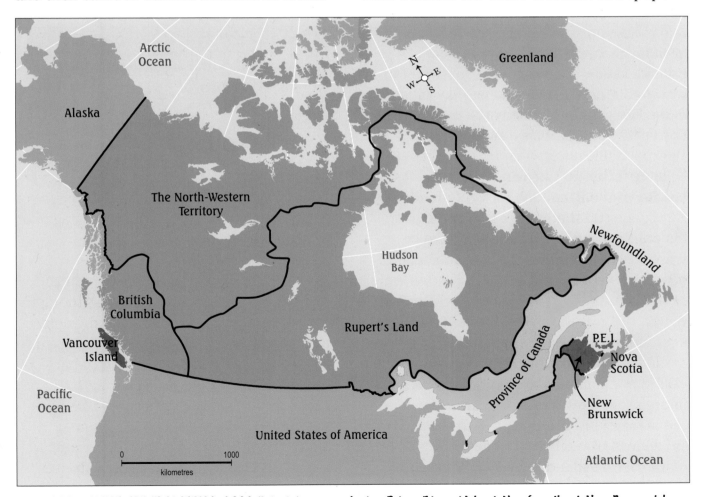

Figure 13.9 BRITISH NORTH AMERICA, 1860. Britain's seven colonies: Prince Edward Island, Newfoundland, New Brunswick, Nova Scotia, Canada, British Columbia, and Vancouver Island

Brown believed that the Canadas should have **representation by population**. That meant that the more people there were in the province, the more people they had to represent them in the Assembly. Brown also wanted the country to expand to the west, and to separate religion and politics. He did not want the church to run schools or dominate government decisions. He also believed the French should keep their special rights.

Brown was first elected in 1851 as a Liberal candidate. By 1864, after losing his seat and then regaining it, suffering from ill health, and marrying Anne Nelson, George Brown came back to politics hoping for real change for the country. He worked hard for the next few years, bringing about Confederation and promoting representation by population. In 1867, he lost his seat and moved on to other businesses, including his Toronto newspaper, the *Globe*.

George-Étienne Cartier
Leader of the Bleu Party from Canada East

George-Étienne Cartier was born in Lower Canada in 1814. His family had been financially successful in the years following the British conquest of Quebec (after the Seven Years' War). They had no quarrel with the British. Cartier was even named after the British king,

Figure 13.10

George III. His father had fought in the War of 1812, and his grandfather had been a member of the elected assembly.

Cartier became a lawyer in 1835, and fought for the Patriotes in the 1837 Rebellion, after he became disappointed in Britain's refusal to grant Responsible Government. He had to escape to the United States for a short time, but when things settled down, he returned to Quebec and was elected to the Legislature of Canada West in 1848.

The people of Lower Canada had great respect for him, and by the mid 1850s, he decided to join forces with other Conservatives so that the British colonies could unite. He and John A. Macdonald became political allies and friends. They were so close that Macdonald said that they had never had a disagreement.

Letter written by Cartier to his wife, during Confederation talks

Quebec, March 15, 1865.

I am so glad you will allow me to get the bird for baby. What shall it be – a parrot, or a parrot and some canaries? I am glad she likes animals. By and by we shall have rabbits for her, and pigeons, and a pony, and all sorts of things to make her kind and gentle. Do you know, I think the care of little creatures has a most softening effect on all children. I recollect how I petted my rabbits, and ever since I have been unable to see, without extreme horror, even any rough usage of dumb creatures.

Since writing the above we have had a vote of want of confidence, and the government has been sustained by a majority of 93 to 23. We are now on the second motion. Rose has just spoken, and Street is firing away on the defence question, and I must close and take part in the debate.

Don't for a moment fancy that what I am now doing will unfit me for a quiet settled life. On the contrary, every day makes me more anxious to get quit of politics forever. I don't like it, and would with all my whole heart abandon it finally tomorrow.

In 1857, George Cartier and John A. Macdonald were co-premiers of Canada. They worked together for the next decade to bring about Confederation, and after that to strengthen the country. Cartier oversaw the purchase of Rupert's Land from the Hudson's Bay Company, laid the foundations for Manitoba and British Columbia to enter Confederation, and ensured the railroad would be built from the Eastern Maritime provinces to the Pacific Ocean.

When Cartier died in 1873, John A. Macdonald cried and held his empty chair. His political "twin" was gone.

Thomas D'Arcy McGee
Leader of the Reform Party from Canada East

Figure 13.11

D'Arcy McGee was an Irish immigrant, a refugee of the potato famine. He had supported Irish independence as a young adult, but he soon began to believe that Ireland should work within the British system. He was a **compelling** speaker, and the Irish community in Montreal elected him in 1858 to represent them. He joined the Great Coalition (see p. 212) because he believed that Canada could achieve independence within the British system.

McGee wanted to ensure that Catholics and other minorities had their rights protected. He spoke out against the Fenians. He said they were worthy of the death penalty and that they should stop their raids in Canada. The Fenians tried to scare him by sending him threatening letters, and then they offered money for his assassination.

"The Hangman's Eyes"

They hung young Paddy Whelan back in 1869
For the murder of D'Arcy McGee
It was his shadow in the doorway but the hand upon the gun
Was a Fenian conspiracy

Chorus:
The snow began to fall that morning
Just as the sun began to rise
It went drifting across the gallows and freezing on the rope
Swirling in the hangman's eyes

It seemed like every man in Ottawa and half the township too
Were gathered there along the gaol-yard wall
With the pickpockets and the peddlers and the papists and the prayers
Of the Orangemen that the trap door wouldn't fail
[Repeat Chorus]

For forty days and forty nights the stormy winds did blow
And the snow drifts piled high on each fence line
And they huddled in their kitchens and they stoked the fires high
And they watched the grey skies for some rainbow sign
[Repeat Chorus]

This song, by the band Tamarack, talks about the last public execution in Canada. It was held in Ottawa in 1869 for the alleged assassin of D'Arcy McGee. It drew a crowd of over 5000. A snowstorm started on the day of the execution and lasted over a month. People called it the Year of the Deep Snow. The jail (spelled gaol in the song) is now a hostel, and the scaffold is a popular tourist attraction.

The Fenians succeeded. D'Arcy McGee was shot in the back of his head on April 7, 1868. Patrick Whelan, an Irish immigrant, was found guilty of the shooting. But mystery surrounds the circumstances of McGee's death. Some people think it was a plot of the Fenians and that Patrick Whelan was innocent.

Charles Tupper
Premier of Nova Scotia, Conservative Party

Figure 13.12

Charles Tupper first ran for office as a Conservative and won against Liberal Joseph Howe in 1855. He was a medical doctor who kept his medical bag under his chair in the House of Commons. Tupper believed in public education and campaigned to build a cross-country railroad.

By 1864, when he became premier of Nova Scotia, Charles Tupper was a firm believer in Confederation. But when it seemed like it would take too long, he began to push for a Maritime union of New Brunswick, Nova Scotia, and Prince Edward Island.

Samuel Leonard Tilley
Premier of New Brunswick, Reform Party

Figure 13.13

Leonard Tilley was a successful pharmacist. He was also interested in politics, and in 1850, he won a seat in the New Brunswick Assembly. He supported temperance, which would make alcohol illegal. He also wanted a railroad, public schools, and Responsible Government.

Tilley believed strongly in the benefits of Confederation and even lost an election because of his pro-Confederation stance. Just in time for Confederation, voters changed their minds and voted him back in. They were frightened of being invaded by the Fenians, and they knew that they would not have the resources to protect themselves without help from other colonies.

Tilley is credited with calling Canada a **dominion**, and for coming up with Canada's motto, "from sea to sea."

John H. Gray
Premier of Prince Edward Island, Conservative Party

Figure 13.14

Colonel John Hamilton Gray was in the military for 20 years before he ran for the Prince Edward Island Assembly in 1858. He wanted to settle the problem of absentee landlords in Prince Edward Island. Absentee landlords were landowners who lived somewhere else. They owned large areas of land that could not be worked or settled by others, and lay unused. This inhibited Prince Edward Island's growth for many years.

At first, Gray was a supporter of a Maritime Union, but he became a supporter of Confederation, which would include the province of Canada as well. He faced strong opposition to Confederation in his province. He became disappointed, and resigned in 1864. He returned to military life and led the Island's volunteer army.

John H. Gray was also the name of another Father of Confederation, a politician from New Brunswick.

DID YOU KNOW?

Opponents of Confederation

Not every politician of the time thought that Confederation was a good idea. Below are two of its most **outspoken** opponents.

Joseph Howe
Leader of the Reform Party from Nova Scotia

Figure 13.15

Joseph Howe might have misjudged Charles Tupper, his political rival in Nova Scotia. In 1852, Joseph Howe said, "Let us hear the little doctor by all means. I would not be any more affected by anything he might say than by the mewing of yonder kitten." Three years later, Howe suffered his first political defeat in 20 years when Tupper ran against him. If Tupper was a kitten, then maybe Howe was a mouse.

Joseph Howe was born in Nova Scotia in 1804. He did not attend school for long, but apprenticed in his father's printing shop when he was 13. By 1828, he purchased the *Novascotian*, a newspaper, and became the editor. He used his newspaper to expose government corruption, and was charged with **libel** in 1835. He defended himself in court and won. The case made him famous.

He was first elected to goverment in 1836. He immediately began working toward Responsible Government. Nova Scotia achieved it in 1848, largely because of Howe's leadership.

Howe spoke out against Confederation in Nova Scotia and rallied the population to oppose it. Like many people in the Maritimes, Howe believed that things were good in the Maritimes. The economy was strong, and trade was increasing. He thought Confederation would reverse the region's fortunes. He even travelled to London, hoping that he could stop the passage of the British North America (BNA) Act, the government act that would form the new country of Canada. After it passed, he worked to **repeal**, or undo, the act. All his efforts failed, however, and when Howe realized he could not undo Confederation, he worked on getting a "better deal" for Nova Scotia.

Antoine-Aimé Dorion
Leader of the Rouge Party from Canada East

Antoine-Aimé Dorion was educated as a lawyer. He was elected to the reform-minded Rouge Party in 1854. He believed in colonizing the West and keeping the church out of government. Dorion was opposed to Confederation because he believed that it would not give individual provinces

Figure 13.16

enough power. He also felt that some of the smaller provinces would have more power than they should. He believed the costs would outweigh the benefits, and the general public should be consulted about it. He spoke out regularly against Confederation, but was unable to generate opposition to it.

He sat in the House of Commons after Confederation, but quit politics in 1874, when he became the chief justice at the court of Queen's Bench in Quebec.

Hammering Out Confederation

Once George Brown broke the political deadlock and united his opponents, there was much work to be done on the road to Confederation. Where would the provinces' representatives meet? Which colonies would become provinces? How would they be represented in a new federal government? How would the government operate, and what powers would be assigned to the federal and provincial governments? There was a great deal to discuss.

Charlottetown Conference

The Charlottetown Conference was originally planned by the Maritime provinces to discuss a union among themselves. However, the Canadians asked if they could come and present their idea of a larger federal union. Tupper, Tilley, and Gray from the Maritime provinces welcomed Macdonald, Cartier, and Brown from the Canadas.

The conference barely made the news. Everyone was more interested in seeing the circus that was in town. Because of the circus, hardly anyone was working at the dock when the delegates from Canada arrived. One representative from Prince Edward Island rowed out in a little fishing boat to greet them. None of the Canadian delegates were able to find a hotel room in town, either. They ended up sleeping on their ship each night.

The meetings started on Thursday, September 1, 1864, and George Brown said that the union had been decided after lunch on Saturday. There were still several days of meetings and parties, however.

Figure 13.17 This painting, *Fathers of Confederation*, by John David Kelly, shows delegates at the Quebec Conference. This textbook mentions only some of the Fathers of Confederation. Can you find out who some of the others are?

The week wrapped up the following Thursday with a gala ball, fancier than anything Charlottetown had seen before. The delegates arranged to meet again to work out the details of Confederation.

Quebec Conference

On October 10, 1864, delegates from Canada and the Maritimes met again to discuss the ideas raised at the Charlottetown Conference the month before. This meeting was a lot of work. Delegates had to decide on how they would run the new country they were creating. After much discussion and disagreement, the founders compromised. They drew up a document known as the 72 Resolutions from which they would form the laws and foundations of a new country.

The resulting agreement, known as the Quebec Resolutions, became the basis for the British North America Act (BNA Act), Canada's founding constitution. Now the delegates had to return home and convince their assemblies to agree to the resolutions.

The London Conference and the BNA Act

The first meeting of the London Conference was held in December 1866. Confederation was officially declared on March 29, 1867. The legislative assemblies of Canada West and Canada East, Nova Scotia, and New Brunswick had agreed to Confederation. Prince Edward Island and Newfoundland chose not to join. With Confederation, Canada West would become the province of Ontario and Canada East would become the province of Quebec.

Throughout the previous conferences, it was John A. Macdonald who led the meetings. He convinced and cajoled the other delegates until they came to agreement. Macdonald also led the meeting that wrote the British North America Act that would bring the new country of Canada into existence.

The British North America Act outlined everything from how to deal with criminals, to the laws governing marriage and divorce. It said that people would have rights "similar to those in the United Kingdom," but it did not specifically outline those rights. It established how the provinces would work together (for example, people would not have to pay a fee to trade across provincial boundaries). It stated that Parliament had to make laws for the "peace, order and good government" of Canada. One of the most important clauses gave Quebec and New Brunswick rights for Roman Catholic schools.

The BNA Act made Canada a full-fledged, self-governing country, instead of a group of British colonies. The type of government set down in the BNA Act is known as **representative democracy**. That means that representatives who the citizens voted for as members of Parliament would represent their interests. The country would collect its own taxes and decide how to spend its own money. Britain still controlled the constitution, however, and Canada could not make changes to the rules in the BNA Act without British permission.

Q and A: *The British North America Act*

Q: What in the world is the British North America Act?

A: The BNA Act is Canada's first constitution.

Q: What is a constitution?

A: A constitution is the rules and principles of a country. It outlines the key laws that will govern a country, and what a country is allowed to do in order to enforce and use those laws.

Q: According to the BNA Act, what are some of those rules for Canada?

A: The BNA Act outlined the powers that the federal and provincial governments would have. For instance, provinces were to be in charge of local matters like schools, prisons, and hospitals. The federal government was in charge of things affecting the entire country, such as the army and trade with other countries. The Fathers of Confederation wanted a strong central, federal government, and so they said that any powers not specifically mentioned in the BNA Act would fall under federal control.

Q: Why was that significant?

A: The Fathers of Confederation were influenced by what they saw happen with the civil war in the United States, when the southern states wanted to form their own country. They believed Canada might have the same trouble in a few years. They believed a strong central government would make strong provinces that were committed to being part of Canada.

Figure 13.18 Dominion Day celebrations, 1880

The whole process of Confederation was a good example of the representative democracy that was to come. Many ordinary people did not agree with it, but their representatives pushed it through. The representatives felt they were acting in the best interests of the people, even if the people did not agree with what they were doing. The people could vote them out in the next election, but they could not undo Confederation.

Dominion Day

Queen Victoria decreed that Canadians should celebrate each July 1, the day the laws of Confederation were to take effect. Early Dominion Days were celebrated with 21-gun salutes, speeches by ministers and politicians, and activities like boat, running, and sack races. Sometimes a band would play, and sometimes there would be fireworks in the evening. In 1982, the name "Dominion Day" was changed to "Canada Day."

Baboo

John A. Macdonald was a successful politician, but he experienced many personal tragedies. His first wife became sick and was an invalid for many years before she died. One of his two sons born to her died as an infant.

Figure 13.19 Agnes and Mary Macdonald

Years later, his second wife, Agnes, gave birth to a girl, whom they named Mary. Mary was born with water on the brain. Because of this, her head was very large, and she was unable to walk or speak clearly. Still, in a time when many people with disabilities were shunned, John A. loved his daughter. He took her to Parliament, called her by an affectionate nickname, Baboo, and rocked her to sleep. When she was older, he wrote her letters, and she replied to them. She died in England at the age of 65.

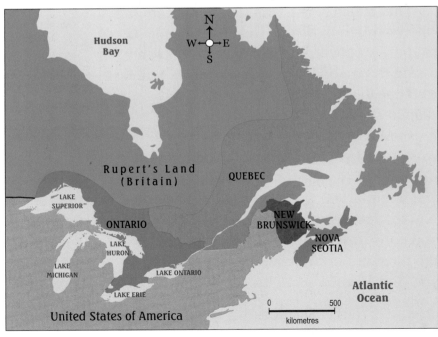

Figure 13.20 CANADA AFTER CONFEDERATION, 1867. Following Confederation, Canada was made up of Nova Scotia, New Brunswick, Quebec, and Ontario.

Canada's First Day

Today shall be a glorious day! Queen Victoria has decreed that we should have a special day today because of the Confederation of Canada! There is to be a parade and a picnic. Mama said that she will buy me an ice cream. That must be the most delightful of treats!

There will be races of all sorts. I hope Mama will let me enter the races. She said that it's not becoming for a young lady to enter races and such, but perhaps she will let me if there are other parents allowing their daughters to race.

I'm excellent at sack races, and I know that Nellie and I could beat all the boys at a three-legged race. We did at school! But Mama and Papa think that Miss Norton has radical views about those kinds of things, and they asked that there be no more races between the boys and the girls. Well, for today, even if I am not allowed to race, I know I shall be able to watch.

Papa has said that he will not go. He actually wanted to hang out black mourning crepe! Mama would not hear of it. She said that perhaps Confederation is not in the best interests of our colony, but it will not be undone and so we must make the most of it. Papa grumbled and **tamped** down his pipe, and he said not a word in reply.

It is so funny when Mama puts Papa in his place! She does this so rarely, but I was relieved that she stood up on this account. Imagine!

Willard MacDonell has to miss the celebrations because his father is against them, and his mother would never breathe a word to **retaliate**. Willard's been imagining how he could sneak out to enjoy the day, but his father will watch him like a hawk, he says. I heard Mama say that Mr. MacDonell may be opposed, but he will not be above opening his pharmacy to sell all the fountain drinks the crowds will buy.

Perhaps even Papa will not be able to resist the wonderful fireworks they are talking about setting off when it gets dark, and he always loves a cricket match. I do hope he decides to come, as it will be a glorious day. It would be exciting to celebrate this first birthday of Canada with our whole family.

Figure 13.21

Reactions to Confederation

Reactions to Confederation varied across the colonies.

Aboriginal peoples. No Aboriginal peoples were among the Fathers of Confederation, and their concerns were not discussed. Although the French and English languages were both mentioned in the BNA Act, nothing was said of Aboriginal languages or Aboriginal rights.

In 1857, The Gradual Civilization Act had given the Province of Canada the right to decide who had **Indian status**. It also told Aboriginal men how to give up their status, become citizens, and gain European-style ownership of their land. Aboriginal peoples with Indian status could not vote (until 1960), and Aboriginal peoples who moved off the **reserve** and owned land lost their special rights. As well, in the late 1850s, the Indian Department (as it was called) introduced new measures that made sure the government, and not Aboriginal peoples, controlled minerals, timber, and oil.

Quebec (Canada East) and Ontario (Canada West). With the division of the Province of Canada into two provinces, the political deadlock was broken, and each could run its own affairs. Because Confederation brought in representation by population, and both provinces had large populations, they had more influence than the smaller provinces.

Figure 13.22 Construction of Parliament Buildings, Ottawa, 1865. Canada's Parliament Buildings were completed in 1866. However, a fire in 1916 destroyed all but the library and the northwest wing. The structure was rebuilt in 1922, and still serves as the home of Canada's government.

Nova Scotia. Nova Scotia had excellent trade relations with the United States, and many people there did not want anything changed. In fact, they feared that Confederation would hurt their economy. Because Charles Tupper had a majority within the government, he was able to push Confederation through before the elections. For several years afterward, an anti-Confederation movement worked to repeal the British North America Act. It blamed Confederation for many of the financial problems the province faced in the late 1800s, including drought, border and trade troubles, and a downturn in the economy.

New Brunswick. Many people in New Brunswick were against Confederation. John A. Macdonald and others had argued for a strong central government, but people in New Brunswick wanted a stronger provincial government. Business people worried that they would have to pay more taxes and tariffs, and that they would have to deal with increased competition because of Confederation. Ethnic minorities, like the Acadians and Irish Catholics, did not trust the Protestant Tilley and his followers. Others, however, saw the benefits of Confederation, particularly the security it offered.

Prince Edward Island. Prince Edward Islanders, whose hospitality had made the Charlottetown Conference such a success, declined to join in 1867. They felt that they would have little impact in the united colonies and were concerned that they would have to fight in Canadian battles. They also worried that they would have to pay higher taxes.

However, only six years later in 1873, railroad debts, continuing frustration with absentee landlords, and the promise of an efficient steamship service to the mainland persuaded them to join Confederation. In addition, Prince Edward Island was able to send six representatives to Parliament instead of five, and received $50 per person for joining Confederation. From Canada's perspective, bringing Prince Edward Island into Confederation kept more land from falling into the hands of the Americans.

Newfoundland. Newfoundland opted out of Confederation and only sent a few observers to the Quebec Conference. The observers were excited by the idea of Confederation, but when they brought the idea back to the colony, people were not interested. Roman Catholic leaders felt that they might be subject to anti-Catholic laws, and merchants were afraid of new taxes that would not benefit them. Newfoundland did not join Confederation until 1949.

Other provinces and territories. Later arrivals to Confederation included Manitoba in 1870, when it seemed as if the Manitoba Act would deal with Métis concerns. British Columbia joined in 1871, lured by the promise of a railroad and Canada's willingness to pay its debt. The vast North-Western Territory would become part of Canada in 1870. Renamed North-West Territories, then in 1912, Northwest Territories, it would continue to be carved up over the years. In 1898, Yukon gained territorial status. In 1905, the provinces of Alberta and Saskatchewan were created. In 1999, Nunavut was formed.

Conclusion

In this chapter, you learned about some of the reasons for Confederation, the people who came together to create a new country, and how they created it.

The decisions made during the time of Confederation continue to affect us. Many of our laws are based on the founding principles outlined in the BNA Act. Peace, order, and good government are still Canadian ideals, and many of us cannot imagine a Canada that does not include all the provinces.

In the next chapter, Ben and Sara explore what it meant to be a citizen of Canada in 1867 and what it means today.

14

Citizenship Then and Now

The Alvarez family had just become Canadian citizens. Sara, Ben, and their parents had been invited to the citizenship ceremony. Now, they were on their way to a party at the Alvarez home.

The ceremony had been held with many people from countries all over the world, including Ghana, South Korea, Mexico, Sudan, and El Salvador. At one point, everyone stood up and said an oath:

"I swear that I will be faithful and bear true allegiance to Her Majesty Queen Elizabeth the Second, Queen of Canada, Her Heirs and Successors, and that I will faithfully observe the laws of Canada and fulfill my duties as a Canadian citizen."

After receiving their citizenship certificates from the judge, Mr. and Mrs. Alvarez were smiling from ear to ear. Mrs. Alvarez even had tears in her eyes, she was so happy. "Ten years ago, I would never have dreamed I would be living in such freedom. Canada has been very good to us. I am proud to be a citizen."

The party was wonderful. Music played; people laughed; there was cake, ice cream, *pupusas*, and fruit to eat. When Ben and Sara got home later, though, Sara wondered why Mrs. Alvarez was so happy. What did she mean about living in freedom? After all, she and her husband had to go to work every

day and pay bills like everyone else. Sara asked her mother.

"In Canada, we can vote for whomever we want, and speak out when we see injustice. In the Alvarez's country, you could be put in jail, and sometimes even killed, for speaking out against the government or supporting a certain political party. I think that is why living in a free country means so much to the Alvarez family. Yes, they have many responsibilities. They must work, pay taxes, and obey the law. But they also have many rights – things they can do freely – that they did not have before."

What Is Citizenship?

Throughout history, both the history of Canada and the history of humankind, people have lived together. We depend on each other for many things, and without the care of a loving community, a child cannot grow into a healthy mature adult.

As you have seen throughout this book, sometimes people work together to grow food and build communities. They look after one another and protect each other. Being a citizen means you are a member of a group. As a member of that group, you will get help and support. At the same time, you

Figure 14.1 Greek and Roman citizens

are expected to do your part for the well-being of your community.

The idea of being a citizen has been around for a long time. Thousands of years ago, Greek and Roman city-states developed the concept of citizenship. Being a citizen meant that you had privileges like the right to vote and to own land. It also meant that you had responsibilities like paying taxes and serving in the army.

In these city-states, serving as a political leader was seen as the highest good you could do for your community. In ancient Greece, not everyone was allowed to serve and equally participate as a citizen. Women were not considered citizens, nor were slaves or foreigners. A person had to be born in Rome to be a Roman citizen or else buy citizenship at a high price. Citizenship was valued by those who had it, and coveted by those who did not.

In North America, early Aboriginal groups did not necessarily talk about citizenship. However, there were rights and responsibilities that went with being a member of their communities. Everyone had a role to play within a family group and larger society. Rights were unique to different groups as well. For instance, in some groups, women were seen as equal partners in their society. In others, women were given many responsibilities, but few rights.

Being a citizen is still something that brings rights and responsibilities.

You can think of it as a balancing act. If everyone in a society had only rights and no responsibilities, the society would not thrive. People would enjoy the benefits their rights would bring, but may not contribute or care for their society.

A society in which people have responsibilities but no rights is equally unhealthy. For instance, people in these types of societies can be imprisoned for many years, even if they have not done anything wrong. There are still many societies around the world where people may have responsibilities but have no rights, because of their gender or race or religious beliefs. Imagine how your classroom or your family would function if it lacked a balance between rights and responsibilities.

Figure 14.2 Lamia Kabir, left, takes an oath of citizenship with her mother, Nasima, and sister Ushmi, age two. The Kabirs, originally from Bangladesh, were among 52 people from 20 different countries who were sworn in as Canadian citizens at this ceremony in May 2004.

As you read, think about

- **what it means to be a citizen**
- **who was considered a citizen in 1867**
- **who can claim citizenship today**
- **some of the rights and responsibilities of citizens in Canada**

Responsibilities and rights

A responsibility is a duty, something that you should do. In Canada, you have a responsibility to treat other people fairly whether or not you agree with them.

A right is a privilege that you are given. In Canada, you have the right to be treated fairly by others, no matter your age or gender or opinions.

If you are a Canadian citizen, here are some of your rights and responsibilities:

RIGHTS	RESPONSIBILITIES
Freedom of thought, speech, and religion.	Let other people express their thoughts and religion.
Anyone accused of a crime must have a fair trial. Everyone deserves to be treated in the same way by police and the law courts.	Follow Canadian laws.
Everyone must be treated fairly without discrimination.	Treat others fairly.
Canadians can live wherever they want to within Canada. They can also leave and come back to Canada.	Look after our country and its environment so that it will be a good, healthy place for others to live.
All Canadian citizens who are at least 18 can vote in elections. Their vote is allowed to remain secret.	Vote in elections at age 18 and older.
Any Canadian citizen of voting age can run for public office.	Vote for politicians who are honest and accountable.

Citizenship in 1867 and Today

Being a citizen of Canada in 1867 was different from being a citizen of Canada today. For many years, being a Canadian citizen meant that you were a British subject. A person's first allegiance was to the British monarch, not to the Dominion of Canada. For a rousing display of patriotism, people sang "God Save the Queen," not "O Canada." Canada did not have its own official flag. Instead, Britain's flag flew over the land.

Citizenship and legal status were often limited because of race, gender, religion, or birthplace. Citizenship meant different things to different people at the time of Confederation, and it can still mean different things to people today.

WHO HAS CITIZENSHIP?	1867	TODAY
Anglophone property owners	Yes	Yes
Anglophones who do not own property	No	Yes
Francophone property owners	Yes	Yes
Francophones who do not own property	No	Yes
Aboriginal peoples	No	Yes
Asian people	No	Yes
African-Canadian people	No	Yes
Women	No	Yes
Children	No	Yes

Citizenship and Aboriginal Peoples

Aboriginal peoples were not treated as citizens at the time of Confederation. Although their treaties stated that they had a right to their lands, it was not the land they had always lived on. Their traditional lands were taken by the government. The Aboriginal peoples were confined to smaller parcels of land called reserves. They did not have a right to use their own languages, and many of their traditions were discouraged or even made illegal. Aboriginal peoples may have been allies and partners with the European settlers in the past, but by the time of Confederation they had been pushed to the **edges of society**.

The federal government viewed the Aboriginal peoples as subjects who were not able to take care of themselves. The government decided to make laws that would control them and assimilate them. Most Aboriginal peoples were not allowed to vote.

Today, Aboriginal peoples are legally entitled to rights and privileges as citizens of Canada, including voting and running for public office. They also have exclusive rights, including hunting and fishing rights. However, the real experience of citizenship for Aboriginal peoples is not always the same for others in Canada. Aboriginal peoples still struggle with injustices, such as poverty, racism, and discrimination.

Aboriginal peoples continue to work toward self-government. Some of them have a declaration (see below), which is similar to an oath of citizenship.

Figure 14.3 This couple (c. 1878), from the North-West Territories, would have been caught between two worlds. Their old way of life was ending, and they had to move to reserves. Yet they were not considered Canadian citizens, so could not vote for the laws and policies that decided their future.

We the Original Peoples of this Land know the Creator put us here.

The Creator has given us Laws that govern all our relationships to live in harmony with nature and mankind.

The Laws of the Creator defined our rights and responsibilities.

The Creator gave us our spiritual beliefs, our languages, our cultures, and a place on Mother Earth that provided us with all our needs.

We have maintained our freedom, our languages, and our traditions from time immemorial.

We continue to exercise the rights and fulfill the responsibilities and obligations given to us by the Creator for the land upon which we were placed.

The Creator has given us the right to govern ourselves and the right to self-determination.

The rights and responsibilities given to us by the Creator cannot be altered or taken away by any other Nation.

Figure 14.4 *Upper Town Market, Quebec.* Although people of many backgrounds and classes would meet in this busy market, only some of them were considered citizens.

Citizenship and the French

Until the 1800s, the population in Canada of French people was greater than the population of the English. After the Seven Years' War, when Britain defeated France in North America, there were few French settlers. More settlers began to come from Britain, especially during the Loyalist period and the Great Migration following the Irish potato famine.

As the British began to outnumber the French, the French recognized that they would need to do something to protect their language and culture. By the time of Confederation, the French language had "protected" status. French and English have always been the official languages spoken

in the government, and Article 133 of the BNA Act of 1867 states that all official documents must be written in both languages.

Within provinces with large French populations – Quebec, New Brunswick, and Manitoba – the French were assured of schools that would teach French children in their own language and were administered by their Roman Catholic Church.

Today, French people in Canada are assured of their rights to language and to their unique cultural practices. However, some still fear assimilation, so they want to separate from Canada. The Canadian government continues to seek a balance between Quebec's unique society and the rest of Canada.

Citizenship and the British

At the time of Confederation, men of British descent had the most power and the most freedom as citizens in society. Men who were wealthy and owned land, or who had important family connections, had more rights and privileges than men who were poor. Men who were wealthy, owned land, had important family connections, and belonged to the Church of England (Anglican) were the most privileged of all.

Today, people from all ethnic backgrounds, religions, races, and walks of life have the same rights and responsibilities. Canada's population has grown, not just from people of British or European descent, but from people from all over the world.

Figure 14.5 In 1869, when this family portrait was taken, a woman's success was measured by her role as a wife and mother. Women were not expected to be concerned about matters outside the home, so the right to vote was thought unnecessary. Although the woman in this picture could not vote or own land, she would have been considered successful and a valuable asset to her husband's status in society.

Citizenship and Women

Women and men were treated very differently by the law at the time of Confederation. Women were not allowed to vote, and they had few rights. Unmarried women were under the control of their fathers, and married women were under the control of their husbands. Most married women were not allowed to own property, and only the father, not the mother, had a legal right to their children. Many people did not believe that women needed much education, so it was very difficult for most women to go to school beyond the first few grades. Society felt it was more important for a woman to learn how to work around the home and care for children and the family.

Today, women are equal to men under the law, and they are able to participate fully in government, as well as own land and possessions.

Figure 14.6 These children enjoy celebrating Canada Day on a camping trip. As Canadian citizens, they are entitled to security, health, and education. Children in 1867 (Figure 14.7, at right) were not protected from such things as abuse or neglect, nor did the government have to provide them with an education.

Citizenship and Children

At the time of Confederation, children who were under 21 had no rights as citizens. They were under the legal care of their father, or if they were orphans, the government. It was not against the law to abuse children, and children did not have the right to an education.

Today, Canada has agreed to the United Nations statement about the rights of children. Some of those rights include

- the right to adequate standards of living, such as shelter, nutrition, medical treatment

- the right to reach their fullest potential, through such things as education, play and leisure, cultural activities, access to information, and freedom of thought, conscience, and religion

- the right to participate in their communities, express opinions, and have a say in matters affecting their own lives

- the right to be safe from abuse, neglect, and exploitation

Conclusion

Children living in Canada are in a position that is unique in the world. There are other countries where children are valued and allowed to participate in society, but there are also many countries where children are not given the rights and responsibilities to be involved in their community.

Many Canadian children have worked to make a positive difference within and outside Canada. Equality, respect for cultural differences, peace making, and freedom of expression are some of the values that many Canadian children can promote within their homes, schools, and communities.

Although you may not be able to vote until you are 18 years of age, you may write your Member of Parliament in Ottawa, or your Member of the Legislative Assembly in your province. You have a right to have

Kids who make a difference

Some children collect food at their birthday parties rather than gifts from their friends. Over the years they have donated hundreds of kilograms of food to a local food bank.

One child collects money for hungry children living in famine-stricken countries rather than getting gifts from his friends. He has collected over $500 for children who would otherwise go hungry, and has never missed the gifts — he still gets plenty from his family!

Hannah Taylor was upset when she saw a man eating out of a garbage can. She talked to her parents and her teacher and began to collect money for homeless people. Over the years, her organization has raised thousands of dollars to help homeless people in Manitoba and across Canada.

Craig Kielburger (above right) was only 12 years old when he started "Free the Children," which speaks out against child labour around the world. Over the years his organization has

- built 400 Free the Children schools around the world, providing education to more than 35 000 children every day

Figure 14.8 Craig speaks with Mother Teresa, who spent most of her life helping the poor.

- delivered 200 000 school and health kits to students around the world
- shipped $9 million in medical supplies to 40 countries
- provided health care centres and community funding to help 500 000 people
- provided access to clean water and improved sanitation to over 125 000 people

your concerns heard and to receive an answer from your representatives.

As a citizen of Canada and the world, you have the right to raise awareness about issues that may bother you. Whatever your concern – homelessness, the environment, or world hunger – you can make a difference. Where would we be today if the people mentioned in this book had not taken a stand?

You can do something, too. As a Canadian child, you have the right to make a difference. The history of our country is based on shared values of cooperation and working together, despite our differences. As we work together, we can accomplish a lot for the good of our country and the good of our world.

Canada was populated and created by people who were willing to take risks and improve their society. Throughout our history, people have stood up to protect our country and the people who live in it. They have spoken out for those who are less fortunate, and they have made their lives better. Are you willing to follow in their footsteps?

Glossary

A

adapt to change to fit new conditions

adze axe-like tool used for cutting and shaping wood

alliance friendly but formal agreement, usually between nations, to work together

allies people, groups, or nations that join together for a common cause

amulet any object used for adornment, protection, or good luck

ancestor person who is directly descended from another person who lived many generations ago

angakok Inuit medicine man or shaman, either male or female. In traditional Inuit society, the *angakok* was doctor, advisor, and spiritual healer

appoint to choose someone or something

aquavitae kind of liquor

archaeologist person who investigates the past by digging up artifacts and other remains, then studying and interpreting them

arquebus early type of gun used in the 1500s and 1600s

artifact object, such as a tool or weapon, that was made or used by people in the past

assimilate to absorb into a larger group of people by causing a minority group of people to take on the characteristics of the larger group

atlatl short stick with a handle at one end and a hook at the other end to which a dart was attached. The atlatl served as an extension of the thrower's arm, allowing him to throw the dart farther and with more force. Atlatls were used before the invention of the bow and arrow.

B

band group of people who usually share common values, traditions, and practices of their ancestors

banish to send someone away from a place and order that person not to return

benefactor person who gives support (usually money) to another person or a cause

Beringia bridge of land, about 1600 kilometres long, that joined present-day Alaska and eastern Siberia during the last ice age. It is now covered by water known as the Bering Strait.

bounty reward offered for the capture of a criminal

bubonic plague disease, carried by fleas from rats, that spread through Europe in the 14th century and killed approximately a third of the continent's population

C

cairn pile of stones placed as a marker

census official count of a country's population

charter formal document that states the rights or duties of a group of people

chinking material used when building to seal the gaps between logs

civilization society marked by arts, sciences, and advanced political and social institutions

clan group of people who are descended from a common ancestor

cloistered closed off from the rest of the world, usually for religious reasons

colony territory controlled by a distant country

compelling forceful

confederacy union of persons, organizations, or states

confederation a union of political organizations

Confederation in Canada, the union of certain colonies of British North America to create the Dominion of Canada

consensus agreement reached among all the people in a discussion or a meeting

constitution basic laws of a country, including the powers and duties of its government

convent building where nuns live and sometimes work

convicted proven guilty of a crime

culture learned behaviour of people, which includes their belief systems and languages, their social relationships, their organization, their art and music, and their material goods, including food, clothing, shelter, and tools

czar Russian emperor

D

dialect way a language is spoken by a particular group of people in a particular place

diplomat person who represents his or her country's government in a foreign country

dominion large area of land controlled by a single ruler or government

dowry money or property that women in some cultures bring with them when they marry

durable strong and lasting for a long time

E

eccentric odd or strange

edges of society state of living apart from, and usually with less than, other people in a society

egalitarian having equal rights and opportunities

Elders Aboriginal persons who are respected and consulted due to their experience, wisdom, knowledge, and understanding of the communities they come from

elite group of people who have special advantages and privileges that others in a society do not

empire territory ruled by a king or queen

entrench firmly establish

environment physical surroundings

exile to send someone away from his or her own country and order that person not to return

extended family family group that includes parents, children, and other close relatives such as grandparents, aunts, uncles, and cousins

F

factor person in charge of a Hudson's Bay Company trading post

First Nations descendants of the first people who lived in Canada, and whose ancestors lived here for thousands of years before explorers arrived from Europe

flint knapper person who made stone tools

free Blacks African-Americans who were no longer slaves. Some were born free; others bought their freedom.

G

generation average amount of time between the birth of parents and that of their children. A generation is approximately 30 years.

glacier huge sheet of ice that forms when snow falls and does not melt, because the temperature remains below freezing

gorget necklace

Great Law of Peace founding constitution of the Iroquois Confederacy created around 1500 CE. It is an oral tradition that defines how the Iroquois nations can solve disputes among themselves and maintain peace.

H

habitants people in New France who farmed along the St. Lawrence River. They worked the seigneur's land in exchange for part of the crop.

hierarchal type of society with different classes, ranging from the lower class to the elite

Homo sapiens sapiens modern human beings

I

ice ages periods of time in history when large areas of Earth were covered with ice

Indian status individual's legal status as a First Nations' member, according to the Indian Act

iniskims ceremonial stones used to attract bison

innovative idea or invention that is new

intendant official assigned by the king of France to look after finances, justice, and police in a colony

Iroquois Confederacy group of Iroquois nations that created the Great Law of Peace. The nations were the Seneca, Mohawk, Oneida, Onondaga, and the Cayuga. In 1720, the Tuscarora joined the confederacy.

L

land bridge dry land, exposed during periods when sea level is low, that connects large masses of land

l'Habitation settlement built by Samuel de Champlain in 1608 on the site of present-day Quebec City

libel published or broadcast statement that is untrue and that damages someone's reputation

linguist person who studies the structure and development of a language and its relationship to other languages

longhouse Iroquoian communal dwelling that is much longer than it is wide

Lower Canada British colony in North America, at the downstream end of the St. Lawrence River in the southern portion of the modern-day province of Quebec. The colony was one of two created by the Constitutional Act of 1791 by the partition of the British colony, the Province of Quebec.

M

Manifest Destiny idea that God intended all of North America to belong to the United States

marksmen people who can shoot at a target with great accuracy

merger joining together of two or more companies to form a single company

missionary person who is sent (usually to a foreign country) by a church or religious group to teach that group's faith and do good works

modified changed slightly

monarch ruler, such as a king or queen, who usually inherits his or her position

monopoly complete control given to a company to make or sell something

O

oath of allegiance promise of loyalty to a specific country

oral tradition stories and beliefs that are passed on by word of mouth from one generation to the next

order (religious) community of people living under the same religious rules, including monks, friars, nuns

ornate elaborately decorated

outspoken honest and frank when giving opinions

P

pacifist someone who believes that war and violence are wrong and who, for those reasons, refuses to fight in wars

palisaded fenced around something to protect it from attack

parlay discussion usually between enemies, to come to an agreement

persecution act of treating someone cruelly and unfairly because of that person's political or religious beliefs

point of view what a person thinks about a certain situation, event, or someone else's opinion

portage carrying of boats and supplies overland between two waterways

potato blight harmful disease that causes potatoes to rot in the ground

pound fenced area into which animals are herded

privateer private ship (or its captain) authorized by a country's government to attack and seize cargo from another country's ships

projectile point arrow, dart, lance, or other pointed hunting tool made from bone, stone, or metal

Protestant Christians and churches that separated from the Roman Catholic Church after 1517

Puritans English Protestants who wanted the Church of England to get rid of all Catholic influences

Q

quarantine when a sick person, animal, or plant is separated from everything else to stop the spread of a disease

R

rebellion armed fight against a government

rebound rise of land masses that were depressed by the huge weight of ice sheets during the last ice age

reform to change something for the better

regalia colourful clothing and items of adornment worn during ceremonies

repeal to do away with something officially, such as a law

representation by population idea that the larger the population in a governed area, the more representatives the voters can elect to the government assembly

representative democracy type of government in which citizens vote for members of Parliament or an assembly to represent their interests

reserve land for Aboriginal peoples to live on that was set aside by treaty or the Indian Act

Responsible Government form of government where the executive or cabinet, made up of members of the party with the most seats in the assembly, must answer to the elected representatives of the people. The elected representatives must represent the wishes of the people.

retaliate to do something unpleasant to someone because that person has done something unpleasant to you

retreat shrinking of a glacier caused by melting or erosion by water

revolt to rebel against the government

revolution 1. uprising by the people of a country that changes the country's system of government 2. large, important change

S

sanction to give approval to or permission for

scurvy disease caused by the lack of vitamin C that resulted in bleeding gums, loss of hair and teeth, weakness, and eventually death

seigneurial system form of land distribution in New France in which land was granted to a seigneur

seigneur in New France, a man of the upper class who owned land granted by the king of France

shareholder person or organization that owns part of a company

siege surrounding of a place, such as a castle or city, in order to cut off supplies and capture it

skirmish short battle

sovereign independent of others

spawning producing a large number of eggs

symbolize to stand for or represent something else

T

tamp to pack something down tightly (tobacco in a pipe, for example) using a series of taps

taxes money that people and businesses pay to support a government

tenant person who rents space that belongs to someone else

theory idea or opinion based on evidence that explains facts or events but does not prove them

till soil, rocks, and other material deposited by glaciers

trade particular job or craft done by a person

travois frame used to carry cargo, made of a platform atop two poles, that was pulled by a dog or horse

tribal council people who have been elected to meet, discuss, and make decisions about matters concerning a tribe

U

Upper Canada British colony created in 1791. It extended south of Lake Nipissing and north of the St. Lawrence River and lakes Ontario and Erie to the eastern shoreline of Georgian Bay and the northern shoreline of Lake Superior, and is now the southern part of present-day Ontario.

V

values person's or groups' beliefs about what is right and wrong and how people should behave

village council people who have been elected to meet, discuss, and make decisions about matters concerning a village

W

weir enclosure (often made of wood) used to trap fish

Pronunciation Guide

Key

a	at, cat, mat, snap
ah	father, bother
ahr	lard, yard
aw	jaw, saw, all, caught
ay	[long "a"] day, pay, obey, weigh
eh, e	bed, pet, peck
ee	[long "e"] beat, easy, seem
er	error
I	[long "i"] tie, sky, side, buy, eye
i, ih	it, tip, active
ihr	ear, fear
o	cot, hot, not
oh	[long "o"] bone, go, know, toe
oo	boot, rule, youth
u	book, foot, put, pull, wood
uh	[schwa] ago, alone, banana, linen

Algonquin	al GONG kwin
angakok	ANG uh kok
Anishinabe	a nish uh NAH beh
Assiniboine	a SIN uh boin
Athapaskan	a thuh PAS kan
atlatl	AT lat ul
Atsina	AT see nuh
Beothuk	beh OH tuhk
Cayuga	kay YOO guh
Chilcotin	chil KOH tin
Dene	DEH nay
dodem	DOH duhm
Domagaya	DOH muh *gi* uh
Donnacona	DAHN uh KOHN uh
Gitskan	GIT skan
Gros Ventre	GROH vawnt
Haida	H*I* duh
Haisla	H*I* sluh
Haudenosaunee	how den uh SHOH nee
Heiltsuk	H*I*L tsuk
Hidatsa	hee DAWT saw
Hochelaga	HOSH eh LAG uh
Innu	IN oo
Inuktitut	i NUK tih tut
Inuvialuit	in OO vee AHL oo it
Iroquois	EE ruh kwa
Kainai	K*I* n*i*
komatik	kahm uh TIK
Kutenai	KOO tuh nay
Kwagiulth	KWA gee ulth
Lakota	la KOH tuh
Lillooet	LIL oo wet
Mandan	MAN dan
Mi'kmaq	MIK mak
Mohawk	MO hahk
Montagnais	mawn tuh NYAY
Monte Verde	MAWN tay VER day
Nakota	na KOH tuh
Nanabozho	NA nuh bo shoh
Naskapi	nas ki PEE
Nehiyawak	nuh HEE a wik
Netsilik	NET sil ik
Neutral	NOO truhl
Nicola	nee ko LAW
Nisga'a	NIS guh
Nisichawayasihk	ni SEECH a WAY a seek
Nlaka'pamux	ing klah KAP muh
Nootka	NOOT kuh
Nuu-chah-nulth	nootsh NAW looth
Nuxalk	NOO halk
Odawa	OD uh wah
Okanagan	o kuh NAW guhn
Oneida	o N*I* duh
Onondaga	awn uhn DAW guh
Opaskwayak	oh PAS kwee ak
Oronhyatekha	oh roo nyuh DEH kuh
Peigan	pee GAN
Petun	puh TOON
Piikani	pee KAH nee
Sadlermiut	sad LER mee oot
sagamite	SAG uh m*i*t
Salish	SAY lish
Sarcee	sahr SEE
Seneca	SEH nuh kuh
Shanawdithit	shah nah DITH it
Shuswap	SHOO swap
Siksika	SIK sik uh
Stadacona	STAD uh KOHN uh
Taltheilei	tal TEEL ee
Thanadelthur	tah nah DEL ter
Thompson	TAWM suhn
Taignoagny	tay nyoh AN yee
tikanagan	TIK an uh gin
Tlingit	KLING kit
Tsuu T'ina	TSOO tuh nay
Tunit	TOO nit
umiak	OO mee ak
Wendat	W*I* uhn dawt
windigo	WIN dih go
Yamozha	yuh MOH zuh

Index

Image credits

The publisher has made every effort to acknowledge all sources of illustrations, and photographs that have been used in this book, and would be grateful if any errors or omissions were pointed out so that they may be corrected. The following illustrations are identified by figure number or page reference.

1.4 Natural Resources Canada, image produced with permission of Natural Resources Canada. Her Majesty the Queen in Right of Canada; 1.6 © The Manitoba Museum; 1.10 Courtesy B. Kooyman, University of Alberta; 1.12 © The Manitoba Museum.

2.3 © The Manitoba Museum / Courtesy of the Royal Alberta Museum, Edmonton, Alberta; 2.7 © The Manitoba Museum; 2.8 Courtesy: John Brumley in Liz Bryan's *Stone by Stone: Exploring Ancient Sites on the Canadian Plains.* Surrey, B.C.: Heritage House, 2005; 2.9 Courtesy: Liz Bryan. *Stone by Stone: Exploring Ancient Sites on the Canadian Plains.* Surrey, B.C.: Heritage House, 2005; 2.11 © The Manitoba Museum; 2.12 Stone Knife © Canadian Museum of Civilization, artifact number KkLn-4:380, photo Harry Foster, image number 80-578 / Taltheilei Stone points (Composite photograph) © Canadian Museum of Civilization, image number 2001-82; 2.14 © The Manitoba Museum; 2.15 © The Manitoba Museum; 2.16 © The Manitoba Museum; 2.17 Vancouver Museum Canada (QAD 1692); 2.18 Sid Kroker, courtesy of Quaternary Consultants; 2.19 © The Manitoba Museum; 2.23 © The Manitoba Museum; 2.26 Photo by Len Minor, courtesy of Pam Goundry; 2.27 © The Manitoba Museum; 2.29 Post Holes. Reproduced by permission of the London Chapter, Ontario Archaeological Society, from The *Archaeology of Southern Ontario to AD 1650* edited by Chris J. Ellis and Neal Ferris; 2.30 Iroquoian village outline. Reproduced by permission of the London Chapter, Ontario Archaeological Society, from *The Archaeology of Southern Ontario to AD 1650*, edited by Chris J. Ellis and Neal Ferris; 2.31 Iroquois Ceramic Pipe © Canadian Museum of Civilization, artifact number III-I-1114 a, b, image number D2004-20742 / Iroquois Pottery © Canadian Museum of Civilization, artifact number III-I-1938, image number D2004-20778; 2.32 © The Manitoba Museum; 2.33 © The Manitoba Museum.

3.9 © Jason Bowers.

4.1 LAC / C-036350; 4.3 © P. John Burden; 4.5 © Parks Canada / A. Cornellier / H.01.11.06.01 (02); 4.6 © Parks Canada / J. Steeves / H.01.11.01.04 (40); 4.7 Giovanni Battista Ramusio / LAC / NLC-000700; 4.8 © Portage & Main Press; 4.9 *The Ambassadors*, 1533 (oil on panel), Holbein, Hans the Younger (1497/8-1543) / National Gallery, London, UK, / The Bridgeman Art Library/

BAL 122676; 4.10 AKG-images / 1SP-90-E1502; 4.12 The British Library / 3522 / Shelfmark C.114.C.15; 4.14 LAC / C-003278.

5.5 Samuel de Champlain / LAC / C-001137 (detail); 5.8 Samuel de Champlain / LAC / C-003354; 5.12 John Lambert / Library and Archives Canada / C-001703; 5.13 Frank Craig / LAC / C- 010622; 5.14 Pierre le Ber / Musee Marguerite-Bourgeoys; 5.17 © Gary Evans; 5.18 © Gary Evans.

6.2 Public domain. From: Diderot's *Encyclopédie*; 6.3 After Herman Moll / LAC / C-003686; 6.4 Shanawdithit / LAC / C-028544; 6.6 LAC / C-001090; 6.7 LAC / NMC-811; 6.8 Public domain. From: *Picturesque Canada*, vol. II, 1882; 6.9 Charles William Jefferys / LAC / C-069903; 6.10 Nova Scotia Archives & Records Management; 6.13 *Acadian lighthouses at Cheticamp.* Nova Scotia Tourism, Culture and

Heritage; 6.14 LAC / C-027665 (detail); 6.15 Joseph Highmore (attributed) / LAC / C-003916 (detail); 6.16 LAC / C-146340; 6.18 LAC / C-002834; 6.19 Newfoundland & Labrador Tourism; 6.20 A. Bobbett (engraver) / LAC / C-011250; 6.22 LAC / C-002833.

7.2 Historic Period Trade Goods, Slide #30 from Vol. 45 of Canada's Visual History © Canadian Museum of Civilization, image no. D2006-11056; 7.3 Hudson's Bay Company Archives, Archives of Manitoba, *Modifications of the Beaver Hat from "Castorologia"* by H. T. Martin, 1892; 7.4 LAC / C-007300; 7.5 Public domain; 7.7 Chiedel / LAC / C-041881K; 7.8 LAC / C-099259; 7.9 Cornelius Krieghoff / LAC / C-000053; 7.10 Samuel de Champlain / LAC / C-005750; 7.12 LAC / C-075209K; 7.18 From the Hudson's Bay Company Corporate Collection, used with permission of Hudson's Bay Company; 7.19 © The Manitoba Museum; 7.20 I.B. Scotin (attributed) / LAC / C-010891; 7.21 Henri Beau (attributed) / LAC / C-017059; 7.22 Hudson's Bay Company Archives, Archives of Manitoba, HBCA P-228; 7.28 Arthur H. Hider /LAC / C-006896; 7.30 I.B. Scotin (attributed) / LAC / C-012005.

8.2 Frances Anne Hopkins / LAC / C-002774; 8.3 LAC / C-008711; 8.4 Frances Anne Hopkins / LAC / C-002773; 8.5 LAC / C-000164; 8.6 LAC / C-095779; 8.7 British Columbia Archives / PDP2244; 8.8 British Columbia Archives / A-01926; 8.11 William Armstrong / LAC / C-010512; 8.13 Hudson's Bay Company Archives, Archives of Manitoba, *Mr Samuel Hearne, Late Chief at Prince of Wale's Fort, Hudson's Bay* (Churchill); 8.15 William Armstrong, *Dr. John Rae (1813-1893), Arctic Explorer*, Collection of Glenbow Museum, Calgary, Canada; 8.19 British Columbia Archives / A-0259; 8.20 John Webber / LAC / C-006642; 8.21 British Columbia Archives / PDP2252; 8.22 John Webber / LAC / C-088489; 8.26 H. A. Ogden / LAC / C-082974; 8.27 William Armstrong / LAC / C-010500; 8.28 John James Audubon / LAC / C-041808.

9.2 Hudson's Bay Company Archives, Archives of Manitoba / HBCA P-1169.2.1; 9.3 George Gipps (attributed) / LAC / C-996049; 9.4 William Armstrong / LAC / C-010502; 9.5 With permission of the Royal Ontario Museum © ROM; 9.6 LAC / C-00026; 9.8 Hudson's Bay Company Archives, Archives of Manitoba / HBCA 1987/63-P-80-S/6; 9.9 Hudson's Bay Company Archives, Archives of Manitoba / HBCA P-388; 9.11 LAC / C-000624; 9.16 Archives of Manitoba, Arnett, Margaret 22 (N16983); 9.13 Hudson's Bay Company Archives, Archives of Manitoba, HBCA P-378 (N-87-8) ; 9.17 LAC / NLC-008796; 9.18 Hudson's Bay Company Archives, Archives of Manitoba / HBCA 1987/363-S-25/T78; 9.19 Peter Rindisbacher / LAC / C-001934; 9.20 William Henry Edward Napier / LAC / C-001065.

10.2 James Erskine / LAC / C-011209; 10.3 © Library of Congress, Washington, D.C., USA; 10.5 Going to Meeting in 1776 / The Bridgeman Art Library; 10.6 *George Washington* / Library of Congress LC-USZC4-2968; 10.7 The Colonial Williamsburg Foundation; 10.9 Henry Sandham / LAC / C-000168; 10.10 W. Booth / LAC / C-040162; 10.11 James Peachey / LAC / C-002001; 10.12 Samuel Wale /LAC / C-114468; 10.13 Shelburne County Museum, Shelburne, Nova Scotia; 10.14 Courtesy Linda McDowell; 10.15 Shelburne County Museum, Shelburne, Nova Scotia; 10.16 Shelburne County Museum, Shelburne, Nova Scotia.

11.2 Phillip John Bainbridge / LAC / C-011831; 11.3 LAC / C-143393; 11.4 William Steele / LAC / C-000796; 11.5 Public domain. From *Pictorial Field Book of the War of 1812*, by Benson John Lossing; 11.6 LAC / C-036181 (detail); 11.7 19670070-009 / © Canadian War Museum; 11.8 James B, Dennis / LAC / C-000276; 11.9 Mary Ann Knight / LAC / C-123841; 11.11 Henry Francis Ainslie / LAC / C-000518; 11.13 LAC / C-007763; 11.14 *The embarkation, Waterloo Docks, Liverpool*, c.1850 / McCord Museum, Montreal /